SOCIAL SYSTEMS DESIGN

SOCIAL SYSTEMS DESIGN
Normative Theory
and the
MAPS Design Technology

RALPH H. KILMANN
Graduate School of Business, University of Pittsburgh

NORTH-HOLLAND
NEW YORK   OXFORD   AMSTERDAM

Elsevier North-Holland, Inc.
52 Vanderbilt Avenue, New York, New York 10017

North-Holland Publishing Company
P.O. Box 211
Amsterdam, The Netherlands

Library of Congress Cataloging in Publication Data
Kilmann, Ralph H
  Social systems design: normative theory and
  the MAPS Design Technology
  Bibliography: p.
  Includes index.
  1. Organizational research. 2. Social
change. 3. MAPS design technology. I. Title.
H62.K479 301.18'32 76-46466
ISBN 0-444-00198-0

Manufactured in the United States of America

To my father
Martin H. Kilmann
whose influence is now felt
and fully appreciated

Contents

Preface

Social systems design refers to the arrangement of, and the process of arranging, technical and human resources to accomplish various social systems objectives. More specifically, the term "social systems" is meant to include both profit and nonprofit formal organizations, such as business firms, schools, hospitals, and governmental agencies. Also included in the term social systems, however, are more diffuse social settings, such as communities, institutions, temporary groups (e.g., committees), and so forth. Furthermore, we are concerned with the process of designing social systems as well as the resultant structural design. The latter includes the particular arrangements of technical and human resources, while the former is the process by which the members of a social system (with the aid of external social scientists) decide upon the need for a new design, formulate such a design, and then implement it in their social system.

This book presents a unique social science technology for effectively designing social systems that is referred by the acronym MAPS—Multivariate Analysis, Participation, and Structure. These properties are essential for the development and application of a comprehensive design technology, as will be discussed throughout the book. Actually, the development of such a technology has been advocated as the sine qua non of social science research: to utilize scientific knowledge in order to make our organizations and institutions more efficient, effective, and responsive to societal needs. Not only have technologies in the social sciences been sparse, however, they have also not been based on contributions from the various disciplines of the social sciences in a systematic and normative manner. To date no other technology purports to do what the MAPS Design Technology does. While much more theoretical and empirical research needs to be done with MAPS, it does represent the potential for a comprehensive and useful technology for designing effective social systems.

As will become evident, the MAPS Design Technology forces the raising and questioning of some of the most important social systems design issues that must be confronted under any circumstance. At a minimum then, examining and debating the properties, assumptions, and values of the MAPS Design Technology can serve as a provocative educational methodology for social science learning. Thus this book is written for the student, the social scientist, and the practitioner concerned about the critical substantive, methodological, and value issues in regard to social systems design, as well as to examine a specific technology that can actually assess and change the designs of our organizations and institutions. Consequently, this requires a discussion of the development of normative theory (i.e., guidelines, criteria, and principles to suggest how social systems should be designed) rather than strictly descriptive theory (i.e., describing and explaining how social systems are currently designed).

Perhaps the most appropriate task for this preface would be to provide some of my background which affected the development of MAPS, so that readers may better appreciate the ultimate intention of this technology. Basically, the MAPS Design Technology was not developed solely in some highly formalistic manner (i.e., doing a literature search, noting gaps and shortcomings, developing hypotheses, engaging in research, and then drawing implications for the practical applications of the research). Rather, MAPS has been influenced by my personal background, psychodynamics, and values. Let me suggest briefly some factors involved in the how and why of MAPS development.

I spent six years at Carnegie-Mellon University studying management science. The Carnegie approach to management is highly quantitative. A typical guide to research at Carnegie as I saw it was, "If you can measure it (quantitatively), it must be important." The converse of course was, "If you cannot measure it, then it must not be important!" But I did have the feeling that some things that could not be so assessed might still be the most important elements in research. I did not believe, for example, that one should precisely and quantitatively solve a trivial problem or the wrong problem (Mitroff and Featheringham, 1974). Nevertheless I "played the game" by developing a mathematical model of interpersonal behavior to predict the interactions and outcomes of small groups, only to be told by my professors that interpersonal and small group behavior cannot be measured in this way, and who was I to even try to quantitatively assess such intangible variables?

This brought me to the Ph.D. program in management at the University of California at Los Angeles. Here the emphasis was on T-groups, sensitivity training, and personal growth. I had not even heard of this latter term at Carnegie. At UCLA, the focus was not on management science per se, but on the importance of what was being measured. I was exposed to the values of social change and the change process, and was asked such questions as, "How is the research you are doing an expression of your personal growth areas and the personal struggles you had as a child?" No one had ever asked me a question like this before! So I became involved in T-groups and personal growth as part of my formal Ph.D. program, and it seemed that the school's evaluation of me and my qualifications to become a Ph.D. was based as much on my personal development as on my scientific knowledge and capabilities.

The MAPS Design Technology is an opportunity for me to integrate both schools of management thought—my education at Carnegie Mellon emphasizes the quantitative aspects of science, and my learning at UCLA accentuates the personal growth, values, and social change aspects of science. As the reader will see, the MAPS Computer Program underlying the technology was developed because multivariate statistics and high speed computers can process amounts of information that individuals by themselves cannot even comprehend, let alone calculate, in a short period of time. But computer science to date (and hopefully always) cannot process ethics, values, and clinical skills in diagnosing and defining problems as complex as social systems design and design changes. The latter type of behavioral phenomena must be approached by qualitative means, by the values and practices of organizational development (OD) specialists, for example. Thus the quantitative and qualitative aspects of science demand integration in a technology such as MAPS. This book proposes that this integration has begun, needs to proceed and, perhaps even more importantly, needs to occur in other social science technologies if we as social scientists and practitioners can have a significant impact on the real world.

As in most endeavors, many individuals have been directly or indirectly involved in the creation and expression of this volume. I would like to acknowledge those who had the greatest impact on me and the development of the MAPS Design Technology. To begin with I would like to acknowledge Bill McKelvey who first gave me the opportunity to work with him on a study which led to the initial conception of MAPS, and who then helped foster my motivation to spend the next several years developing these preliminary ideas into a formal design technology, as represented by this book. I would also like to acknowledge the impact of Chris Argyris on my work, but more especially those times when he challenged me on the ethics and values underlying the MAPS Design Technology. I have also been heavily influenced by the values and philosophies of Bob Tannenbaum, who has always confronted me on the right issues, at the right time, and in the right manner. Ken Thomas was and is most supportive of all my research and personal efforts, as is my good friend, Tuck Taylor.

I am indebted to the Graduate School of Business at the University of Pittsburgh for constant support of my research and ideas. Special acknowledgment is due to Dean Jerry Zoffer, who could not have been more supportive and encouraging, and to Associate Dean Andy Blair for providing me with research assistants at many stages of the technology's development. The MAPS group of doctoral students have been my major advocates at GSB and, although their scholarly efforts are acknowledged as collaborators in the chapters of this book, they are the most challenging and sustaining group that I have ever encountered. I hope I have done as much for them. Special thanks to Marjorie Lyles for coordinating the completion of this book; to Walt McGhee for providing technical assistance and continual encouragement; to Grace Ann Rosile for her editing; to Dick Herden for his dependable and special assistance in preparing the final manuscript; and to my secretaries, Valerie Wagner and Cindy Rubinkowski, for their many and varied contributions to this book.

Finally, I wish to acknowledge the one individual who has had the greatest impact on my social science learning and who has been the strongest advocate of MAPS, Ian Mitroff. Ian's contribution to this volume is indicated in several places so I need not repeat them here. What I do want to indicate and acknowledge at this time is Ian's continual support and confrontation of my ideas and feelings. He has fostered my personal growth process greatly, and thus, has done much to encourage my self-reflection as a person and as a scientist.

22 July 1976   RHK
Pittsburgh, PA

Foreword

One can speak of the perspective of the researcher and the perspective of the human being as an actor. The predominant focus of the researcher is to describe reality as accurately as possible in order to understand and predict human behavior; the predominant focus of the human being as an actor is to understand and predict events well enough to realize them.

The kind of on-line learning required of each perspective differs importantly. Human beings as actors are always involved in a learning cycle composed of discovery of problems, invention of solutions to problems, production of solutions in terms of actions, and evaluation and generalization of the production to assess its effectiveness which, hopefully, leads to new discoveries. Social scientists, on the other hand, when following their established practices, tend to focus especially upon discovery (understanding and predicting). They attempt to make the discovery of knowledge as thorough as possible by postponing the invention of solutions until "all" the relevant data are generated and as a result they rarely get beyond the invention of solutions. In other words, they do not test the solutions in terms of actions. Indeed, researchers leave such tasks to what they call demonstration experiments. Researchers assume that systematic knowledge will not result from research that attempts to produce solutions to problems in the world of everyday life.

There is an inherent limitation embedded in this approach. The nature of knowledge obtained will differ depending upon the objective; whether it be to understand and predict or to go beyond and produce knowledge to informed action. For example, the responses that subjects give to questionnaires or the behavior that they exhibit for researchers may vary depending upon whether they are involved for the sake of understanding and predicting or they are involved to generate knowledge about how to take action in their world beyond the research context. More importantly, they may not be aware of the differences of their responses because the information processing rules that they use to search and retrieve information under these different conditions tend to be tacit. To put this another way, human beings as actors in every-day life require knowledge that they can use to understand, predict, and produce actions.

Another difficulty is the tendency of social science to limit research to a description of the existing universe. Such research has the intended consequence of producing knowledge about the status quo but the unintended consequence of neglecting alternatives to the status quo. Genuinely new options require new maps, new concepts, and a dialectic relationship between what is and what might be.

Yet, some readers may respond, research that describes the universe does lead to insights into how the world might be. This is true, but we are learning that its truth is much more limited than we realized. For example, Karl Marx analyzed the state of affairs during his lifetime and made subsequent predictions about the future. Given these predictions, he invented another option for the organization of society. We know that some of the key predictions made by Marx about the plight of the workers under capitalism and state socialism were not realized. They were not realized for the simple reason that there exists in capitalism and state socialism inner contradictions that could not surface until each was produced. In other words, if Marx had attempted to produce state socialism in a microsetting, he would have generated knowledge that would have caused him to question his original analysis.

Scientists who take the requirements of action seriously find themselves faced with complexities much more intricate than those found at the level of discovery. Not only are the variables more numerous and complex, but they rarely can be brought under systematic rigorous control.

The traditional research strategy has been to decompose complexity thereby bringing it under control. But the knowledge produced has rarely been recomposable into a pattern that an actor might use to deal with the problem. The pattern should not be so complex that the actors must spend most of their time "fitting" it to the situation. Furthermore, parts of the complexity are situationally unique and situationally ambiguous. Knowledge about this type of uniqueness and ambiguity is difficult to produce ahead of time in the form of usable generalizations.

Hence, if knowledge is to be applicable it must focus on the fact that human beings always operate with incomplete information, under conditions of high ambiguity, and high time constraints. To take these properties of reality seriously means that the generalizations that social scientists produce must inform human actors how to make events come about under these conditions.

The moment this requirement is taken seriously, then research must place the processes of design at the center of attention. Design includes the processes by which human beings attempt to organize themselves and their organizations in order to achieve objectives, to produce actions. There are very few research investigations that take design seriously. I am glad to say that this investigation is one of the few.

While working in this difficult and unchartered zone, Professor Kilmann adds several more rare attributes to his research. First, he confronts the problem of producing empirically repeatable and publicly verifiable data. Too often researchers who strive to be applicable ignore the importance of systematically produced and tested knowledge. The data that Kilmann's programs produce are not only quantitative but they are usable, correctable and hence controllable by the users. Ralph Kilmann is not only producing knowledge about designing organizations, he is also producing knowledge about how to design design-processes that are systematic and useful.

Ralph Kilmann has yet another concern and that is the development of a design methodology that enables people to produce valid and useful information without deteriorating their free and informed choice, thereby enhancing their commitment to that choice. In other words, science is designed to meet conditions of rigor (e.g., public verifiability) without sacrificing human freedom.

A good book raises questions and does so in an unequivocal manner. I wonder what are the limits of designing organizations based on people's preferences. My concern ranges from how realistic is this to the implicit assumption that individuals may choose their preference over organizational health. Also, what if people change their choices, but these cannot be altered? Will that not bring us back to the original problem of organizations that Kilmann is trying to overcome, namely their apparent unchangeability and unilateral control?

Ralph Kilmann is aware of these questions and he continues the program of research necessary to illuminate them. In the meantime, we must not forget that people are frequently making choices related to preferences. Since such choices are at best quasi-legal, they are usually camouflaged. One consequence is that they become undiscussable. Undiscussable choices are not consciously and planfully alterable. At least with Kilmann's methodology, preferences may become discussable and given a methodology that makes them manageable, they may be alterable.

CHRIS ARGYRIS
James Bryant Conant Professor of
Education and Organizational Behavior
Harvard University

Introduction and Overview

Social systems have been designed over the centuries to obtain objectives that cannot be obtained by separate individuals. Over time, however, particularly this past century, the environment of our organizations and institutions has undergone massive changes, and these changes are now occurring more rapidly than ever before (Toffler, 1970). The political process of nations, economic conditions, technological developments, the information explosion, and changes in cultural values and mores continually pose new problems, contingencies, and constraints on our social systems. Those changes have made it increasingly difficult for social systems to obtain their objectives, particularly if the social systems themselves have not proactively attempted to manage and adapt to these changes.

A major theme of this book is that many, if not most, social systems will find it increasingly difficult to perform effectively if they are not designed appropriately and if their designs are not altered over time to adapt to environmental changes. But the history of social systems indicates not only that designs are altered infrequently, but also that many social systems seem to consider their designs as a given and not subject to redesign. There is actually some evidence to suggest that social systems tend to keep the design they began with, whether these systems be business firms (designed via production, marketing, and finance functions), universities (designed by academic disciplines), health care organizations (designed by medical specialization), or religious institutions or military organizations (Stinchcombe, 1965). It appears that such is the case since social systems design is a most complicated, ill-defined, and ambiguous undertaking. For this reason, and also because of the major role design plays in the effectiveness of social systems, the need for useful methodologies and technologies to approach the design problem becomes perhaps the most important objective of the social sciences, which strive to enhance the performance and satisfaction of our organizations and institutions.

To date, however, there appears to have been little progress in developing sophisticated methodologies and/or technologies to address social systems design problems. In essence, we have not seen large-scale, systematic redesigns of social systems based upon a comprehensive and integrated technology developed from the several social sciences. Without providing extensive support for this observation, it should be evident that each discipline of the social sciences has largely applied its own unique conceptualizations and methods to this area, and each discipline has benefited little from the others. Thus anthropology, sociology, psychology, economics, and the in-

1

formation sciences have not developed interdisciplinary methods and technologies for redesigning social systems.

Furthermore, these disciplines have approached design problems mainly from a descriptive stance (i.e., reporting on how groups, organizations, and institutions have designed resources) rather than from a normative stance (i.e., providing values and guidelines for indicating how a social system should design its resources). A normative approach is needed to create change and to provide methodologies to design for effective social systems change. The descriptive approach merely observes natural change, while the normative approach is needed for planned change (Bennis, et al., 1969).

Since the foregoing perspective provides a most challenging task for the social sciences, a program of research is currently under way to actually meet this challenge: to develop an interdisciplinary, normative technology to mobilize (or remobilize) resources to more effectively define and obtain social systems objectives. This technology, referred to as MAPS (Multivariate Analysis, Participation, and Structure), was initially suggested by Kilmann and McKelvey (1975) to redesign the operational subunits of organizations. Since then, the MAPS Design Technology has been developed for the designing of adaptive organizations (Kilmann, 1974d), task forces for curriculum innovation (Kilmann, 1974c), a community action program (Kilmann, 1975a), and strategic planning systems for multinational corporations (Kilmann and Ghymn, 1974). As these extensions were developed, it became apparent that the MAPS Design Technology could provide an interdisciplinary, normative approach to social systems design.

PLAN OF THE BOOK

This book is divided into three main parts, which in total provide a thorough discussion of the current state of the technology as well as the research ideas and projects under way to develop the technology further. Part I describes the theoretical underpinnings of the MAPS Design Technology: the research on organization design, structural interventions, and the concept of purposefulness (i.e., people can design their own organizations). Part II presents the stages of MAPS, starting from the entry and diagnosis of some social system and ending with the evaluation of an actual design change. Part III provides a discussion of potential applications of the MAPS Design Technology to enhance social and organizational problem solving. This part also contains a summary of the current applications of

MAPS, how these applications pertain to the conceptual models presented in earlier chapters, and how these applications represent the use of various research methodologies to study organization design and the MAPS Design Technology. The book concludes with a chapter on the ethics of using this technology for creating social change and includes an ethical code for change agents.

In order to appreciate how the main parts of the book and the chapters that constitute the parts contribute to to the development of a broad, normative, interdisciplinary technology, the components of the book can be traced to the Diamond Model of problem solving proposed by Sagasti and Mitroff (1973). This model, shown in Figure 1, consists of four nodes: Problem Defined, Conceptual Model, Scientific Model, and Solution. The arrows leading to these nodes represent the processes that the scientist or change agent utilizes in solving a problem: defining the problem, conceptualizing a model, developing a model, solving the model, and implementing the solution. It can be argued that only if some proposed technology explicitly recognizes and addresses each process and state in the model can that technology successfully integrate social knowledge for social action.

Figure 1 shows how the chapters of this book contribute to the development of such a design technology. The introductory chapter seeks to define the scope and nature of the problem for which the MAPS Design Technology has been proposed. Chapters 1 and 2, on organization design and purposefulness, provide the substantive knowledge of the field; that is, the various conceptualizations of organization design problems and the value premises underlying them. Chapter 3 contains the diagnostic phase of applying the MAPS Design Technology—how the change agent enters the social system and chooses the particular variables to focus on for his interventions. Included in this diagnosis is the conceptualization of the design boundaries; that is, the particular subsystems to partake in the design assessment and /or design change.

Chapter 4 discusses the core of the MAPS Design Technology: input, analysis, and output. The input concerns the members of a social system developing and responding to the MAPS questionnaire (i.e., what tasks the members want to work on and with whom they want to work). The analysis concerns the multivariate statistics used to translate member responses to the MAPS questionnaire into alternative organization designs via the MAPS Computer Program (i.e., which group of people should work on which cluster of tasks). Chapter 4 then discusses alternative representations of organization designs (output) to facilitate the decision to choose a particular design.

FIGURE 1 (of Introduction and Overview)   The Diamond Model (Segasti and Mitroff, 1973) Applied to the MAPS Book

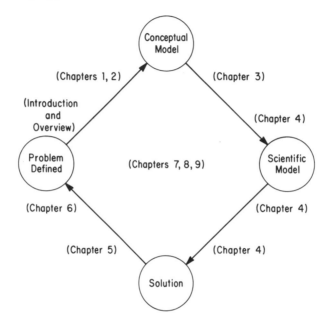

Finally, the chapter presents the derivation, characteristics, and functions of the six scientific models of MAPS (i.e., different combinations of input variables, computer analyses, and output formats).

Chapter 5 is concerned with the implementation process. The first section of the chapter presents the method used to select a single design to implement from the several designs generated by MAPS, or the modification (synthesis) of a design solution by the client system. This includes an extensive comparison between the current social systems design and the MAPS designs. The second section of Chapter 5 outlines several sets of procedures to implement the selected MAPS design. Different procedures are needed to implement different types of designs (e.g., a design for operational purposes versus a design for strategic planning). The third section of the chapter proposes a specific methodology to monitor the implementation process: to assess resistances to change and then to manage the dynamics of change. Chapter 6 provides the theory and methods of evaluating the impact of the design change and, describes the way and the extent to which the implemented design has actually made the social system more effective. Stated differently, Chapter 6 ends where the process first began, by assessing whether a problem that might require additional design changes still exists.

Chapters 7 and 8 address the holistic aspects of the Diamond Model. Chapter 7 considers the philosophical and systems views of design change and how to design effective problem-solving organizations, while Chapter 8 presents specific applications of the MAPS Design Technology that touch upon all the processes and states represented in Figure 1. The book concludes with Chapter 9, with discusses the ethics of applying MAPS to solve social systems problems, and considers the implicit and explicit components of the technology that behoove ethical discussions.

In summary, the primary plan of this book is to provide the reader with a thorough understanding of the MAPS Design Technology: its theoretical underpinnings, the formal steps of the technology, its current and potential applications, and the ethics involved in using the technology to create changes in social systems. While the material in this book is largely theoretical and normative, as opposed to empirical and descriptive, it should be emphasized that this book could not have been written without actual experiences and applications of MAPS in a number of organizational settings. While Chapter 8 presents a summary of the 13 applications to date, what is not so obvious is that these very applications greatly affected the material presented in prior chapters and our general understanding of the MAPS Design Technology. It is only because of a particular "logic" in sequencing the chapters, that is, a reconstructed logic versus a logic in use [see Kaplan (1964)] that the applications and research of MAPS were not presented earlier or even at the very beginning of this book. Basically it was felt that the reader first had to understand the underlying concepts and structure of the technology (even though these were developed as a result of the applications) before the reader could fully appreciate the applications and MAPS research presented in Chapter 8. A forthcoming book that concentrates on empirical research studies with the MAPS Design Technology is currently under way.

HOW THE BOOK WAS WRITTEN: PRACTICING WHAT WE PREACH

Perhaps the most exciting and, at the same time, reflective aspect of writing this book on the MAPS Design Technology was how the book was written. It was not written by one person, or even by a few people, in the traditional manner. Rather, this book is an actual example of applying the MAPS Design Technology to mobilize social and organizational resources to accomplish a specific set of objectives.

Twenty-five students were enrolled in my doctoral seminar on the MAPS Design Technology. Their areas of study include behavioral science, management information systems, accounting, operations research, environmental influences on business, hospital administration, psychological counseling, and public administration. These students were in various stages of their doctoral programs from those just entering to those who had completed their comprehensive examinations. Thus they represented a tremendous amount of resources and expertise that could be applied to a major research undertaking. In essence I expected that these students, through an organization design and development effort and through my leadership and climate-building activities, could make a major contribution to social science literature.

On the first day of class, I proposed that the participants in the seminar would be actively involved in learning MAPS through their own behavior and experiences in designing a learning organization. This organization would be composed of all seminar members, and early in the semester the MAPS Design Technology would be applied to mobilize the diverse and varied resources of the students into a number of subsystems to pursue their learning of the technology. The design of this learning organization would include "team building" of the subsystems formed by MAPS, the development of coordination and integrative mechanisms across the subsystems (i.e., a leadership structure), and an incentive system to motivate students to utilize their resources toward organizational objectives (e.g., an elaborate grading system, including peer evaluations). I also indicated that a major output of the learning organization would be a book on the MAPS Design Technology that would include the individual and /or group papers written by the students in their subsystems. To the extent that students contributed to the development of the book, their names would be acknowledged in the chapters to which they contributed. There appeared to be at least a reasonable expectation among the students that this was a worthwhile activity and objective, although there was considerable apprehension as to the scope of the project and whether the students actually had the expertise (and confidence) to participate successfully. Some of these apprehensions were never completely resolved but had to be confronted throughout the compilation of the book. Nevertheless, the first session concluded with the week's assignment: to read critically the most recent literature on the MAPS Design Technology, with particular emphasis on these aspects of MAPS that the student was most interested in exploring further.

The following week we had an all-day organization design workshop (eight hours). During the first part of the day members listed their names, education, interests, and other personal information on a large sheet of paper. Then each student wore the data sheet (taped to the shoulders) so others could read it, as everyone milled around the room. This gave everybody an opportunity to get acquainted quickly and to learn one another's area of expertise, interests, and interpersonal style. In the afternoon I outlined a general, tentative table of contents for the MAPS book. The students then generated specific task items representing the issues they felt should be written about for each category in the table of contents. This resulted in 60 task items. Each student then responded on a seven-point scale, according to how interested the individual was in working on each task item. The second part of the MAPS questionnaire listed the names of the 25 students (and myself), and asked each individual to indicate on a seven-point scale how well he could interact with each person in pursuit of task activities.

During the next week student responses to this MAPS questionnaire were inputed to the MAPS Computer Program, which transformed the data into alternative organization designs for the class. (The actual steps of the MAPS Design Technology are presented in Part II.) Several design solutions were discussed at the next class session and a six-cluster solution was chosen. Two groups subdivided further as members were given the opportunity to shift in and out of the groups, resulting in eight task groups for the learning organization. Appendix A presents the resulting organization design that was implemented in writing this book (i.e., groups of people working on particular clusters of tasks). The reader can compare this design with the final table of contents.

In the next week, each of the eight groups and each individual were asked to participate in a management by objectives (MBO) process to establish specific objectives for the accomplishment of organizational objectives (i.e., writing the MAPS book). These objectives included the following deadlines for: (a) literature reviews on particular topics, (b) sections of chapters, and (c) revised drafts. Insofar as possible each individual and group detailed the steps necessary for the successful completion of the task items assigned them (via the MAPS Computer Program and negotiated modifications among the groups), as well as the expected completion times. All the group statements were then combined into a Gantt chart—a table of overall tasks and schedules for the entire, organized seminar. During the MBO process a leadership structure developed in the organization. Each of the eight groups consensually chose a group member to represent them in a coordination board led by me (as suggested by members of the seminar). This board was responsible for coordinating the efforts of the various groups, acting as an information-processing link, and attempting to fully generate the commitment and motivation of individuals and groups to accomplish organizational tasks. The board met periodically throughout the semester as coordination issues arose.

The book was produced in three stages. First, extensive outlines of each chapter were due so that potential redundancies, gaps, and integration of chapters could be better anticipated and managed. Second, initial drafts were due several weeks after the outlines, and the coordination board provided detailed reviews to each group. Finally, based on these reviews, the groups submitted their revised chapters and complete bibliographies. To facilitate the review and revision process, the outline and the chapter drafts were entered by each group on a computer tape that contained a program for computerized editing. Thus there was easy acess to what each group had written; copies could be distributed to all groups; and it especially facilitated editing and modifying the chapters for changes without extensive retyping. When all the chapters were completed and edited, the text was right justified, paginated, and printed in upper and lower case. This original was then used to print the first copies of the book, which were sent to publishers for review.

In summary, throughout the semester every effort was made to apply our knowledge of the MAPS Design Technology, organization design and development, leadership behavior, and so forth, to foster a creative, effective, and challenging organization. While unanticipated problems arose frequently, the coordination board and the various groups met to resolve and manage these difficulties, some of which included problems of commitment, expertise, and information flow. To organize and write such a book was clearly a major undertaking, and only through the use of a technology to mobilize and make the most of the available resources could this project have been completed so efficiently. We also anticipated that this book would represent a major research contribution. The extent to which this is actually the case suggests the potential usefulness of the MAPS Design Technology beyond its earlier applications. We at least relied heavily on it for our own organizational needs, and therefore this book represents a test of the technology. Let the readers themselves judge its contribution, character, and style.

Part I
FOUNDATIONS OF SOCIAL SYSTEMS DESIGN

Chapter 1

Conceptual Models of Organization Design: Theory and Research

In collaboration with Afzalur Rahim*

Part I of this book contains two chapters that summarize and explore not only the different approaches to the field of organization or social systems design, but also the value assumptions and intervention strategies necessary to actually design or redesign an organization. First, Chapter 1 provides a conceptual framework for categorizing different approaches to organization theory, behavior, and design that pinpoints the basic kinds of variables (process vs. structure) and the basic value distinctions (Theory X vs. Theory Y) that have been considered by many researchers. Once this framework is used to give a historical perspective to the field, Chapter 1 concentrates on the contingency theory approaches to organization design that represent the major theoretical foundation for developing design technologies in general and the MAPS Design Technology in particular. In the contingency approach, the major issue is the "fit" among four major "elements": the organization's task environment, its technology, its members, and its design. These four contingency elements lead to the specification of a contingency model of organization design.

An analysis of how three of these contingency elements have changed over the past few decades (e.g., task environments, technologies, and people), while designs have largely remained unchanged, strongly suggests the increasing emergence of organization design problems and the need to address these emerging problems explicitly. In essence, because organization designs have not been basically altered as the other contingency elements have changed, an increasing mismatch and lack of "fit" among the four elements has been created. However, although contingency theorists have performed numerous empirical research studies to test and refine their theories, they have payed little attention to developing intervention methods and technologies to create design changes in organizations or in the values that necessarily guide the development and use of such technologies. Extensions of Contingency Theory by Kilmann and Mitroff not only highlight the need for additional organization designs and a more systematic specification of their different design

*This chapter also benefited from the contributions of Rose Constantino and Jerzy Zderkowski.

characteristics, but also emphasize the need to consider explicitly the values that implicitly underlie the development of various organization designs. Yet even with these extensions, the contingency studies have been principally descriptive as opposed to normative.

Chapter 2 focuses on the value issues and design problems raised in Chapter 1 by explicitly emphasizing the concept of Theory Y values and purposeful systems as criteria for developing and guiding structural interventions. Such a value position is taken only after considerable attention is given to the fundamental distinction of top-down versus participative design, and to what extent given research results versus ethical and value positions are to determine the choice of alternative structural interventions. Chapter 2 concludes with the expressed need for a technology that can systematically and efficiently design a variety of purposeful (Theory Y) social systems. Part I thus lays the groundwork for a presentation of the MAPS Design Technology, which is proposed to be highly relevant for addressing the increasing prevalence of organization design problems in a Theory Y (participative) manner.

A DEFINITION AND CONCEPTUAL FRAMEWORK FOR ORGANIZATION DESIGN

Organization design as a field of inquiry received some attention from a few scholars and practitioners during the first half of this century, but did not emerge as an independent discipline for research and study until quite recently. A comprehensive definition of design is proposed as follows: The arrangement and the process of arranging human, technological, economic, informational, and environmental resources to overcome physical, biological, and psychological limitations of any one individual so that various social systems objectives can be accomplished (Barnard, 1938). Stated differently, organization design is "the arrangement and the process of arranging the organization's structural characteristics to attain or improve the efficiency, effectiveness, and adaptability of the organization." (Kilmann, et al., 1976). Thus design is as much a process (designing) as a structure (the resultant design). From these definitions it seems there are several factors, such as people, environment, technology, and so forth, that should be considered in designing an organization.

Furthermore, organization design is distinguished at the microlevel from design at the macrolevel. The former perspective would include such issues as job design, job enrichment, and job enlargement. While these have received considerable research attention

(Davis and Werling, 1960; Davis, 1971; Trist and Bamforth, 1951), issues of job design do not necessarily generalize to the broader, more encompassing features of organization design (Davis and Canter, 1956). We are more interested in organization design at the macrolevel, which includes the process of differentiation and integration, the broadened terms of division of labor, or specialization, and coordination. An organization is differentiated into subunits with specialized objectives, policies, and tasks so that each unit can respond effectively to divergent needs of organization members, technologies, and environments. Effective organizations establish mechanisms of integration to channel specialized activities of different subunits toward the attainment of overall social systems objectives (Lawrence and Lorsch, 1967a). It should be stated that in most cases we will use the term social system as synonymously with organization. If there is a difference between the two terms, the former would include more diffuse social settings (e.g. communities, interorganizational and institutional settings), while the latter would more distinctly represent legal systems (e.g., business firms, schools, churches, government agencies, etc.). Although most of the literature and discussion derives mainly from organization concepts and research studies, we assume that these are applicable to broader social systems as is the MAPS Design Technology.

Although the management of organization design is generally conducted at an intuitive level by practitioners, we believe it needs to be raised above that level to a more scientific activity. This will require the integration and application of knowledge from the several social sciences that pertain to organizational phenomena. It also seems that research on organizational behavior consists mainly of an assessment and description of what organizations do. While these descriptive studies have made a valuable contribution to our understanding of organizational behavior, they need to be translated toward the development of normative organization design theories and technologies if social science knowledge is to be used for social change. To us organization theory and organization behavior are descriptive, while organization design is prescriptive and normative. It is the latter perspective that concerns us here. Thus the objective of this chapter is to facilitate the translation of descriptive to prescriptive theory, in addition to summarizing what organization design research has actually been conducted. The outcome of this chapter is meant not only to provide frameworks and substantive knowledge for furthering organization design, but also to serve as the theoretical and historical foundation for the MAPS Design Technology.

A Conceptual Framework

It is proposed that if one were to conduct a very comprehensive but qualitative factor analysis, or cluster analysis on all the empirical and theoretical research studies in the field of organizational behavior during the past 50 years (all social science disciplines included), two major dimensions would emerge that would help define and categorize fundamentally different types of approaches to this area of study. One dimension concerns the basic types of variables that researchers have emphasized, while the other deals with the basic types of values (i.e., normative guides to behavior) that were assumed explicitly or implicitly about the nature of man.

The concern of the first dimension is whether the causes of some behavioral phenomena are primarily identified as stemming from either process or structural variables (Thomas, 1976). Process variables portray the events, sequences, activities, and so forth, that occur over time, and are therefore a source to explain, predict, or change the behavioral phenomena in question. Structural variables, on the other hand, describe the conditions, forces, circumstances, and so forth, that are relatively constant over a period of time or are temporarily frozen in time. These structural variables are seen as shaping behavior, and hence as causing behavioral phenomena. While process variables place the individual, the organization, or the social systems in a sequence of events, structural variables place these social entities in a web of forces (Kilmann and Thomas, 1974).

Since a major concern of social science is explaining, predicting, and /or changing behavior, some value stance concerning the researcher's view of man or the world is always implicit or explicit in any research study (Mitroff, 1974). In other words, the development of hypotheses, the design of research studies, the interpretation of results, implications for action, and so on, are all influenced to some extent by the basic assumptions and values of the researcher. One value framework that appears to draw out two fundamentally different assumptions of man and world views is McGregor's Theory X and Theory Y. This framework was chosen also because it is phrased in terms of work-related behavior relevant to social systems.

Therefore McGregor's well-known Theory X and Theory Y will be utilized as the other axis in differentiating organization phenomena. These theories are based on the following assumptions (McGregor, 1960):

> Theory X—That an individual inherently dislikes work and will avoid work, and therefore the individual must be coerced, controlled,

directed and threatened with punishment to get him to achieve organizational goals. Further, the average person prefers to be directed, wants security, wishes to avoid responsibility and has little ambition.

Theory Y—That an individual exercises self-direction and self-control in the goals to which the person is committed. Commitment is a function of rewards associated with goal achievement. The average person seeks responsibility and the avoidance of responsibility is generally a consequence of past frustrating experiences. The average person has a high degree of imagination and creativity which is rarely utilized in modern organizational systems.

Chapter 2 will further explore these two different types of values in relationship to other value and personality typologies, small group task dimensions, and other value frameworks at the organizational level of analysis. As we will discover in Chapter 2, Theory X and Theory Y describe two very different orientations to designing social systems, top-down design (Theory X), and participative design (Theory Y).

The two axes (dimensions), Theory X–Theory Y, and Process–Structure, result in the following four approaches to organization design:

1. Theory X–Structure
2. Theory X–Process
3. Theory Y–Process
4. Theory Y–Structure

Figure 1.1 presents a matrix of these four different organization design approaches.

It should be stated at the outset that two of the above approaches to organization design, Theory X–Structure and Theory Y–Structure, relate explicitly to design. The other two approaches, Theory X–Process and Theory Y–Process, are not generally considered as subject matter for organization design because they focus on the events of behavior and not on the conditions. As will be indicated at several points in this book, it is not only difficult to clearly distinguish process from structure, but the two types of variables are highly interrelated and interactive. Processes occur within structures, and structures guide processes. Furthermore, as was indicated by the definitions of design given at the start of this chapter, by "design" we mean the process of designing as well as the resultant organization or social systems design. That is, design is both a verb (process) and a noun (structure). Perhaps the interrelationship of the two is evident

FIGURE 1.1   Four Approaches to Organization Design

Theory X

Scientific Management (Taylor, Gilbreths, Gantt, Emerson)	**Bureaucracy** (Weber, Parsons, Downs)
Functional or Process School (Fayol, Gulick and Urwick, Mooney and Reiley, Koontz and O'Donnell)	**Contingency Theory** (Lawrence and Lorsch, Burns and Stalker, Woodward, Thompson)
Human Relations (Mayo, Roethlisberger, Dickson)	**Socio-Technical Systems** (Trist and Bamforth, Rice, Davis, Emery and Trist)
Behavioral Humanism (Maslow, McGregor, Argyris, Likert)	**The MAPS Approach** (Kilmann and McKelvey)

Process (left axis)   Structure (right axis)

Theory Y

when we realize that any intervention to design or redesign a social system is necessarily a process of designing (e.g., a consultant interacting with a client system to bring about change over a period of time), and therefore only those definitions, concepts, or frameworks of design that are purely descriptive could actually portray design strictly as a structure. However, since this chapter and this book is concerned with normative design (i.e., technologies for changing the design of social systems), we must consider both process and structural approaches to the subject. Incidentally, the distinction between designing and the resultant design will be pursued further in Chapter 2 as paramount for developing a theory of structural intervention.

Behavioral phenomena never fit clearly, neatly, and exactly into the categories of any conceptual framework or taxonomy, whether it is the framework we proposed or some other typology for classifying approaches to organization design. Not only are research approaches not so narrow and well-defined (i.e., most approaches will naturally cut across the boundaries of any typology), but complex phenomena such as social systems design are so multidimensional that it is necessarily a difficult and imprecise task to sort such approaches via only one or two dimensions. Nevertheless, rather than avoiding the issue altogether and consequently not give any order or framework to the field of organization design, we have proposed the Process–Structure, Theory X–Theory Y framework for present purposes. Using this framework, we have categorized each major research approach by what appeared to be its primary focus on variables and values, realizing that aspects of it may also be relevant to some of the other quadrants. Thus the reader will have to assess not only the usefulness of this framework for drawing key distinctions in the organization design field (toward the development of technologies to effectively design and redesign social systems) but also how well the various research approaches have actually been classified and presented by the chosen (intuitively derived) framework.

Theory X—Structure

This approach to organization design subscribes to Theory X values. The design decisions do not take into account the needs, values, and aspirations of the lower level members of the organization. The design decisions are made at the top of the organization and are imposed on its lower level members. The design decisions and their implementation are top-down because it is assumed that the lower level members do not have the expertise, information, or initiative to participate in these decisions and implementations.

Under this approach, design decisions involve mainly structural considerations of member skills, systems of control, hierarchy of authority, and so on. Completely bureaucratic organizations fall into this category. Classical organization designs, of which bureaucracy is one, have dominated management thinking during the first half of this century. It had its origins in the ideas of Adam Smith, who set forth the principles of specialization in his work entitled *An Inquiry into the Nature and Causes of the Wealth of Nations* (1776). But it was not until the beginning of this century that the principles of classical design were presented by Max Weber (see Gerth and Mills, 1958; Weber, 1947).

About 1910, particularly concerned with military, religious, and governmental organizations, Weber suggested that all organizations were moving toward an ideal type of structure called bureaucracy. He characterized bureaucracy as follows: a high degree of specialization or division of work at all organizational levels, a hierarchy of authority, use of a set of rules and procedures for conducting daily organizational functions, and impersonality in decision making.

Weber's theory proposes that human beings can only function in an organization that is highly structured and hierarchical. He also believed in the diminution or even obliteration of human variability from an organization's functions. This approach relies heavily on structure and a static patterning of behavior and functions based upon a rigid set of rules and specialized tasks. Although Weber was aware of the dysfunctional consequences of bureaucratic structures and processes, he maintained that these were appropriate for the efficient functioning of organizations (Weber, 1947: 34). Perrow (1973: 34) gives an account of bureaucracy's entry into organizations:

> At first, with his (Weber's) celebration of the efficiency of bureaucracy, he was received with only reluctant respect, and even hostility. All writers were against bureaucracy. But it turned out, surprisingly, that managers were not. When asked, they acknowledged that they preferred clear lines of communication, clear specializations, and clear knowledge of whom they were responsible to.

Bureaucracy has negative connotations for most people. It suggests rigid rules and regulations, hierarchy, and narrow specialization that can constrain and dehumanize creative and innovative organization members. Yet every organization has a form of bureaucratization to some extent, exhibiting a more or less stable patterning of behavior and order based upon a structure of roles and specialized tasks.

Theory X—Process

This approach to organization design considers mainly the economic needs of organization members. Since the assumptions about human behavior are Theory X, organization decisions, communications, information flow are one way top-down. Lateral and upward communication and information flow are almost nonexistent. Taylor's scientific management and the functional, or process, school of management hold Theory X assumptions about human behavior but have attempted to study some of the process issues that the model of bureaucracy failed to consider.

Taylor (1947) was the founder of the scientific management movement. He emphasized "maximum prosperity" for both employers and workers. He believed that this could be achieved only by bringing about a complete "mental revolution" on the part of management and labor.

Scientific management combines a study of the physical capabilities of a worker with an economic approach that views the individual as driven by fear of physical and mental starvation and the search for monetary rewards. The central tenet of this approach is that if material rewards are closely related to work endeavors, the individual worker will respond with the maximum performance of which he is capable (Etzioni, 1964: 21). Taylor was not alone in the development of scientific management. Associates in the promotion of his ideas were Frank Bunker Gilbreth (1914) and Lillian Mollar Gilbreth, who worked toward improving the totality of man and his environment.

The Gilbreths played a primary role in the development of time and motion studies and task simplification. They were interested in the development of man through effective training, work methods, improved environment and task, and healthy psychological outlook. They believed the individual worker or manager must be directed and tailored toward the attainment of organizational goals. Along with Taylor the Gilbreths believed that employees can be scientifically selected, trained, and taught (George, 1968: 99).

Another promulgator and close associate of Taylor was Henry L. Gantt (1919). Gantt's belief about organization design centered on a task and system for the worker. He contended that a wage system should provide fair remuneration regardless of worker productivity. He developed the Gantt chart, which plots each task planned and completed on one axis and the time elapsed on the other. It is a kind of control system placed upon the individual worker to ensure that all tasks performed are accomplished in accordance with organizational objectives.

As was mentioned earlier scientific management did not provide any means for input of workers or lower level organization members into organization design decisions. Taylor insisted on the separation of planning from doing, the former to be done by management. As a result, the design decisions are top-down (Theory X) rather than participative (Theory Y).

Conceptualization of design approaches aimed at organizational processes were also suggested by Fayol (1949). He suggested that managerial processes such as planning, organizing, directing, coordinating, and controlling are requirements for efficient and effective task fulfillment. Some of the issues inherent in this view of organization design are (Fayol, 1949: 20–40):

1. Division of labor—refers to task specialization.
2. Unity of command—an employee should receive orders from only one superior.
3. Unity of direction—each group of activities having one objective must have one head and one plan.
4. Centralization—everything that increases the importance of the subordinate's role is decentralization; everything that decreases it is centralization.

These design concepts were also identified by Babbage (1969: 73), Gulick and Urwick (1937: 107), and Mooney (1969: 105). Babbage contended that division of labor among workers was the most important principle on which the economy of a manufacturer depended. Gulick and Urwick distinguished between design by function (process specialization) and design by product (according to output). Gulick (1969) identified coordination as the most important principle of organization. Mooney and Reiley (1931) broadened this principle beyond the business world to the state, the military, and the church. Koontz and O'Donnell (1972) have attempted to explain and improve all five managerial functions or processes advocated by Fayol and other writers.

Unlike scientific management, the functional school deals with the macro aspect of organization design, such as the process of dividing the organization into departments, coordinating the departments, managing the hierarchy, and so on. The design decisions are top-down, however, as in scientific management, and therefore a Theory X orientation is suggested.

Theory Y—Process

This approach to organization design concerns processes that may occur in the social system in a Theory Y manner. Thus communication can be two-way, decision making can be participative, leadership or interactions between superiors and subordinates can be collaborative, and so forth. But this approach largely ignores the structures within the organization and how they might limit the extent of Theory Y, discretionary behavior that can be fostered.

Included in the Theory Y–Process is the human relations movement pioneered by Elton Mayo in the early 1930s. Mayo believed that factors related to emotions and feelings were more important than rationality or logic. The major findings of Mayo's Hawthorne studies (1933) were as follows:

1. A work group develops its own norms, values, and attitudes and exerts strong social control upon the individual members of the group and their behavior at work.
2. Physical conditions have little influence on the performance and attitudes of workers in comparison to their need for security, recognition, and belongingness.

Mayo has made important contributions to the understanding of people at work. Although he is criticized for the design of his experiments (Carey, 1967), many of his ideas are still valid today and have been the subject of scholarly discussion.

In reaction to the rapid growth of the classical approaches to design and management of organizations, Walker and Guest (1952), Argyris (1957), McGregor (1960), Likert (1967), Bennis (1966a), and others, began to emphasize change in social systems processes for improving organizational effectiveness. While human relationists (Mayo, 1933; Roethlisberger and Dickson, 1938; Roethlisberger, 1941) sought only to modify classical organization theory, the behavioral humanists are inclined to seek radical change. Argyris explores the conflict between the individual and the organization in psychological terms (1957), and considers the needs of the two to be antithetical. He observes that contemporary organizations expect mature individuals to behave passively and dependently. Argyris views this as dysfunctional and believes that behavioral scientists should promote a synthesis.

McGregor's (1960) model of man had the greatest impact on the value systems and change programs of the behavioral humanists. His two cosmologies (Theory X and Theory Y) have been the basis for one dimension in Figure 1.1. While McGregor prefers the Theory Y cosmology, he admits that organizational and other constraints may make Theory X management more appropriate. Therefore, unlike those of other humanists, there is an element of contingency in McGregor's model.

Likert (1967) states that all organizational systems fall into one of four categories:

System 1: Exploitive
System 2: Benevolent authoritative
System 3: Consultative
System 4: Participative

Systems 1 and 4 are comparable to McGregor's cosmologies of Theory X and Theory Y. But while Likert believes that effective organizations must function near the democratic extreme of System 4, McGregor, as indicated above, takes a contingency view of his cosmologies.

The beliefs of the humanists about effective organization design follow from their models of man. The humanists believe that organizational processes should be characterized by Theory Y, two-way communication and information flow, and democratic leadership. They prefer that organization designs promote generalist skills, flat hierarchies, informal procedures, temporary states, need-oriented jobs, fluid careers, and so forth.

The major programs for organizational change developed by the humanists are the organizational development (OD) methods (Bennis, 1966; Bennis, et al., 1969; French and Bell, 1973; Margulies and Raia, 1972; Schein, 1969) among which T-group or sensitivity training is the underlying discipline (Argyris, 1962, 1970b; Bradford, et al., 1964). Sensitivity training is designed to bring about individual change through a group method. Viewed in another way, the goals of the T-group are the individual attainment of what Argyris (1970b) calls "pyramidal values." He believes that these values influence organizational performance to a great extent. In a way the T-group focuses on a person as Theory Y, capable of change toward greater achievement. Primarily it emphasizes processes of members' trust in leadership, members taking leadership roles, and members' decreasing reliance on authority and increasing reliance on task ability.

The OD programs are based on Theory Y values and are oriented mainly to process issues rather than structural ones. OD programs are not generally formulated to address the structural design problems of an organization. For example, in an article on unresolved problems facing OD, Bennis (1969b) has stated:

> Organization development pays lip-service to structural (or technological) changes while relying only on a change in organizational "climate"...This is no mean feat, of course, but again - related to the preceding point - it is seriously restrictive. The Organizational Development literature is filled with vague promises about "restructuring" or "organization design" but with some exceptions few outcomes are actually demonstrated.

Theory Y—Structure

Much has been learned from the foregoing approaches to management and organization design: Theory X–Structure (bureaucracy),

Theory X–Process (scientific management and the functional school), and Theory Y–Process (human relations and behavioral humanism). However, three major criticisms can be leveled against the first two (classical) approaches:

1. Design decisions are top-down because it is assumed that people at the lower level of the organization do not have the expertise, information, or willingness to make design decisions.
2. Values, feelings, and attitudes are not taken into account in design decisions. In other words, it is assumed that people's feelings and values should not enter into the process of decision making-decisions should be entirely rational.
3. The classicists attempted to develop one "best" design for all organizations by considering the forces internal to the organizations, especially the task variable. They did not give attention to the effect of environment or technology on organization design.

A major criticism of the Theory Y–Process approach, however, is that processes are expected to take place in a Theory Y manner within the given Theory X, bureaucratic organization design. This approach states in effect: Take care of the needs, values, and feelings of the organizational members; processes will be more effective and this will assure the effectiveness of the entire organization. But a largely Theory X, bureaucratic organization design (structure) will necessarily limit the degree of freedom or discretion that members have to actually engage in Theory Y processes. In fact it may be quite difficult to have two-way communication, trusting and open interpersonal interaction, and participative decision making when the bureaucratic design has rules and procedures that stifle such processes.

In order to overcome the limitations and constraints of Theory X structures on Theory Y processes, as well as to requestion the assumptions and limitations of the Theory X–Structure and Theory X–Process approaches, the structural design of organizations has recently re-emerged as a distinct area of study (Kilmann, et al., 1976). Research in this area has taken three directions: Socio-technical Systems, Contingency Theory, and the MAPS approach. Socio-Technical Systems and the MAPS approach assume Theory Y values about people and designs, and are concerned mostly with the structural aspects of an organization.

The concept of sociotechnical systems was first developed by the Tavistock Institute of Human Relations in England. The initial study by Trist and Bamforth (1951) demonstrated how a change in job design (i.e., the interrelationships of human and technical resources) had significant effects on member performance and satisfaction and on subunit productivity. Since then studies by Rice (1958), Davis and Canter (1956), Conant and Kilbridge (l965), and Davis and Werling (1960) have provided further documentation and elaboration on the nature of changing the structural properties of sociotechnical interfaces. These studies concentrate on the design of jobs within a given department or section as opposed to major structural changes for the entire organization, but they do imply a Theory Y orientation. As Davis suggests, however: "As regards the design requirements for larger organizational units with more complex interactions, it would be hazardous to draw any conclusions for the studies reviewed."

Broader structural studies have been performed by Lawrence and Lorsch, and others (Lawrence and Lorsch, 1967a, 1967b, 1969; Lorsch and Lawrence, 1970; Morse and Lorsch, 1970). As shown in Figure 1.1, however, Contingency Theory is largely a Theory X approach to structure since, as we will discuss, it implies top-down design decisions and implementation, and little attention is given to actually developing Theory Y systems. Even a recent addition to Contingency Theory in design (Morse and Lorsch, 1970) that explores the Theory X and Theory Y dispositions of organizational members, still implies a Theory X design process to bring about a Theory Y type of design. (See Chapter 2 for a more detailed discussion of this point.) However, since the development of Contingency Theory is quite recent, it seems more appropriate for purposes of discussion to present the concepts and issues of contingency theory with those of sociotechnical systems and the MAPS approach rather than presenting it along with the classical bureaucracy theory discussed under the Theory X–Structure category in Figure 1.1. In other words, the actual concepts of contingency theory fit better with the two Theory Y–Structure approaches shown in Figure 1.1, even though there is a difference in value orientation (Theory X vs. Theory Y).

Because of the importance of these recent approaches to organization design in general and to the MAPS Design Technology in particular, the remainder of this chapter will concentrate on the contingency theories. To a large extent the latter serve as the impetus to the MAPS approach, although there are differences in value orientation. Since this entire book focuses on the MAPS approach we will not review it at this time, but merely indicate that it is primarily a Theory Y–Structure technology although it heavily relies on Theory Y–Process for its application.

CONTINGENCY THEORIES OF ORGANIZATION DESIGN

Contingency theorists, as best exemplified by Lorsch and Lawrence, assert that "the internal functioning of the organization must be consistent with the demand of the organization's task, technology, or external environment, and the needs of its members, if the organization is to be effective" (1970: 1). In other words, instead of finding the one best design for all organizations, the researchers have examined the functioning of organizations in relation to their internal conditions and member needs (Theory X or Theory Y) and the external conditions facing the organization (stable or dynamic). To state it more concisely, this approach leads to the development of a contingency model of organization design: the design of an organization is contingent upon both internal needs and external requirements.

Several other management and organization theorists have implied bipolar or contingency approaches to organization design. For example, Bennis (1966a) differentiated between the bureaucratic and the organic-adaptive design; Burns and Stalker (1961) distinguished between the mechanistic and organic structure; Katz and Kahn (1966) discussed the differences between the hierarchical and democratic types of organization design; Parsons (1960) differentiated the general bureaucratic from the professional organization; and Stinchcombe (1959) described the bureaucratic versus the craft form of organization. Some of these behavioral scientists explicitly indicated that the design of an organization should be organic-adaptive or democratic rather than mechanistic or bureaucratic (Argyris, 1957; Bennis, 1966). However, as the contingency theorists suggest, the type of structure suitable for an organization depends on the situation. In the following paragraphs, two important lines of research that have examined major situational factors will be discussed. The first deals with the relationship between technology and organization design. The second investigates a relationship between environment and organization design. From these two lines of research, an overall model of contingency theory will be proposed.

Technology and Organization Design

Studies by Burns and Stalker (1961), Woodward (1965), and Perrow (1967) reported technology as a major determinant of organization design. Burns and Stalker studied the difficulties faced by twenty

British firms in introducing electronic development work and found that organizations can move between "mechanistic" and "organic" designs depending on the situation. Organization units that have tasks which are stable and well defined and hierarchical authority pattern are classed as mechanistic. Classified as organic, on the other hand, are organization units that are flexible, have less specifically defined tasks, and relationships and communications that are informal (nonhierarchical) rather than formal. The conclusions of the study were that in firms in which innovation is in constant demand, the organic type of design is appropriate. The mechanistic type of design is most appropriate for an organization that is preoccupied with maintaining the status quo. Burns and Stalker characterized whole organizations as mechanistic or organic. As will be seen later, an organization is likely to contain both organic and mechanistic units simultaneously.

The most extensive study on the relationship between technology and organization design was conducted by Joan Woodward (1965) and her colleagues on a number of industrial enterprises in the South Essex area of England. They found that organization design differences were not explained by company size, type of industry, or executive personalities. Instead the study found that technology is a major link to organization design and effectiveness. Specifically, Woodward classified the firms she studied into three major categories of unit, mass, and process production along a scale of "technical complexity." Whereas successful firms (defined in terms of profits and growth rates) with mass production technologies tended to have mechanistic organization designs, successful firms with unit or process production technologies tended to have organic designs.

These results can best be understood by analyzing natural business functions: product development, production, and marketing. In job-order or unit firms the cycle begins with marketing, that is, finding a customer to secure an order. Development of the product is a critical activity because the product must meet customer specifications. Production comes last in the cycle. The organic structure is most effective for promoting the necessary communication and integration of activities to meet the requirements of job-order or unit production. In the middle of the technological continuum is mass production. The market exists for a more or less standardized product, and the task is to deliver the product. Marketing comes last in the cycle. Woodward found the mechanistic design to be appropriate for such a technology. She observed that the classicists apparently had considered only mass-production technologies in formulating principles of organization. The process production is at the other end of the technological continuum, where the cycle starts with the development of a product. But the critical function is marketing because success depends on continuous demand for the product(s). Production comes last in the cycle. Woodward observed that the design of the organization in this case is unimportant insofar as the success of the firm is concerned.

In essence Woodward's results suggest that a curvilinear relationship exists between technology and design. Perrow (1967) reexamined Woodward's categories, which led him to propose to fold her scale in the middle. This produced a technological continuum from routine to nonroutine work. Using the new scale, the relationship between design and technology became linear rather than curvilinear. However, Perrow used the term technology to mean characteristics of information used in work process, which is different from the production technology referred to by Woodward.

Several other studies have been undertaken to test the relationship between technology and design since the publication of Woodward's work (Hage and Aiken, 1967; Harvey, 1968; Hickson, et al., 1969; Mohr, 1971). While some of these studies found relationships between the two types of variables, others did not. Lack of a commonly accepted definition of technology and differences in measurement and sampling are probably the sources of discrepancy. As a consequence, knowledge in this area has not advanced much further.

The major problems with the studies by Woodward, Perrow, and others are that these researchers fail to take into account the existence of multiple technologies within an organization, and offer little insight into the process of change by ignoring the importance of the internal and external environments of an organization.

Environment and Organization Design

The foregoing studies attempted to establish the relationship between technology and organization design. Another approach has been pursued by a number of researchers, who examined the relationships of the organization to its environment (Chandler, 1962; Dill, 1958; Galbraith, 1970; Lawrence and Lorsch, 1969; Morse and Lorsch, 1970; Thompson, 1967).

In a broad sense the environment of an organization is the universe of elements (e.g., other organizations, the culture of the society, political rules and regulations, technological developments, clients, etc.) that surround the organization (Dill, 1958). One cannot comprehend the effects of all these elements on an organization; one can only consider the relevant objects of the environment that are significantly related to the elements or objectives within an organization (Bobbitt, et al., 1974: 13). This concept of relevant environment is very close to what Dill (1958), and Thompson (1967) call the task environment.

Lawrence and Lorsch (1967a) used a slightly different approach in conceptualizing environment. They found that one useful way to conceive of the environment of an organization was to look at it from the organization outward. This approach is based on the assumption that an organization is an active system which tends to reach out and manage its otherwise overly complex surroundings. This is accomplished as the organization becomes differentiated into various subsystems, where each subsystem is expected to address a different segment of the organization's environment (Lawrence and Lorsch, 1967b). Lawrence and Lorsch suggest that industrial organizations segment their environments into three basic parts: a market subenvironment, a scientific subenvironment, and a technical-economic subenvironment, and require the different organizational subsystems to manage these subenvironments. Data about the environmental uncertainty facing these subsystems, sales, production, and research, were collected from ten organizations. This was done by considering (1) different rates of change of information, (2) different time span of feedback about results, and (3) different certainty of information at a given time.

For example, the scientific subenvironment (managed by the research and development subsystem) was found to have low certainty of information, longer time span of feedback about results, and greater rate of change than the market subenvironment (managed by a sales subsystem) and the technical-economic subenvironment (managed by a production subsystem). Only the rate of change in the scientific subenvironment was not found to differ from the market subenvironment.

Lawrence and Lorsch also found that the degree of certainty in different subenvironments was related to the degree of differentiation among different subsystems. Differentiation was defined as "the differences in cognitive and emotional orientation among managers in different units and the differences in formal structure among units" (Lorsch and Lawrence, 1970: 6). Lawrence and Lorsch measured differentiation in terms of the following variables:

1. The formality of structure (formal rules and procedures vs. the opposite condition).

2. Goal orientation (concern with market goals vs. concern with cost, quality, and efficiency goals, vs. concern with specific goals).
3. Time orientation (long term vs. short term).
4. Interpersonal orientation (concern for task vs. concern for people).

Since each subsystem must respond effectively to its relevant subenvironment, the subsystem tends to become more differentiated in heterogeneous or uncertain environments than in homogeneous or certain ones. This creates, however, the problem of attaining integration, defined by Lawrence and Lorsch as "achieving unity of effort among the various subsystems in the accomplishment of the organization's task" (Lawrence and Lorsch, 1967a: 4). Differentiation and integration are antagonistic states; the more differentiated an organization is, the more elaborate the integrative devices must be. Lawrence and Lorsch found that subsystems which operate effectively in different environments have different degrees of differentiation and integration (Lawrence and Lorsch, 1967b). Executives in the functional subsystems responsible for managing dynamic environments develop greater degrees of differentiation than those who face more stable environments. Differences in degrees of integration are also accounted for by differences in environments. It is important to emphasize that the effective organizations not only attained more effective integration among the subsystems requiring interdependence than the less effective organizations, but they also accomplished greater differentiation among these subunits (Lorsch and Lawrence, 1970).

While not expressed explicitly as a contingency approach, the concepts and propositions by Thompson (1967) complement the notion of an organization being designed into particular subsystems to address elements in the environment. Specifically, Thompson focuses on types of interdependencies and costs of coordination. He distinguishes among three types of interdependencies: pooled (independent combinations of subsystem outputs), sequential (ordered input-output transactions among subsystems), and reciprocal (mutual, simultaneous interactions). Thompson stipulates that various costs arise as a result of the need for coordination of input and output transactions among subsystems. He assumes that interdependencies grouped within a subsystem do not entail coordination costs, whereas coordination between or among subsystems requires certain additional integrative mechanisms to facilitate the handling of the interdependencies. Consequently, Thompson suggests that organizations should differentiate their subsystems (i.e., group activities) so that the more costly forms of interdependencies are contained within these subsystems, while the less costly forms can be coordinated between the subsystems.

Galbraith (1970) found some illustrative empirical support for Thompson's approach. Galbraith defines the design problem as "one of balancing the benefits of process specialization against the costs of coordination. Process specialization is important for effective performance on subsystem tasks while coordination is important for integrating all the subsystem tasks for effective completion of the whole task." (Galbraith, 1970: 119). This design objective implies concurrent emphasis on both differentiation and integration.

The studies mentioned above all support the contingency approach to organization design. They were conducted in business organizations, using different research methodologies: case study, historical analysis, questionnaire survey, and interviews. A recent study in a nonbusiness situation by Blau and Schoenherr (1971) supported the findings of Lawrence and Lorsch. This study of 53 state employment offices of the United States and its territories found: (1) increasing the size of an organization creates design differentiation along various dimensions at decelerating rates; (2) design differentiation increases the need for managerial manpower; (3) differentiation (i.e., hierarchical, vertical, and occupational) is positively related to environmental diversity.

A Contingency Model of Organization Design

The contingency theories grew out of a Theory X–Structure approach (especially from the findings of Burns' and Stalker's research). While Theory X–Structure, or bureaucracy, was considered by the classicists as the best design for all organizations, and Bennis (organic-adaptive) and Likert (System 4) implied that Theory Y–Process and Structure was always best, the contingency approach suggests that each may be appropriate depending on the situation. The important point is that contingency means the consideration of alternative design configurations and that this theory is developed to help specify conditions, such as technology, people, task environment, and so on, that determine which type of design would be most effective. However, as we will discuss shortly and again in Chapter 9, it would be rather impersonal and uninvolved to suggest that fitting the subsystem characteristics to its subenvironment on certain design (structural) variables is the same as fitting certain value orientations to the design process. The latter is not based on impersonal, objective research alone, but is also based (or should be) on the type of value orientation we would like to see (i.e., a Theory X or a Theory Y world). It is through structural interventions (discussed in Chapter 2) that we can alter not only the fit of structural variables but also the attitudes and values of organizational members. As behavioral scientists and change agents, we cannot separate our values from our interventions, so we might as well be explicit concerning the value orientation that underlies our interventions, all "research" aside.

Figure 1.2 represents an integration of the various contingency approaches to organization design. The model illustrates the various interrelationships among the following:

1. The organization's members (i.e., whether Theory X or Theory Y better describes their motivational tendencies).
2. The organization's task environment (i.e., whether it is stable and homogeneous, or complex, turbulent, and dynamic).
3. The organization's technology (i.e., whether it is routine or nonroutine).
4. The design of the organization (i.e., whether it is mechanistic or organic).

It is anticipated that the more these four factors are compatible and consistent with each other, the greater the potential and likelihood of effective organizational performance. For example, if the members of an organization (or some departments) wish to operate by Theory Y principles, then the organization design representing organic forms would be most likely to create the conditions under which Theory Y behavior could be manifested. However, if the task environment in which the organization (or department) exists is most compatible with a rigid and highly formalized design (e.g., a stable environment requiring programmed, technical efficiency of operations with extreme specialization), then a design based on Theory Y conditions might not result in organizational behavior that best satisfies its task environment. Thus in a given situation a trade-off might have to be made between utilizing a particular design to address the task environment and the nature of the technology, while simultaneously attempting to develop a design that supports the behavioral tendencies and desires of organizational members. Also, if the various departments of the organization are designed differently to address differentiated task environments and technologies requires, as Lawrence and Lorsch (1967a) found, special integrative mechanisms to coordinate the departmental activities into a functioning whole.

FIGURE 1.2   A Contingency Model of Organization Design

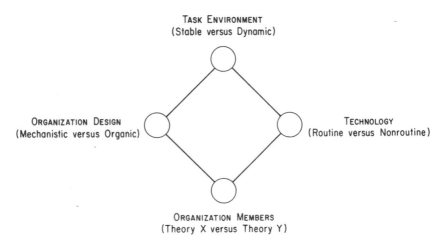

TASK ENVIRONMENT
(Stable versus Dynamic)

ORGANIZATION DESIGN
(Mechanistic versus Organic)

TECHNOLOGY
(Routine versus Nonroutine)

ORGANIZATION MEMBERS
(Theory X versus Theory Y)

The extent to which the various elements in Figure 1.2 do not fit or are not congruent with each other limits the potential for organizational effectiveness. For example, if the design of the organization were mechanistic or bureaucratic in a dynamic task environment, the organization would have highly specific rules and procedures to control organizational behavior. As the environment changed, however, the rules and procedures would quickly become outdated and irrelevant. As soon as the organization developed another set of highly prescribed rules and regulations, these too would become more and more irrelevant over time. Therefore to maintain the bureaucratic design in the face of a dynamic and changing environment, the organization would spend most of its time changing rules and role specifications rather than engaging in effective task behavior. In contrast, if the task environment were stable, an organic organization design would be inefficient, since there would not be prescribed rules and regulations for addressing the well-defined and stable task requirements. Instead the discretion that organizational members would have in such a design might very well be misdirected and not properly guided to the correct set of routine tasks.

THE EMERGENCE OF ORGANIZATION DESIGN PROBLEMS

It is interesting to observe that there have been some characteristic changes in several elements shown in Figure 1.2. In particular, the environments of organizations have been becoming increasingly complex and dynamic over time. Thirty or forty years ago the environment was much more stable. Product cycles were longer, the time between innovation and the resulting product was also longer, less resources were directed to research and development (R & D), and technologies were not yet developed that fostered an information-processing revolution. In the last two decades this situation has changed drastically. The economy, the political scene, technological developments, information processing, and research and development, among other things, are fostering more dynamic and changing environments. Toffler's (1970) *Future Shock* is an excellent portrayal of these developments. While some subenvironments may always be more stable than others, the environment as a whole has become increasingly dynamic. In addition, technologies available to organizations have become more complex and nonroutine.

At the same time individuals in our society have also been undergoing changes. While there will always be individual differences, on the whole American society has become more affluent over the past forty years, and consequently individuals have become motivated more by higher order needs such as esteem, autonomy, and self-actualization than by strictly economic and security needs (Maslow, 1954). The former situation is more Theory Y, while the latter is predominantly Theory X. Furthermore since the level of individual education has also been increasing over time, individuals on the whole have come to expect more responsibility, involvement, and challenge on their jobs (Theory Y characteristics) and are less willing to be satisfied with simple and routine work. The recent uprisings of workers on the assembly line lend support to these arguments (Wall Street Journal, 1971). The literature on work motivation, satisfaction, and performance, is another indicator of this trend (Bucklow, 1966; Vroom, 1965). Mainly older, less educated, and individuals of lower economic status are willing to work under Theory X conditions, which suggests the occurrence of a value change in our society.

What is particularly relevant to the preceding discussion, and an indication that the environments, technologies, and individuals in our society are moving toward dynamic, nonroutine, and Theory Y conditions, is that many organization designs have remained largely bureaucratic and mechanistic! Some research supports the view that not only have organization designs not tended to change, but that their form is actually predicted by the circumstances and the period in which they were first formed (i.e., by capital investments, given technologies, assumptions about culture, stereotyped notions of whether an organization should be designed by product or by function, etc.) (Stinchcombe, 1959). Basically there have been few dramatic changes in the designs of large-scale organizations. The changes that have been seen are largely evolutionary, without planned action steps.

This situation has important implications for the contingency model shown in Figure 1.2, for it suggests that on the whole a greater imbalance or lack of fit has occurred among the four contingency elements, assuming that at some earlier time, say thirty or forty years ago, there actually was a better fit. This is likely, however, since at that time "everything" was generally stable, simple, routine, and economic /security needs were paramount. At present, environments, technologies and people have changed in the direction of greater complexity and needs for autonomy and self-actualization are more pervasive. It will therefore not be surprising to find the greater presence of organization design problems; problems that stem from a mismatch among the elements in the contingency model because organization designs in general have not been altered and adapted to changing internal and external conditions.

In a sense the very motivation to write this book and to develop the MAPS Design Technology was the perception and perhaps the recognition that problems of organization design will necessarily increase, and that knowledge, methods and technologies to approach this problem are therefore essential. To ignore such design problems and to devote time, energy, and resources to solve other problems (i.e., to enhance the fit among the contingency elements excluding organization design) would increase the likelihood of a Type III error: the probability of solving the wrong problem when one should haved solved the right problem (Mitroff and Featheringham, 1974). This Type III error is applied to organization design in later chapters of this book: here, however, it was important to suggest why organization design problems are likely to become increasingly salient. It should be added that organization design variables can be altered much more readily than attempting to change the environment of the organization, the state of the technology, or the personalities of individuals. While these can be changed in the long run (e.g., by changing consumer attitudes, technological developments, education and training programs, etc.), the design of the organization can be changed in the short run because it contains variables that are under the direct and immediate control of top management and the members of the organization or social system. Therefore design problems are not only becoming increasingly pronounced, but the solution or management of these problems is feasible in the short run to improve individual, organizational, and societal effectiveness. Chapter 6 will present an overall model of organizational effectiveness and will suggest how design changes can address each component of effectiveness.

With the foregoing discussion on environmental and societal changes in the United States as they pertain to the fit of elements in the contingency model, it is interesting to note that there have been very limited tests of the contingency theory of organization design in the context of cultures other than those of the United States and the United Kingdom. Dill (1958) found in his study of two Norwegian firms that managers operating in relatively dynamic environments had more autonomy than those operating in fairly stable environments. The study by Negandhi and Reimann (1972) in India suggested that a slightly modified version of this theory is appropriate in the context of a developing country. The authors could not say with certainty that 'organization effectiveness requires decentralization under stable, noncompetitive conditions. Rather we would suggest that dynamic, competitive market conditions make decentralization more important to organizational effectiveness than do stable, noncompetitive conditions' (Negandhi and Reimann, 1972: 144).

Ruedi and Lawrence (1970) conducted an in-depth study of a German plastics firm to make comparisons with a group of six U.S. firms operating in the same highly technical and dynamic industry. Results show that there is a contingent relationship between culture, the nature of tasks, and task effectiveness. The implications of the study as observed by the authors are that "given conditions of a free world market, nations will either have to specialize in industries whose technological complexity 'fits' their culturally determined approach to organization or they will have to change their culture. The only other logical alternative would be to step back to trade restrictions and the formation of cartels which protect less efficient industry" (Reudi and Lawrence, 1970: 83).

Thus it seems that the basic aspects of the contingency model are applicable to different cultural settings, although the concept of culture itself might have to be included in the model for cross-cultural design considerations and to make the model itself more dynamic by highlighting cultural as well as value changes that can take place within a given culture.

EXTENSIONS OF CONTINGENCY THEORY

One of the major problems of the contingency theorists discussed earlier is that they provide limited options for organization designers to create new organizations or redesign existing ones. The contingency theorists assume that organizations are either mechanistic or organic, people are either Theory X or Theory Y, task environments are either stable or dynamic, and technology is either routine or non-routine, that is, either of the two extremes is implicitly expected to exist in an organization. It is conceivable that a designer will face more of a continuum. Another problem with the model is that it makes assumptions about the values of organizational members and, as stated earlier, that the choice of Theory X or Theory Y is simply a matter of fitting organizational member characteristics appropriately to a given organization design, and so forth. The choice of value orientation, however, is most relevant to the process of designing and not just to the resultant organization design. Again, the reason that the contingency theory approach has been labeled Theory X–Structure (see Figure 1.1) is because the contingency theorists imply top-down, Theory X design decisions and implementation, even though they have actually given very little attention to the design process.

The Kilmann and Mitroff Contingency Model

To overcome some of the problems of the contingency approach, Kilmann and Mitroff (1977, 1976) formulated a contingency model of organization design based on the personality typology of C. G. Jung (1960, 1923). The Jungian personality typology has two basic advantages over the previous classifications:

1. Its dimensions are directly related to various managerial and organizational styles, and hence it allows creation of an appropriate basis for comparison between different personality and organizational types.
2. The Jungian typology emphasizes only each type's major strengths and weaknesses without considering any one as superior or better in general.

Since the Jungian framework as it relates to organization design is utilized throughout this book, a thorough discussion and consideration of this framework is given here. Two particular dimensions of Jungian typology were considered in a study by Mitroff and Kilmann (1976). The first concerns the kinds of input data an individual usually prefers to absorb from the environment. The second dimension refers to the person's preference in decision-making processes that interacts with his preferred kind of input data.

According to Jung, individuals can absorb data from the outside world either by sensation or intuition but not by both simultaneously. Thus individuals tend to develop a preference for either mode of input. Sensation refers to those individuals who typically take in information via the senses, who are most comfortable when attending to the details of any situation, and who prefer hard, concrete facts. In contrast, intuition refers to those individuals who typically absorb information by means of their imagination, by seeing the whole, or the gestalt, of any situation. These persons typically prefer the hypothetical possibilities in any situation to the "actual" facts. It should be stressed that all individuals perceive with both of these functions at different times. Jung argues, however, that individuals tend to develop a preferred way of perceiving, and cannot actually apply both types of perception or data input at the same time.

According to Jung there are two basic ways of reaching a decision: thinking and feeling. Thinking is the process that is based on impersonal, analytical modes of reasoning. Feeling, on the other hand, is the process that is based on personalistic value judgments that may be unique with the particular individual. Thus however one takes in data (by intuition or sensation), an individual may come to some conclusion about the data either by a logical, impersonal analysis (thinking) or by a subjective, personal process (feeling).

Combining the two data-input modes (sensation and intuition) with the two decision-making modes (feeling and thinking) in all possible ways results in the following four Jungian personality types, as illustrated and elaborated in Figure 1.3:

1.   Sensation–Thinking (ST)
2.   Intuition–Thinking (NT)
3.   Sensation–Feeling (SF)
4.   Intuition–Feeling (NF)

Mitroff and Kilmann (1976) conducted a study to relate the Jungian personality concept to the analysis of organization design problems. The subjects were management students of an executive MBA program. A short personality test was administered to the managers using the Myers-Briggs Type Indicator (Myers and Briggs, 1962). Immediately after completion of this test each subject was asked to write a short story that expressed his or her concept of an ideal organization. Upon completing this task each individual was placed in one of four different discussion groups depending upon the individual's personality type; that is, the particular personality test

FIGURE 1.3   The Jungian Dimensions (Adapted from Kilmann and Mitroff, 1976)

Thinking (T)

(1) logical
(2) analytical
(3) scientific
(4) dispassionate
(5) cold
(6) impersonal
(7) concerned with matters of truth
(8) unconcerned with people's feelings
(9) theoretical
(10) concerned with rationality
(11) concerned with theories

Sensation (S)

(1) careful
(2) concerned with parts
(3) lives in present
(4) specialist
(5) factual
(6) precise
(7) concrete
(8) realist
(9) likes to develop a single idea in depth rather than several ideas
(10) practical
(11) conventional

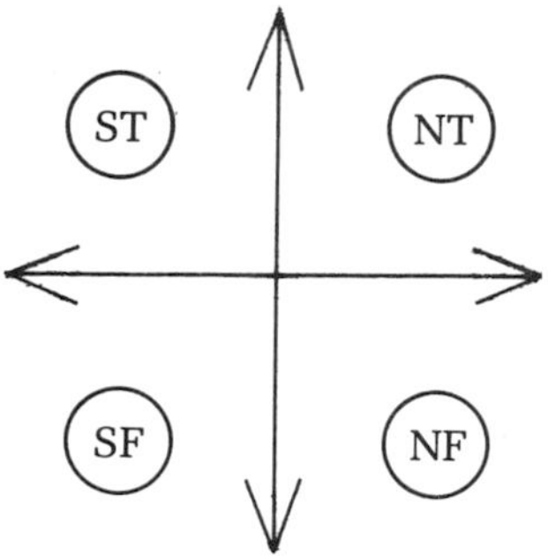

Intuition (N)

(1) risk-taker
(2) concerned with whole
(3) lives in future
(4) generalist
(5) hypothetical
(6) vague
(7) speculative
(8) idealistic
(9) likes to produce many alternative ideas
(10) inventive
(11) unconventional

ST   NT

SF   NF

Feeling (F)

(1) alogical
(2) poetic
(3) artistic
(4) passionate
(5) warm
(6) personal
(7) concerned with matters of ethics
(8) concerned with people's feelings
(9) atheoretical
(10) concerned with justice
(11) concerned with uniqueness and individuality of all things

that was used sorted individuals into one of the four personality type groups (ST, NT, SF, and NF): each discussion group contained only those individuals whose type was the same. The groups were then asked to express their concepts of an ideal organization in the form of stories.

The content analysis of the individual stories and the stories of the four Jungian discussion groups showed: (1) a remarkable similarity between the stories of those individual who had the same personality type (e.g., NT); (2) remarkable differences among stories of the four personality types. Actually the variations in the stories of different types were so great that one is tempted to say that the ideal of one type is the absolute hell of the other, and vice versa.

The stories of ST individuals (and groups) are characterized by an extreme emphasis and concentration on specifics, on factual details. ST types are extremely sensitive to the physical features of their work environment. For example, the stories of ST types display an extreme preoccupation with environments that are neither "too hot" nor "too cold" but "just right." The ideal organization of STs is characterized by complete control, certainty, and specificity. In their ideal organization everybody knows exactly what his or her job is. There is no uncertainty as to what is expected in all circumstances. Further, ST organizations are impersonal. The emphasis is on work and work roles, not on the particular individuals who fill the roles. Thus it comes as no surprise that the ideal organization of STs is authoritarian. There is a single leader at the top and a well-defined hierarchical line of authority that extends from the top down to all the lower rungs of the organization. In an ST organization individuals exist to serve the goals of the organization. Finally, the goals of an ST organization are realistic, down-to-earth, limited and, more often than not, narrowly economic.

The stories of NTs are marked by extreme emphasis on broad, global issues. In describing their ideal organization, NTs neither specify the detailed work rules, roles, nor lines of authority, but focus instead on general concepts and issues. To put it somewhat differently, if the organizational goals of STs are concerned with well-defined, precise microeconomic issues, then the goals of NTs are concerned with fuzzy, ill-defined, macroeconomic issues such as "an equitable wage for all workers." NT organizations are impersonal like ST organizations. However, where STs focus on the details of a specific impersonal organization, NTs focus on impersonal concepts and theories of organization. For example, they are concerned with concepts of efficiency in the abstract. Likewise, whereas in an ST organization individuals exist to serve the particular organization, in an NT organization they exist to serve the intellectual and theoretical concept of the organization in general. In a word, if ST organizations are impersonally realistic, then NT organizations are impersonally idealistic.

The stories of NFs are also marked by an intense preoccupation with broad, global themes and issues. NFs also show extreme disdain toward getting down to specifics. NFs are similar to NTs in that both take a broad view of organizations. However, NFs differ from NTs in that the emphasis of NTs is on the general theory or theoretical aspects of organizations, while the emphasis of NFs is on the most general personal and human goals of organizations. Thus, NF organizations are concerned with "serving humanity; with making a contribution to mankind." NFs differ from both STs and NTs in that for both STs and NTs the individual exists to serve the organization, whereas for NFs the organization exists to serve the personal and social needs of people. Since in Jungian personality theory the NF type is the extreme opposite of the ST type (as the SF type is the extreme opposite of the NT), it is not surprising to find that the ideal organization of NFs is the exact opposite of STs. Thus if an ST organization is authoritarian with well-defined rules of behavior, then an NF organization is completely decentralized with no clear lines of authority, with no central leader, and with no fixed, prescribed rules of behavior. The stories of NFs incessantly emphasize "flexibility" and "decentralization." As a matter of fact, many of the stories of NFs contain diagrams of their ideal organization that show them to be circular or wheellike in structure rather than hierarchical. NF organizations are also idealistic rather than realistic. In essence NF organizations are the epitome of organic, adaptive institutions.

If the ideal organizations of STs and NFs are extreme opposites, then the organizations of NTs and SFs are also extreme opposites. If NTs are concerned with the general theory of all organizations but not with the details of any particular organization, then SFs are not concerned about theory at all or issues in general. Instead SFs are concerned with detailed human relations in their particular organization. SFs are like STs in that both are concerned with details and facts, but they differ from STs in that the latter are concerned with detailed work rules and roles whereas the former are concerned with the human qualities of the specific people who fill the roles. In this sense SFs are similar to NFs. Both SFs and NFs are concerned with the people in the organization. SFs differ from NFs in that while NFs are concerned with people in general, SFs are concerned with individuals in particular. SF organizations are also realistic as opposed to idealistic. Like STs, SFs are also concerned with the detailed work environment although for STs the environment of concern is physical and for SFs it is the interpersonal environment that is of concern.

The foregoing discussion has presented a conceptual framework for studying important organizational phenomena in a manner that capitalizes on man's inherent ability to create stories, emphasizing that these stories derive from basic psychological processes. We turn now to the issue of how the Kilmann and Mitroff approach provides an alternative basis for studying some of the contingency issues of organization design.

Jung and Contingency Theory

One of the major shortcomings of the contingency theorists is that they have not provided a general conceptual framework for the explicit definition of different organization designs. The design often labeled as "bureaucratic" or "mechanistic" implies a fixed hierarchy of authority, a highly specified set of rules and procedures, and rigid control over behavior, whereas the design generally labeled as "organic" represents just the opposite, namely, a design that is somewhat fluid (organic), changing (adaptive), and conducive to the unique development of each individual. It is our contention that the Jungian framework just introduced provides a set of underlying dimensions and hence a systematic rationale for defining the basic characteristics of these fundamentally different organization designs. In particular, the first design represents an ST organization whereas the second portrays an NF organization. Recalling the stories of STs and NFs concerning their ideal organizations illustrates well the primary distinctions between the two basic organization designs that have been studied, if not conceptualized, by contingency theorists. Thus the bureaucratic design emphasizes specific rules, procedures, and data (i.e., sensation) and the formal, logical ordering of the organization's hierarchy (i.e., thinking). In contrast, the organic design explores the global, long-term goal orientation of the organization (i.e., intuition), and the informal, social, human resource potential of the organization's members (i.e., feeling).

To reiterate an earlier point: this Jungian framework for defining different organization designs is based on two different information systems (sensation and intuition) and two different decision-making systems (thinking and feeling). A diverse and abundant literature attests to the validity of these two types of system concepts as central to investigating organizational behavior (King and Cleland, 1973; March and Simon, 1958; Mason and Mitroff, 1973; Murdick and Ross, 1971; Simon, 1957). Furthermore, the adoption of this framework provides additional benefits. It permits the specification of two additional types of organization designs: the NT and the SF. These designs have been overlooked in the design literature, which has described only the ST and NF designs. While the NT and SF designs have not received explicit research attention, the stories by NTs and SFs provide a tentative basis for defining the nature of these two designs. The NT design emphasizes the global, long-term goal orientation of the organization while maintaining a loosely structured set of roles in order to accomplish these goals. Thus the members have some discretion in defining their function in the organization. The SF design, on the other hand, specifies the hierarchy and role set of organization members while emphasizing that these roles and management hierarchies are for the benefit of the members, namely, to promote their needs and their desires to communicate openly with one another.

The use of the Jungian framework also permits a more systematic conception of contingency issues. For example, instead of referring to the organization's or subunit's task environment as simply dynamic or stable, we can conceptualize and study different environments with different information and decision-making requirements. A task environment can impose an ST problem (e.g., specific, stable, well-defined, short-time horizon, fitting an existing model or technology, etc.), an NF problem (e.g., diffuse, unstable, ill-defined, long-term, complex, undifferentiated, requiring appreciation, etc.), or an NT or SF problem (e.g., abstract and analytical vs. a unique value-laden issue). Likewise, an alternative to referring to individuals as either Theory X or Theory Y is to assess each individual's psychological type by means of the Myers-Briggs Type Indicator (1962). We may then speak of an ST or an NT individual, and so on.

Contingency issues a la Lawrence and Lorsch are then translated thus: design an ST subunit to address ST problems (task environments) staffed by ST individuals, or design an SF subunit to address SF type problems staffed by SF individuals, and so on; and finally, design various mechanisms to coordinate the subunit efforts of these different subunit designs into overall organizational effectiveness. Such contingency design objectives, however, mask the nature of the kinds of conflicts that are seen in any real situation. For example, a typical intrarole conflict issue is: how does an NF individual adapt to an ST design? Or, more generally, how is an individual to be integrated into the organization when that person's psychological type is different from the design of the organization? At the subunit level, the issue can be stated thus: how can an NF subunit be integrated with ST subunits? The issue here is one of resolving intergroup conflict (Blake and Mouton, 1961; Seiler, 1963).

Not only can these issues be approached more explicitly via the Jungian framework than with more traditional frameworks, but they can also be approached explicitly as value issues. To recall an earlier point: the Jungian framework does not refer to any one type as generally better, more relevant, or more mature than the other types. There is not a connotation that an ST or NT is superior to an SF or NF, and so on. The traditional design literature, on the other hand, does imply that one type is better than another. For example, Argyris (1957) refers to the individuals who function in bureaucratic organizations (ST) as passive, dependent, and subordinate, who work under conditions leading to psychological failure. As another case in point, the contingency theorists mentioned earlier implicitly value the NF design. Their very labels for the different kinds of organizations give them away. NF organizations are labeled as "democratic" or "professional," versus the labels of "bureaucratic" and "hierarchical" for ST organizations. As a result of the Mitroff and Kilmann studies with the Jungian typology, we are tempted to say that those researchers who implicitly value NF designs are NFs themselves. Similarly we are tempted to assert that those who were instrumental in formulating and promoting ST approaches, for example, Weber (1947) and Taylor (1947), had strong components of ST within their own personalities. In other words, our visions—our stories if you will—as social scientists are as much a description of us (i.e., of our psychological type) as they are of the things we study.

Another advantage of the Jungian framework is that it helps to make clear that conflicts between STs and NFs (or NTs and SFs) or between ST and NF subunits will probably be biased in favor of the more socially acceptable or desirable perspective. Mitroff and Kilmann indicate that the majority of organizations are designed in an ST format and tend to attract ST individuals. This means that it will be most difficult for NF subunits and individuals to be integrated with the status quo of ST. Consequently, a framework such as the Jungian one is needed to confront explicitly these value issues and to provide support for those individuals and subunit designs that run counter to the prevailing mood of ST. Unless this is done, NF individuals and NF designs will be both underrepresented and undermined.

The need for SF and NF attitudes and people is growing stronger. During the past few decades, as discussed earlier, task environments (i.e., problems) as a whole have become more dynamic, turbulent, and have changed more rapidly than ever before. In addition, child-rearing experiences such as the "open" classroom are encouraging more individuals to develop the SF and NF sides of their per-sonalities, not to mention the phenomenon of T-group experiences which have a similar objective (Bradford, et al., 1964). Furthermore, there is evidence to suggest that the higher one rises in an organiza-tion the more SF and NF skills are required (Lawrence and Lorsch, 1967c) to confront problems that cannot be easily defined, and that traditional methodologies such as those supplied by operation re-search and management science are simply not applicable (Mitroff and Sagasti, 1973). These themes and the need for different social systems design to address these issues (i.e., ST, NT, SF, and NF designs), will be discussed throughout this book.

SUMMARY AND CONCLUSIONS

This chapter has described the major approaches to organization design as distinguished by the basic types of variables studied (pro-cess vs. structure) and the basic types of value differences underlying the research studies (Theory X vs. Theory Y).

As a way of summarizing the four major approaches, it is interest-ing to note that the historical development of this field can be sum-marized by a particular sequence across the four major categories shown in Figure 1.1. Specifically, the first notable approach was that of bureaucracy as presented by Max Weber, which is largely rooted in the Theory X–Structure quadrant. The bureaucratic organization, however, was seen to have several problems, particularly an inability to shape all aspects of work-related behavior by structures such as rules, procedures, chain of command, and job descriptions. As a consequence of this, it seems that the Theory X–Process approach was developed to specify further the actual sequencing of behavior ex-pected of employees in the bureaucracy by the time and motion studies and the scientific management approach of Frederick Taylor.

After the first quarter of this century, however, the combination of Theory X–Structure and Theory X–Process did not seem to resolve all problems (i.e., organizations were still not completely effective). As a consequence of this, research by Mayo "discovered" that people had motives other than strictly economic ones and developed the notion that people may be motivated by such things as affiliation and social needs. The human relations movement picked up on this theme and further developed the notion of participative management, member involvement in work, two-way communication, and openness and trust. However, this approach also did not resolve all organizational problems since the Theory Y type of processes were still being conducted within Theory X structures, greatly limiting the benefits of the Theory Y approach. What emerged was the Theory Y–Structure studies whereby the actual design or structure of the social system (both job design and organization design) was created to reflect Theory Y values. Thus Theory Y process could occur better under conditions of Theory Y structure.

But is Theory Y best for all situations? This question was discussed by the contingency theorists, who eventually came to argue that for certain types of environments (i.e., stable), the Theory X–Structure and the Theory X–Process approach would be best, while for other types of organization environments (i.e., dynamic), Theory Y–Structure and Theory Y–Process would be preferable (Morse and Lorsch, 1970). While empirical research has provided some tentative support for this contingency notion (although it contains a number of methodological shortcomings), the issue is not simply whether to accept one research approach or another based on strictly "scientific" investigations. Rather, value and ethical positions and considerations can override research results.

For example, one might advocate that Theory Y approaches should be utilized instead of Theory X approaches, since the former are more consistent with the type of world we wish to create. It is our contention, in fact, that research alone can never resolve this dispute. Any resolution to such a distinction in values is rooted in more than "objective" research; it is rooted also in the values themselves. So while the following chapter will present what research evidence there is regarding the design and development of Theory Y, purposeful social systems, we must recognize that our value bias toward this orientation is heavily affecting our discussion and conclusions. Yet it seems better to state this explicitly than to give the impression that values do not enter into research investigations or their interpretations. The Kilmann and Mitroff model of organization design utilizing the Jungian framework highlighted this relationship between contingency designs and the values underlying them. We move on now to Chapter 2 and the discussion of research on Theory Y systems and structural interventions, but we will return at various times to this issue of research evidence versus ethical and value positions.

Chapter 2
Purposefulness, Values, and Structural Interventions

In collaboration with Afzalur Rahim and Dorothy M. Hai*

In the previous chapter, various concepts, models, and the theories of management and organization design were presented. Special emphasis was given to the contingency theories of organization design that can be used as a framework to develop a theory of structural intervention. However, the contingency theories do not explicitly explain the locus of design decision (i.e., who should design or be involved in the design of the social system). Instead the contingency theorists generally assume a top-down design process. In this chapter a thorough discussion will be provided to consider who should be included in design decisions and whether top-down or participative design is most appropriate for various design objectives. Also considered are the underlying values of change agents and organizational members, and which value positions would most foster the design and development of effective social systems. With this end in view, purposeful systems, values, and various models (perspectives) of man will be discussed in order to formulate a theory of structural intervention. The latter will serve as a basis for the types of structural interventions (as well as process interventions) to be performed by the MAPS Design Technology.

PURPOSEFULNESS AND VALUES

As discussed in Chapter 1, writers have distinguished different types of organization design. For instance, Burns and Stalker (1969) differentiate between the mechanistic, which is stable and well defined, versus the organic type, which is seen as more dynamic and able to adapt to an uncertain environment. The distinction between mechanistic and organic will be discussed, using more general terms—deterministic and purposeful systems. Four types of systems are identified by systems theorists: deterministic, goal-seeking, purposive, and purposeful (Ackoff, 1971). A deterministic system is one

*This chapter also benefited from the contributions of Steven E. Bangert, David Breyer, and Hugo M. Schmidt.

47

in which its future state is determined by existing initial conditions. A goal-seeking system is one that can respond to certain stimuli within or outside itself in pursuit of a specific goal. A purposive system can pursue a number of goals while striving for some purpose, but it cannot choose its overall goal. A purposeful system, on the other hand, is one that exercises freedom not only in the selection of its functional purpose but also in its more detailed goals, and it exercises will (Ackoff, 1971: 665–66).

A deterministic system, at one extreme, is like a mechanistic, bureaucratic organization that is necessarily designed as a highly ordered social system with a Theory X value orientation. At the other extreme, a purposeful system is like an organic–adaptive organization that is characterized by its ability to change with an orientation toward Theory Y values; that is, if environmental or other conditions suggest some modification, the system can decide to change not only its overall goals but the characteristics of its subsystems as well. The definition used here for a purposeful system is one that contains one or more purposeful subsystems (Ackoff, 1971: 670). (See McKelvey and Kilmann 1975, for a more extensive discussion on purposefulness and organizational behavior.)

Purposefulness can be used as an objective to design large-scale social systems or some of their parts (subsystems). The advantage of using purposefulness as an objective of organization or subsystem design is that it puts high priority on creating conditions for the organization's or the subsystem's own decision making or exercise of will (Ackoff, 1971). This is in extreme contrast to determinism as a design objective, in which emphasis is on "outside" forces (outside of the defined organization or subsystem) for decision making, including the very design of the social system. But can such a contrast of underlying social systems design objectives, and particularly choosing one approach over the other, be resolved by strictly objective considerations (i.e., by extensive empirical research as to the impact of deterministic vs. purposeful systems on social systems effectiveness)?

Empirical research applied to this question necessitates that relatively pure cases of deterministic versus purposeful systems be easily created, and their impact on a number of outcome variables be easily measured. This does not seem to be the case. While it might be fairly straightforward to design a deterministic system (and there are many examples of these), how to create a purposeful system is less apparent. The latter cannot be formed by a direct experimental treatment or by an outside intervention, since this would be the appropriate strategy for creating a deterministic system. A purposeful system requires that the system itself defines its goals and designs the means of attaining its goals. This violates many criteria of "good" experimental research (Campbell and Stanley, 1963). In fact, it seems quite interesting that a well-designed research experiment is an excellent example of a deterministic system in operation! And yet social scientists have neither developed nor actually accepted in essence the notion of a purposeful research design. Even assuming that such a research methodology existed and was accepted by the scientific community, how would one compare the results of the deterministic system (i.e., the research approach as well as the social systems being researched) with the results of the purposeful system? Not only would this be comparing apples to oranges, but it would not be entirely evident that the "oranges" (i.e., purposeful systems) were actually created. Thus purposefulness is basically an objective to strive toward, whereas determinism is more readily a description of initial or existing conditions of the system.

Alternatively, the type of design and design objectives that social scientists, change agents, or practitioners feel should be fostered depend very much on their values. Similarly the manner in which an organization or group goes through the design process is related to certain values inherent within the system. Rokeach (1969: 5) defines a value as an enduring belief that a particular type of behavior or end state of existence is more desirable than other behaviors or end states on either the personal or social level. In the same vein, he defines a value system as an enduring organization of beliefs or values (as defined above) along a continuum of relative importance. Rokeach (1969: 7–9) further distinguishes two main types of values, terminal and instrumental. Basically, terminal values relate to desirable end states of existence, such as salvation, peace of mind, and world peace. On the other hand, instrumental values specify desirable modes of behavior that are presumably directed toward the attainment of terminal values. For example, instrumental values include such desirable modes as being honest, loving, forgiving, logical, imaginative, and polite.

Both terminal and instrumental underlying values have a significant influence on types and processes of organization design. Conflicting terminal and instrumental values tend to produce an inconsistent system (Etzioni, 1965). In particular, a social system whose instrumental values do not support or are inconsistent with its terminal values is likely to manifest ambivalence, hypocrisy, and mistrust among its members. Figure 2.1 shows the relationships between

FIGURE 2.1   Values and Organization Design

Resulting Design
(Terminal Values)

		BUREAUCRATIC	ORGANIC-ADAPTIVE
Process of Designing (Instrumental Values)	THEORY X	Top-down organization design (Congruent)	(Incongruent)
	THEORY Y	(Incongruent)	Participative organization design (Congruent)

terminal and instrumental values, vis à vis bureaucratic (mechanistic) and organic-adaptive designs, and Theory X and Theory Y values, respectively. For the purposes of this discussion, Theory X values emphasize manipulation, control, and noninvolvement, values related to a top-down organization design. Theory Y values emphasize those listed by Argyris (1970a): valid information, free choice, and commitment, values related to participative organization design. In this context instrumental values are part of the ongoing processes of designing organizations, whereas the terminal values refer to the end product of design itself.

For example, if top management manipulates and in a sense dictates that the organization is to be flexible and open, there is a clash of terminal and instrumental values, hence an inconsistency. In addition, a participative group could decide to have a highly programmed and controlled organization that would take away their participation and "freedom," which would also create an inconsistency of values. One might argue that the off-diagonals shown in Figure 2.1 represent situations that cannot exist effectively over time or even be created in the first place. Can one dictate flexibility, commitment, and trust? Will people participate to eliminate their freedom? However, if top management controls and manipulates for a highly programmed, inflexible environment, then a consistency of instrumental and terminal values produces a Theory X (deterministic) organization. Similarly a participative process of choosing an open, flexible environment (it may be highly structured, but have built-in options for change when needed) creates a Theory Y (purposeful) organization design. This suggests how fundamental values are to social systems design. Therefore to design a social system towards certain ends perhaps necessitates a particular process of designing the social system consistent with the desired end state.

MODELS OF MAN

Whether one believes people can and should participate in design decisions and the implementation of designs relates to underlying values and concepts of man. Such questions as: What motivates man? What are his ultimate goals? Is he responsible?—lie at the root of this issue. A model is proposed to help address these questions that distinguishes between top-down design and participative design at the individual, small group, and organizational level of analysis, as shown in Figure 2.2. Top-down design refers to whether the design of a social system or subsystem is determined by outside authority (such as top management) or, as in the case of participative design, whether the members in the social system or subsystem are actively involved in the design process. Models of man refers to the basic motivational tendencies of individuals, the characteristics of groups, and the work attitudes of individuals in organizations that foster particular types of instrumental and terminal values, and thus to whether top-down or participative design is to be applied in social systems.

The following discussion about the models of man shown in Figure 2.2 relies on empirical research evidence if available; otherwise the discussion reports the value positions taken by social scientists in regard to these issues. As discussed before, even the available "research" is affected by the values of the researcher, especially when interpretations are offered, or when the social scientist gives an "objective" summary of many research results. Recognizing this, we do not expect the results and statements to be invalid, but only maintain that values cannot be easily separated from scientific investigation (Mitroff, 1974), and that this should be fully considered.

Individual Level

Psychologists provide several different views of man, but those of Freud and Skinner have probably been most influential. Perhaps the Freudian tenet most important to this discussion is the pleasure

FIGURE 2.2   Models of Man Differentiated on the Basis of Locus of Design
Decision and Level of Analysis

	Top-Down Design	**Participative Design**
Individual Level	Freud (pleasure principle) Skinner (S-R) Maslow (lower needs) Jung (inferior functions)	Maslow (higher needs) Jung (superior functions) Rogers (self-directed growth)
Group Level	Julian and Perry; Collins and Guetzkow; Raven and Eachus (high degree of structure)	Taylor, Berry and Bock; Bouchard; Campbell (low degree of structure)
Organization Level	Herzberg (hygiene factors) McGregor (Theory X) Argyris (adolescence)	Herzberg (motivation factors) McGregor (Theory Y) Argyris (adulthood)

principle. Freud (Viola, 1973: 2–3) sees this as the beginning of the
source of motivation, meaning that man is mainly motivated to seek
pleasure and to avoid pain, that is, to satisfy lower order or deficiency
needs. Therefore the motivation is toward achieving a homeostatic
state equilibrium in which tension is reduced and gratification is
achieved. Skinner, unlike Freud, belives that man is motivated by
forces outside himself. He argues that man is not free but is shaped by
evolutionary forces determined by his environment. In his recent
work, Skinner suggests that man can no longer afford freedom and
dignity; he is beyond those values (Skinner, 1971). However, both the
writings of Freud and Skinner emphasize deficiency needs and
hedonistic responses as the basic motivational tendencies of individuals. If these models of man are accepted, then the general mem-

bership of the organization should not be involved in designing their systems. On what viable basis would individuals design their social systems if their behavior is largely unconscious (Freud), and if their unconscious objective is to design a system to minimize tensions and simply satisfy their own pleasure-seeking?

In contrast, Maslow, Rogers, and other writers in the area of humanistic psychology suggest different models of man than do Freud and Skinner. Maslow (1962) looks toward a psychology of health and growth rather than one of pathology. He makes a distinction between deficiency and growth needs. In Maslow's hierarchy of needs, the first four (physiological, security, love, and esteem) are classed as deficiency needs. Failure to satisfy these needs over a long period of time may lead to physical illness, neurosis, or some other form of emotional disturbance. The growth needs are desired and welcomed by a self-actualizing person. Whereas the gratification of growth needs produces health, the gratification of deficiency needs only prevents illness (Mogar, 1969). The need for self-actualization is never satisfied. In the case of deficiency needs, however, when one need level is relatively satisfied, the next higher need becomes salient.

There is general agreement on the optimal environmental and psychological climate in which self-directed growth is most likely to occur (Mogar, 1969). In his analysis on the dynamics of change processes that result in a meaningful self-directed sense of identity, Coons (1967) points out that "in an atmosphere of safety, protection, and acceptance, the boundaries of self-organization relax." With regard to any process of facilitating self-growth, the necessary external conditions have been well stated by Rogers (1961). Like Maslow, Rogers sees man as striving toward self-actualization, toward the "tendency to express and activate all the capabilities of the organism..." (Rogers, 1961: 35).

Jung's model of man was explained in the previous chapter. Jung (1960) argues that each individual is characterized by a preferred mode of perceiving and a preferred mode of judging (superior functions). The alternative functions are dormant in most people and they are uncomfortable in using these modes (inferior functions). Jung elaborated the adverse consequences of prolonged suppression of an individual's natural propensities to environmental demands. If social conditions make a strong demand on a person's inferior functions, prematurely or for prolonged periods, undesirable consequences are likely to occur. The ST mode is strongly emphasized in contemporary administrative and organizational systems. The feeling mode is strongly discouraged in our society although it is mainly related to creativity and self-actualization. Jung, as other humanistic psychologists, would propose that in order to achieve balance individuals should be encouraged to develop and express their feeling function in organizations. This would necessitate their involvement in designing their social systems to correspond with their unique needs and values (feeling function).

In summary, whether one endorses the values and perspectives of Freud and Skinner or those of Maslow, Rogers, and Jung makes the great difference in the individual's attitude toward man and hence toward the management of organization design. Freudian and Skinnerian views would tend to produce a rigid, deterministic social systems design. Little freedom or responsibility would be given to the lower organizational members, since they are believed to be seeking only the satisfaction of deficiency needs. Thus the system would be directed toward rewards and punishments to motivate people to work. Maslow, Rogers, Jung, and other humanistic psychologists would involve the individuals in designing their own social systems, which would be congruent with their assumptions about man's growth needs.

Group Level

DeLameter (1974) defines a group in terms of the following properties: interactions between individuals, perception of other members and the development of shared perceptions, the development of affective ties and the development of interdependence of roles (i.e., group structure). A purposeful social group is defined by Ackoff and Emery (1972) as a system whose members are intentional coproducers of a common objective. This discussion considers the dimensions of group design to determine the various sets of conditions that maximize the results of group effort. A review of small group literature provides support that man can be viewed not only as an individual problem solver, but also as a designer of groups for the purpose of accomplishing chosen objectives.

Research indicates that task structure is a salient variable in determining the basic nature as well as the task activity of the group. This is quite consistent with the contingency theories presented in the previous chapter. It is argued here that the task structure and the motivational tendencies of group members determine the effectiveness of group design.

Roby and Lanzetta (1958) suggest that a task be analyzed in terms of its critical demands: "We may expect that the most useful method of classifying group tasks will be with reference to those aspects of group behavior or procedures which these tasks bring to the foreground." Shaw's (1962) framework is useful for classifying tasks as to degree of structure. Specifically it is expected that for tasks characterized by a high degree of structure the information will be processed by the group through a logical sequence, and that the quality of the group output will approach that of the most capable individual. Therefore maximum group effectiveness will be found in work environments that stress the importance of individual effort. This notion, in addition to being supported in a number of research studies —Julian and Perry (1967), Collins and Guetzkow (1964), Raven and Eachus (1963)—is suggested, although untested, by Deutsch (1951).

For tasks characterized by a medium degree of structure, a group of persons working cooperatively may produce the greatest results. The rationale here is that it is not expected that a given individual will be familiar with all possibilities (e.g., perspectives, information, skills, etc.); therefore the probability is greater that a group of persons working cooperatively could more effectively assess the available information and select the solution perceived to be the "best." The "critical demand" in this instance is the group's superior ability to evalute information. Supportive research was done by Smith, Madden, and Sobol (1957), Hammond and Guildman (1961), Haines and McKeachie (1967), and Wheeler and Ryan (1973).

For tasks characterized by a low degree of structure, it is exceedingly more difficult for the groups to evaluate information. It is possible at this point that there is an information overload and that groups will be unable to effectively assimilate all of the available information. Membership behavior may take the form of self-defending, blocking, and aggression. Such behavior hinders process and thus undermines the effectiveness of the group structure. This would suggest a more formalized group which emphasizes task activity rather than group structure. Taylor, Berry, and Block (1958), Bouchard (1969), and Campbell (1968) all report findings that support this line of reasoning.

Taken together, the small-group literature concerned with the degree of task structure provides a relevant perspective for the design of organizations. In particular, there are value and motivational implications to be derived from the three levels of task structure that were discussed. For highly structured tasks reliance is on individual effort, which suggests that the design of the group and the process of designing are not critical determinants of the group's success. Instead the output of the most capable individual is the prime determinant. Consequently the design of a group that is working on tasks with a high degree of structure can be viably done by those other than the group members. This would not be expected to affect the motivation or the output of the group.

For groups that are engaged in tasks of medium structure, however, the design of the group becomes a more important determinant of successful performance, particularly since the design affects the motivation (cooperation) of group members. For such tasks it may be necessary to involve members in the design of their group to maximize their commitmnnt and motivation. However, for groups working on tasks of low structure, the value and motivational components of group behavior are of prime importance: the design must be able to manage not only the complexity and the large amount of information, but it must also creatively and functionally manage the considerable amount of conflict that such task structures can easily generate. Only by carefully and explicitly considering the particular needs, dynamics, and interactions among group members can a viable design be formulated. The essential issue here is whether some outside person alone can assess all the intricacies involved in designing an effective group to address tasks of low structure, or whether only the group members themselves can accurately reveal and consider all their motivational and informtional requirements. It seems unlikely that the former would be sufficient; rather it seems that the latter is necessary.

In summary, the lower the degree of structure of group tasks, the more the group should be involved in actually designing its own behavior since the group's motivations, informational requirements, and capabilities are most understood by the group and its involvement becomes increasingly important to gain commitment of its members to engage in complex tasks (i.e., those of low structure). Such implications will now be explored for organizational level, where the same value issues have been considered.

Organizational Level

There are several theories of motivation that specifically involve organizational behavior. While Maslow was interested in a general theory of motivation, Herzberg (1968) was interested in identifying factors that motivate people at work. Through a series of studies he was able to attribute positive job attitudes to job factors such as achievement, recognition, responsibility for one's own and others' work and advancement. In short, job satisfaction resulted from satisfaction of Maslow's higher level needs, namely, esteem and self-actualization. These motivational factors can be classed as growth needs, as in our models of man. Factors found to result in negative job attitudes were called hygiene factors, similar to deficiency needs. Although hygiene factors (e.g., relations with superiors, working conditions, company policies, etc.) were considered necessary, they did not lead to positive job satisfaction but merely to the experience of dissatisfaction or no dissatisfaction (no dissatisfaction is not the same as satisfaction). To motivate employees, hygiene factors should be maintained at an acceptable level and motivational, or growth, factors should be increased as much as possible. In the words of Herzberg, Mausner, and Snyderman (1959):

> Improvement in the factors of hygiene will serve to remove the impediments to positive job attitudes...when these factors deteriorate to a level below that which the employee considers acceptable, then job context can be characterized as optional, he will not get dissatisfaction, but neither will he get much in the way of positive attitudes...

Another model of man at the organizational level has been provided by Argyris (1957) and is referred to as personality and organization (P and O) theory. Argyris's model portrays the continuous conflict that takes place between an individual and the organization in which he or she works. He points out that from birth an individual begins to develop from a state of infant passivity to adult activity, from a state of infant dependence to adult independence, from being single faceted to becoming multifaceted. His list continues, but the end result is that an individual progresses from infancy to a mature, complete personality. However, all these characteristics of the healthy individual are inconsistent with the principles of most formal bureaucratic organizations. In organizational situations employees are: (1) provided minimal control over their work, (2) expected to be passive, dependent, and submissive, (3) expected to have a short time perspective, and (4) induced to work under conditions leading to psychological failure. Argyris argues that failure is inevitable where organizations thwart the individual desire for development and maturity. He suggests that integration is needed between human personality and formal organizations so that growth as well as deficiency needs of individuals may be manifested.

McGregor's model is supportive of the humanists' model of man discussed earlier (1960). His model is not based entirely on personality development like those of Maslow and Argyris, but is formulated explicitly for the administrators of organizations. McGregor's two cosmologies (Theory X and Theory Y) of assumptions about man, organizations, and leadership styles have been discussed in Chapter 1, where it was suggested that these two value differences are fundamental to the study of social systems behavior. While McGregor prefers Theory Y cosmology, he admits that organizational and technological constraints may make Theory X a preferred system. Theory Y is supportive of the humanists' model of man at work as it emphasizes the ability of organizational members to satisfy higher level needs in their daily work, while Theory X seems to reflect an orientation toward deficiency and lower level needs in the work setting.

It was stated in the previous chapter that the contingency theorists emphasize that organizational effectiveness is achieved when there is a proper fit among task environments, technologies, motivations of the organizational members, and organization design. Morse and Lorsch (1970), in their article "Beyond Theory Y," propose that certain task structures are not suited to a Theory Y philosophy. These researchers conclude that enterprises with highly predictable tasks perform better with Theory X organizations characterized by highly formalized procedures and management hierarchies of the classical type. Similarly highly uncertain tasks that require more extensive problem-solving efforts suggest a Theory Y organization characterized by a less formal design, which emphasizes self-control and members participation in decision making. However, if we accept the basic notions of Theory Y, we are confronted with a conflict of values with this notion of contingency theory (a conflict of theory vs. perscriptive behavior). Specifically, Theory Y emphasizes individual self-actualization, responsibility, and growth, while the prescriptive aspects of contingency theory imply a top-down, Theory X design process even for developing the organic-adaptive, Theory Y design (see Figure 2.2). Thus the contingency theorists attempt to design an organic-adaptive organization (or subunit) by Theory X means (i.e., an inconsistent match between instrumental and terminal values).

Yet the implication of Theory Y is that the organizational members themselves are capable of participating effectively in the design of their own work organization. In The Human Side of Enterprise (1960), McGregor concludes: "the essential task of management is to arrange organizational conditions and methods of operation so that people can achieve their own goals best by directing their own efforts towards organizational objectives." He suggests a management by objectives approach as a solution to the problem. The format for the

MBO system suggested by McGregor himself, however, is again top-down design. The individual is responsible for developing specific courses of action from broad, general objectives from management. Many MBO programs that have been implemented are of this type (Reddin, 1972). This is somewhat different from the approach outlined by Peter Drucker (1954), who states:

> By definition, a manager is responsible for the contribution that his component makes to the larger unit above him and eventually to the enterprise. His performance aims upward rather than downward...This requires each manager to develop and set the objectives of his unit himself. Higher management must, of course, reserve the power to approve or disapprove these objectives. But their development is part of a manager's responsibility; indeed it is his first responsibility. It means, too, that every manager should responsibly participate in the development of the objectives of the higher unit of which he is part.

Drucker's approach suggests that objectives, decisions, and even the design of the organization can meet with success when the process involves organizational members rather than being a top-down design. Thus even McGregor, who contrasted Theory X and Theory Y to begin with and apparently endorsed the latter, overlooked the inconsistency in attempting to bring about a Theory Y end state by a Theory X model of implementation. There are many other examples in the literature revealing the inconsistency in trying to dictate trust, openness, or a participative management system.

The whole body of literature on participative management (Kilmann, 1974e; Leavitt, 1975; Likert, 1961; Vroom, 1965), for example, indicates that commitment and satisfaction will be highest when the organizational member has had an input to the decision-making process on task or policy issues that affect him (both providing information and joining in the actual decisions). Generally this approach has proved to be fairly effective, but failures are often cited (Vroom, 1965). In most cases failure may be attributed to faulty implementation of a participative approach or to homage to a participative label which, in reality, is the traditional Theory X style of management. An excellent example of this is the Non-Linear Systems case, in which top management (shortly after learning about Theory Y) dictated that a Theory Y organization would be developed (Business Week, 1973), did not involve the members in the decision or in the change process, and disbanded the Theory Y approach several years later. To this day the case is cited as a prime example of participative management failure (Malone, 1975), while in reality it was never implemented!

VALUES VERSUS RESEARCH

The reader is referred back to Figure 2.2, where the organizational as well as the group and individual perspectives on top-down versus participative designs are summarized. As can be seen from the figure, at each level of analysis the same basic value distinction emerges: Can and should individuals design their own organizational subsystems (and groups)? Can individuals be motivated by growth needs or only by deficiency needs? However, instead of seeing the distinction as one of either /or, it might be more realistic to consider the conditions under which each is appropriate and not to assume that either one would be best under all circumstances. The latter suggests a contingency approach similar to the Morse and Lorsch (1970) "Beyond Theory Y," discussed earlier. This contingency approach would, however, have to be modified so that an organic-adaptive organization would be actually designed in a Theory Y, participative manner (i.e., to make instrumental values consistent with terminal values), while, as before, a mechanistic organization would be designed in a Theory X, top-down manner. The position taken here is that even if research supported such a contingency view, values can override research findings. Consider the following.

Research findings actually reflect empirical relationships determined in the past. In other words, statistics such as correlations, means, main effects, and so on, of and among variables were created by particular individual and management assumptions, attitudes, and behaviors. Social science phenomena as opposed to physical science phenomena are not independent of time, but are time-dependent (although Einstein's Theory of Relativity suggests otherwise for certain aspects of the physical sciences). Thus as individuals and managers acquire social science knowledge, as their values and attitudes are questioned and perhaps changed, and as change agents intervene in organizations to change the process and structure of organization subsystems, subsequent empirical research studies will necessarily find different correlations, means, main effects, and so forth. Actually, not only will such statistics change (as descriptions and explanations of organizational behavior), but the need will develop to measure other variables not previously assessed, namely, variables within some newly developed conceptual framework. These conceptual frameworks are proposed and developed over time as new ways of describing and predicting social behavior that requires "new" variables to measure and relate empirically to other variables. Such a sequence of research studies, new conceptual frameworks, new research studies, and so on, continues for the development of social science knowledge. But to suggest that such a sequence leads toward finding the ultimate truth or grand theory of social science is a myth. Instead new variables, concepts, and empirical studies are needed in each generation to address new and changing social systems problems (Kilmann and Mitroff, 1977).

We propose that the explicit or implicit values of the researcher and /or change agent determine what problems are to be conceptualized and researched, and toward what purposes the research is interpreted. Consequently, instead of emphasizing the validity of reactive, scientific investigations as determining prescriptive guides to changing social system behavior (e.g., top-down vs. participative design), one could just as well take a proactive stance and suggest prescriptive guides to changing social systems as based on particular value positions (i.e., to foster participative design because we believe social systems should be designed that way to develop purposeful systems). The latter approach is supported by one's values, while the former is supported strictly by research findings (although, as has been suggested, it is difficult to separate out values from supposedly "objective" research investigations). Furthermore, if we do not take the future as given or make the possibly invalid assumption that social science theories are time-independent, then values can serve to foster intervention strategies that would actually change the future and the subsequent empirical relationships that would be found. Stated differently, current interventions to change social systems affect the research results of the future. Consequently unless one values science for science's sake and is largely unconcerned about the future, it seems more appropriate to choose to develop the future in a particular way with a particular value position than to simply allow past research to dictate the future.

Ironically then, as social scientists and as change agents we can choose to operate in a purposeful, Theory Y manner with our research and change technologies, or we can follow the deterministic, Theory X model to pursue our scientific investigations. We prefer the model of purposefulness for science as we prefer participative design for social systems intervention. This is our value position. We will rely on current research knowledge only to better foster our aims: to develop purposeful, Theory Y social systems. We believe that to see the world as deterministic and to conduct all research studies and social system interventions accordingly develops a self-fulfilling prophecy. Social systems will become deterministic if they are conceptualized and approached that way (i.e., reality is in the eyes of the observer). On the other hand, to see the world as purposeful and to intervene and study phenomena with this perspective, might actually bring about purposeful social systems. It is a matter of preference and values, coupled with the use of existing research knowledge, that determines the path to follow.

As indicated, we prefer and value purposeful systems, and the remainder of this chapter and this book emphasizes this value position. Chapter 9, however, will again raise and discuss these important issues and will further explicate our ethical and value positions specific to the MAPS Design Technology. Now we propose a framework for structural interventions based on the notion of purposeful systems.

STRUCTURAL INTERVENTIONS

Argyris (1970a) maintains that older and more complex organizations in our society appear to be in a state of "deterioration." The human and material costs of their activity tend to increase while results either remain the same or decrease. There are numerous causes for the deterioration of organizations. The most important ones, however, are built into the organization's structural design, technology, and various management processes. To overcome this so-called "organizational entropy" (Argyris, 1970a), the society needs new organization designs, technologies, and management processes that will help organizations to become more productive, effective, and self-renewing, which will encourage the fulfillment of growth needs of organizational participants.

To illustrate how the deterioration or impending deterioration of organizations follows from basic problems in organization design, the reader is referred back to Figure 1.2 in Chapter 1. There it was proposed that organization designs have remained largely unchanged while other contingency elements, such as the organization's task environment, its technologies, and its people, have changed considerably during the past few decades. Consequently the fit among these four basic variables has decreased, and leads to the increasing prevalence of organization design problems.

Another way of illustrating the deterioration of organization designs is to consider the following historical progression. As has been suggested, an organization's design is heavily rooted in its past (Stinchcombe, 1965). Take the industrial organizaion as an example. This type of organization is often designed by product or by function, but even the product divisions are usually subdivided into functional areas such as production, marketing, finance, and research and development (R & D). Even assuming that these design categories were appropriately matched to their respective task environments, people, and technologies several decades ago, it does not follow that these same design categories are still functional and appropriate today. As the environment has changed, so has the nature of interdependencies among these design categories, which suggests that the design of subsystems no longer contains the important interdependencies (Thompson, 1967).

For example, as the environment has become more complex and dynamic and as new technologies have developed more rapidly, the life cycle of products has greatly decreased (i.e., the length of time the same product is demanded by consumers) and /or changes in technologies alter the way in which the products are produced. Consequently there are greater interdependencies among the traditional design categories. R & D develops new product ideas as the environment (consumer tastes) changes, and asks the marketing department if the product can be sold in sufficient quantities with various advertising campaigns; the production department decides whether it can produce the product at a reasonable cost and if new technologies are needed to accomplish this; and finally the finance department is asked if the new technologies can be financed at an acceptable cost. This cycle holds true for several products, especially in diversified firms operating in increasingly dynamic environments. Because of all these cross-departmental interactions, some members may spend most of their time communicating with those in other departments rather than with those in their own sections.

At some point the question arises as to the effectiveness of the given design categories if as much as 80 percent of members' time is spent interacting between departments and only 20 percent within departments. Such a situation does not suggest that the given design categories contain the important interdependencies (Thompson, 1967). As in the hypothetical case noted above, perhaps some combination of various R & D, production, marketing, and financial functions might be better contained in a different kind of subsystem design to better manage these important interdependencies. Moreover, research on intergroup and interdepartmental conflict suggests that since members remain loyal to their own departments, identify with their departmental goals, and devalue the other departments' outputs (Blake and Mouton, 1961; Seiler, 1963), the interactions across departments are not likely to be exceedingly effective and supportive of overall organizational goals. This phenomenon further compounds the basic design problem even with the use of special integrative mechanisms suggested and empirically researched by Lawrence and Lorsch (1967a).

As has been stated at several points thus far, organizations have not only retained their original designs but are reluctant to question and change these designs. Thus rather than redesign itself to better contain the changing nature and types of interdependencies, the organization tends to develop more integrative mechanisms. In particular, in order to manage the many interactions across the given design categories (e.g., R & D, production, marketing, and finance departments), the organization supports managers to coordinate the interdependencies between two or more departments. Thus there may be a manager to coordinate marketing and R & D, a manager to coordinate production and finance, and so forth. As the interdependencies increase, however (as the task environment changes more frequently and in different ways), more managers are needed to coordinate the interdependencies between departments. This may continue almost indefinitely as more managers and administrators are hired to coordinate interdependencies across departments, as more managers are hired to coordinate these managers, and as even more managers are hired to coordinate the coordinating managers, and so forth. In essence several research studies support this sequence of increasing managerial staffs by noting that as organizations increase in size, the proportion of administrators or managers to "workers" increases (Starbuck, 1965).

Although one might suggest that this increase in managerial activities and managers is merely a consequence of having larger organizations (i.e., more managers are needed in greater proportion to manage such large-scale, complex organizations), such an explanation does not seem very compelling. One cannot easily ignore the observation, as summarized by Argyris, that older and more complex organizations in our society are deteriorating: their costs increase while their results stay the same or decrease (as discussed earlier). It is our contention that this problem of deterioration is deeply rooted in the design of these organizations. It seems much more compelling to note that continually increasing the relative proportion of managers to manage the increasing interdependencies between departments is attempting to compensate for increasingly ineffective organization designs! Instead of adding increasingly integrative mechanisms (i.e., the managerial hierarchy) to make up for a deficiency in basic organization design, it seems appropriate to consider explicitly confronting, and perhaps changing, the underlying cause of the design problem.

To ignore the latter and to pursue symptomatic manifestations of deficient design is to be solving the wrong problem (Mitroff and Featheringham, 1974).

It should be stated that there have been attempts to solve the design problem although they have not been widespread. The matrix organization design overlaps product or project groups with the functional areas to facilitate the changing composition of interdependencies as changes in task environments are manifested (Galbraith, 1973). Thus as new products require development and implementation, individuals from the various functional areas (e.g., R & D, production, marketing, etc.) are selected to work on a particular project. These individuals remain working on these projects until they are completed and then return to their functional area for possible assignment to some other emerging project. Although this dual design creates certain problems (e.g., switching of roles can confuse the authority system in the organization: is the individual loyal to his project group or to his functional area?), it does foster greater flexibility to a changing task environment. The issue is still, however, the usefulness of the functional "backhome" design categories, for these may require considerable integration and management support activities if they do not reflect changing skill definitions, especially if members remain more loyal to their functional areas than to their project teams, which seems to be the case.

Other attempts at addressing the basic design problem have emphasized the need for a distinct PROBLEM-SOLVING or STRATEGIC PLANNING DESIGN to coexist and support the OPERATIONAL DESIGN of the organization. Zand (1974) describes a collateral organization as one that has two such distinct designs, one for day-to-day activities and the other for long-term problem-solving considerations. Again, if the OPERATIONAL DESIGN for performing daily tasks contains outdated design categories, then there is just so much that the separate PROBLEM-SOLVING DESIGN can do to compensate for OPERATIONAL DESIGN deficiencies. In the extreme case, the problem-solving or collateral organization would spend all its time working on the symptomatic problems that result from having the wrong design categories for the OPERATIONAL DESIGN. At some point the latter design would have to be questioned. One might argue that deficiencies in the OPERATIONAL DESIGN are resolved by the INFORMAL DESIGN of the organization (i.e., informal interactions across formal design categories), but this seems to be avoiding the issue. As has been noted (Roethlisberger, 1941), the INFORMAL DESIGN, while serving as an information flow, is probably most related to social relationships among members, and therefore does not rigorously and proactively seek to resolve fundamental OPERATIONAL DESIGN problems.

The preceding paragraphs suggest the need for diagnostic and intervention methods to explicitly confront the greater emergence of design problems in our society. The various designs mentioned above were capitalized not only to emphasize them as designs versus processes, but also to underscore the attention devoted to them throughout this book. Thus, in the following chapters, these various organization designs (i.e., OPERATIONAL PROBLEM-SOLVING, STRATEGIC PLANNING, and INFORMAL) are continually discussed and related to the issue of solving social systems design problems. Incidentally, the four Jungian designs discussed by Kilmann and Mitroff (1977, 1976), which were presented in Chapter 1, relate directly to these four organization designs: ST is the OPERATIONAL DESIGN; NT is the PROBLEM-SOLVING DESIGN; NF is the STRATEGIC PLANNING DESIGN and SF is the INFORMAL DESIGN. However, before discussing these different designs, the various processes of creating them, and the actual problems that these designs confront, we shall provide basic concepts and principles of intervention that underlie the planned change of social systems. The main emphasis will be on structural interventions that have been largely neglected by both academicians and practitioners.

Principles of Intervention

Intervention may be defined as a process of planned change aimed at helping an ongoing social system to become more effective in determining its purposes, and designing its problem-solving, decision-making, and operational tasks to achieve these purposes. Interventions, of course, may also be implemented for a newly formed social system. The basic assumption of intervention theory is that the social system exists independently of the intervening change agent. Although there are certain interdependencies between the interventionist (considered here as synonymous with change agent) and the system, the level of autonomy of the client system must be maintained or even increased. In other words, the client system (i.e., a social system that has expressed a need for diagnosis and /or change to an interventionist) must be considered as an ongoing, independent entity that controls its own future (i.e., the social system is viewed as having the potential to be a purposeful system), and the boundaries of the client system are clearly distinguishable from those of the interventionist, or change agent.

There are three fundamental requirements or principles that must be fulfilled to achieve effective intervention and to move the social system to further purposefulness: (1) valid information, (2) free choice, and (3) internal commitment of the members of the client system, as formulated by Argyris (1970a).

1. Valid and useful information is the foundation of every purposeful intervention process. Valid information is necessary to enable the client system to engage in the process of searching and defining its problems. The information must not only be accurate and reliable, but the members of the social system should also be able to make some practical use of the data (i.e., the information should be relevant to their problems as well as being valid in its own right).

   The information needed for interventions is generally collected through a process of organizational diagnosis, which starts by gathering data about organizational phenomena such as conflict, trust, job satisfactions, motivation, leadership, differentiation and integration, rules and procedures, and so forth. Data gathering can be accomplished with observation, interviews, and/or structured questionnaires (Margulies and Raia, 1972). There are relative merits and pitfalls in each of these methods, and a combination of questionnaires with either interviews or observation may be most appropriate. These data provide the basis for analyzing the organization's strengths and weaknesses or problems that need to be defined and solved (or at least managed). This diagnostic process is important because before any structural interventions are made the diagnosis should reveal the existence of structural design problems. An important implication is the fact that change is not a primary goal of the interventionist. Argyris (1970a) emphasizes that '...change is not a priori considered good and no change considered bad...' Therefore, before any intervention strategies have been applied, the diagnosis should reveal the existence of, or lack of need for, redesign.

2. For an intervention to be successful, the participants must enjoy 'free choice' of various alternatives. This requirement locates the decision making within the boundaries of the client system, thereby fostering its autonomy. On this subject, Argyris (1970a) states:

   > A choice is free to the extent the members can make their selection for a course of action with minimal internal defensiveness;

can define the path (or paths) by which the intended consequence is to be achieved; can relate the choice to their central needs and can build into their choices a realistic and challenging level of aspiration. Free choice implies that the members are able to explore as many alternatives as they consider significant and select those that are central to their needs.

3. Internal commitment means that members of the organization experience some amount of ownership and a feeling of responsibility about their decisions and the consequences of those decisions. They act on the choices being influenced by their own forces (not induced by others) because these choices and actions fulfill their needs and aspirations as well of those of the organization. It seems highly probable that members equipped with valid information and exercising free choice can maintain their commitment over longer periods of time and can be open to change (Argyris, 1970a).

These three principles, as stated by Argyris, are basic to a theory of structural intervention (and /or process intervention) with the overriding objective of designing and developing effective, purposeful social systems and will appear many times throughout this book as the primary criteria for judging the effectiveness of a given intervention or a particular step of the MAPS Design Technology. Since the latter seeks to design purposeful systems, criteria of valid information, free choice, and internal commitment must guide each distinct intervention of the technology. This will be most evident in Chapter 3, where an extended discussion is provided on the diagnostic steps of MAPS, using interviews, observations, structured questionnaires, and survey feedback to foster the three principles of intervention theory. This will also be apparent in Chapter 4, where the membership of the social system participates in development and response to the MAPS questionnaire, a major input to the resulting design of the social system. Again the prime concern is that responses to the questionnaire represent valid information, and so on, otherwise the resulting design may not only be invalid, but may not be accepted by the membership. Chapters 5 and 6 provide a participative, judicial decision process to involve the membership in choosing a particular social system design (one of the several suggested by MAPS or some synthesized design), implementing the selected design, and then evaluating whether the design actually helped resolve or manage the design problem that was diagnosed initially. The more these three principles are applied at each step of the MAPS Design Technology, the more likely will a purposeful social system actually be designed and the the right design be implemented to solve the real problem.

Basic Intervention Types

The basic model developed in the previous chapter to explain the various approaches to organization design will be utilized to discuss different approaches to intervention. Purposeful approaches to organizational intervention, as shown in Figure 2.3, are of two types: Theory Y–Process, and Theory Y–Structure.

Theory Y–Process Intervention

This approach to organizational intervention considers the events, sequences, and behavioral consequences existing in the ongoing organization. The interventionist generally helps a client system as a

FIGURE 2.3   Organizational Interventions

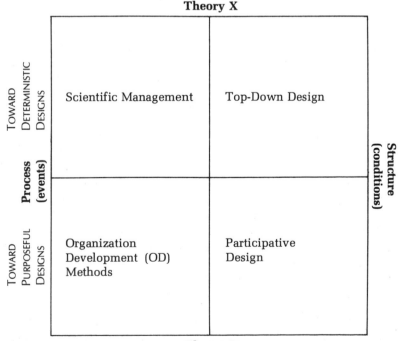

process facilitator who plans and implements change to optimize the system's performance. This type of intervention is directed toward improvement of a system's problem-solving and decision-making activities, communication processes, interpersonal interactions, conflict management, and utilization of human resources. In recent years, organizational development (OD) methods have been developed for Theory Y–Process interventions. Interventions such as the managerial grid (Blake and Mouton, 1964), the confrontation meeting (Beckhard, 1967), the laboratory approach (Golembiewski and Munzenrider, 1973), team building (Beckhard, 1972), and organic problem solving (Davis, 1967) are of this type.

OD interventions are designed to increase the effectiveness of organizations by changing the behavior (processes) of organizational participants. These interventions are useful in managing ongoing subsystems by improving the existing teams, groups, departments, and divisions. The major problem of OD is that it fails to raise the possibility that the subunits it attempts to develop may not represent a useful segregation of objectives, tasks, and people (Kilmann and the MAPS Group, 1976). Therefore spending resources on developing the existing subunits that may possibly be composed of wrong combinations of tasks and people could be an ineffective approach. The management of organization design involves redesigning the existing structure of an organization or one or more of its subunits. Since the process or OD approach does not consider this, we should give proper atention to the development of structural interventions.

Theory Y–Structure Intervention

This approach to organizational intervention has not received the attention it deserves from researchers and practitioners. The literature on structural intervention is scarce and often ambiguous. The theory underlying this type of intervention is largely undeveloped and frequently consultants prefer not to be involved in structural considerations, leaving that problem to the client system.

Structural intervention aims at improving the organization by changing structural characteristics such as differentiation and integration of subunits, rules and procedures, hierarchy, and technology. The principal difference between process and structural interventions lies in their impact on organizational conditions. Structural interventions generate direct changes in organization designs, while process actions can only indirectly influence organizational conditions through modifications in problem-solving activities, decision-making processes, leadership modes, methods of conflict management, and so forth.

Probably the most vital condition affecting the organization as a whole is the overall design or structural differentiation of organizational subsystems. Again, the so-called structural design theory is in its 'status nascendi.' Although some organizational theorists label structural design as one example of the innovation process, the identification and description of intervention steps is rather vague. For example, the Zaltman, Duncan, and Holbek study (1973) suggests the existence of some new structural knowledge that should accelerate a search for structural alternatives, but neither origins nor details of intervention procedures are presented or described. Empirical studies were done by Lawrence and Lorsch (1967a) and other contingency theorists on the overall structural dilemmas of complex organizations. Generally their research findings are central only to the information gathering stage of intervention strategies. Using the differentiation versus integration concept, change agents can monitor the effectiveness of a particular structural design. Although they have been criticized, basic assumptions of contingency theory appear to have practical use in the design of organizations, particularly the diagnostic phase (Lawrence and Lorsch, 1969).

Frequency of Structural Interventions

Before any structural interventions can be made, a proper diagnosis must reveal the lack of effective design(s) for an organization or one or more of its subsystems. In a case where all the important task interdependencies are contained within existing subunits and can be explicitly managed, it is unlikely that participants will perceive problems with the existing structural pattern. Often, however, organizations have designs that demonstrate significant discrepancies between the ideal and the actual situation, and organizational members experience problems because of the design(s). To determine the frequency or need for structural intervention, one must consider the type of environment and the character of organizational objectives. If the design objective is strictly for operational purposes and subunits deal with relatively certain internal or external environments, the need for structural interventions is usually limited and possible directions for change are easily traceable by members of respective subunits (the task interdependencies remain within subunit boundaries and coordination efforts are reduced to a minimal level). Thus we may assume that the use of Theory Y—Process interventions will help to develop the right subunits into a well-functioning whole. However, in a case where organization design objectives involve strategic purposes and a system's adaptability to a heterogeneous and dynamic environment (open systems), the task interdependencies may easily cross the existing subunit boundaries, and much more effort must be made to integrate the various subsystems. Thus the need for more frequent structural and process interventions increases.

The above suggestions may be considered merely as approximations of the complex of factors that have an impact on the frequency of structural adjustments. The changes in technology, spatial dispersion, and expansion of the organization, number and mobility of members, their skills, aspirations, interpersonal orientations, interaction desires, level of stress, and many more unforeseen factors may cause the existing structural design to become outdated and, as a result, the need for Theory Y–Structural intervention increases, as discussed earlier. In view of the plurality of potential change factors, we argue that the social system should institute a periodic review of its structural design (the length of review period should depend on the present and predicted pace and rhythm of change of the various contingency elements; see Figure 1.2 in Chapter 1) and maintain designing as a recurring management process.

CONCLUSIONS

This chapter has considered various models of man at the individual, small-group, and organizational level of analysis to derive important distinctions between the two basic types of structural interventions: top-down design versus participative design. The latter is congruent with a value position and emphasizes the development of Theory Y, purposeful systems, while the former is more supportive of Theory X, mechanistic systems. Although several research studies were cited to suggest the appropriateness and relevance of each type of structural intervention, it was decided to adapt a proactive stance toward the future development of social science knowledge and the future design and development of social systems. In particular, we plan explicitly to assume growth needs, Theory Y, and purposefulness in conducting a diagnosis of social systems as well as in implementing various change programs. Available research knowledge and the development of new research will be pursued with the aim of fostering purposeful (effective) social systems in our society. In line with this proactive stance, three principles of intervention theory suggested by Argyris (1970a) were cited as the basic criteria for intervening in any social system: valid information, free choice, and internal commitment. Specifically it is believed that these three principles, criteria, or conditions need to be generated and acted upon if interventionists (change agents) are actually to design effective social systems.

Some attention was given to exploring the reasons why design problems are emerging increasingly in our society. It was suggested that since task environments, people, and technologies have been changing there is a corresponding need to change the design of organizations so that a better match among these contingency elements would be evidenced (as discussed in Chapter 1). In addition, it was argued that organizations seemed to have addressed these emerging design problems not by redesigning themselves differentially to contain new and changing interdependencies within subsystems, but by increasingly adding on integrative mechanisms in the form of ever more managers to coordinate other managers, and so forth. Although this may alleviate some of the problems, the time may come when organizations will have to requestion and perhaps change their OPERATIONAL DESIGN and/or other designs that might have been planned or have evolved to confront the basic design problem (e.g., STRATEGIC PLANNING, PROBLEM-SOLVING, and INFORMAL DESIGNS).

It is our contention, however, that if social systems continue to conduct cosmetic changes on the design of their systems they will not only be solving the wrong problem, but will also decrease the possibilities of being purposeful systems. The latter condition requires that the membership of the organization partake in defining its destiny as well as the design and design process to strive toward the defined objectives; and that the social system devotes its energies and resources to the right problems. Attention and effort toward the wrong problems will not only divert scarce organizational resources, but will not benefit society in the long run, and hence will hamper the benefits to be derived by the membership of the organization.

What is needed is a comprehensive social science technology that will help a social system define its problems, with particular emphasis on organization design problems, and to systematically and efficiently involve the membership in defining its mission and creating or changing various designs to achieve this mission. To design effective, purposeful social systems, the technology must apply criteria of valid information, free choice, and internal commitment at each stage of the intervention. The MAPS Design Technology is proposed as having the potential for such a comprehensive and purposeful approach, and the remainder of this book attempts to demonstrate this. But the issues raised in this chapter and the preceding one concerning values versus research, solving the right problem versus solving the wrong problem, Theory Y versus Theory X, purposeful systems versus mechanistic systems, and descriptive versus normative theory, will appear many times in different forms for different reasons. These are, however, the critical issues, and how these issues are raised, explored, debated, and managed will determine whether the scientific community will have a valued impact on the real world.

PART II
THE MAPS DESIGN TECHNOLOGY

Chapter 3
Entry and Diagnosis

In collaboration with Frederick J. Slack, David A. Smethers, and Joseph Seltzer.*

The previous chapters of this book have described the theory and concepts underlying social systems design and the MAPS Design Technology. The introductory chapter presented the scope and nature of the organization design problem that MAPS addresses. In Chapters 1 and 2, organization design research and purposeful systems were examined with an emphasis on contingency theory and the increasing emergence of organization design problems. In particular, it was decided to approach such emerging problems in a Theory Y (purposeful) manner, not only as a guide to research but also as a guide to structural (and process) interventions. These chapters have thus provided a substantive knowledge of various organization design conceptualizations and of the values upon which such conceptualizations are based. Using the Diamond Model of problem solving (Sagasti and Mitroff, 1973), the reader has been taken from an overview of the problem to designing possible conceptualizations of the problem. Following the Diamond Model (see Figure 1 in the introductory chapter), Part II will present the actual stages of the MAPS Design Technology. Chapter 3 will address the entry and diagnostic functions of the MAPS consultant: First, the change agent's skills and entry into the client system, the diagnosis of the client system vis à vis organization design concepts, and the choice of the design boundaries for a design analysis via MAPS. Chapter 4 presents the core of the MAPS Design Technology: input (the MAPS questionnaire), analysis (the MAPS Computer Program), and output (alternative organization designs). Also included in Chapter 4 is a discussion of the six scientific models of MAPS (i.e., different genotypic designs for different design objectives). Chapter 5 will address the implementation process and include material on design selection from the computer output, implementation procedures, and a suggested method for monitoring the implementation process. In Chapter 6 the issue of evaluation is explored. This chapter completes the Diamond Model sequence, and asks whether the initial design problem has been resolved or effectively managed and /or if new problems have arisen.

*This chapter also benefited from the contributions of Michael A. Belch, Donald W. Dieter, and Rajendra K. Srivastava.

77

Then the MAPS diagnostic process is again set in motion as new problems are addressed.

A DIAGNOSTIC FLOW CHART

This chapter will outline an interactive model to aid the MAPS consultant in determining the appropriateness, applicability, and boundaries of the MAPS Design Technology for a given client system. Specifically the model provides a systematic method of evaluating (1) the skills of the consultant, (2) the entry point's appropriateness, (3) the problem facing the client in terms of both process and structural issues, (4) a taxonomy of the client system and (5) the boundaries of the intervention. In terms of the Diamond Model, this would result in the conceptual model that aids the MAPS consultant and the client system in selecting one of the scientific models of MAPS discussed in Chapter 4.

An important consideration is to correctly identify the problem before attempting to offer a solution. Here the notion of the Type III error (the probability of solving the wrong problem when one should have solved the right problem) is relevant to the diagnostic process (Mitroff and Featheringham, 1974). Identification of the correct problem for the application of the MAPS Design Technology is critical. Possible reasons for solving the wrong problem include the following:

1. The consultant did not possess the required skills.
2. Entry to the organization was not made at the correct point, or the definition of the client was inappropriate.
3. There was an incorrect diagnosis of the organization's primary problem.
4. The boundaries of the application were set inappropriately.
5. Organization constraints that prevented the complete application of the MAPS Design Technology were not identified and considered during the diagnostic phase.

The intention of this discussion is to reduce the probability of a Type III error by providing a systematic method of entry and diagnosis of organizational problems.

To begin with, MAPS is not the answer to all organizational problems. It is specifically a design technology for the organization or social system and addresses both organization structure and process issues. Structure and process cannot be separated since each affects the other (Kilmann, 1975b; Parsons, 1960; Thomas, 1976). The best design is meaningless if the client system is incapable or unwilling to activate the mechanisms necessary for its implementation; the converse is also true, since good processes are of little value in a poorly designed systems. The interdependence of structure and process must be stressed. In the following, this relationship reappears many times, (See Chapters 1 and 2 for a further discussion of process and structure.)

Since MAPS is a new technology it is tempting to justify its use in any social system from the perspective of the consultant's need for design research data. However, when the decision to use MAPS is made, real people in real organizations will be affected. The application of MAPS will always generate data for the consultant, but at what cost to the client system? In the extreme case MAPS can aid the consultant in research and leave the organization in worse condition than it was before the intervention.

Risk will always be present. To determine the kind of risk involved, a scheme for organizing and systematizing the thinking of both the client and the consultant is necessary. Concern here is with situations in which the consequences of the MAPS intervention are uncertain. Events may occur that cannot be controlled or predicted and whose results will certainly affect the 'final' condition. Thus the decision to use MAPS is thus an important and difficult one to make.

MAPS should be selected because the client and the consultant agree it is the best course of action to follow relative to all considered and feasible alternatives. Personal judgments and preferences affect this decision, and these subjective inputs must be taken into account when a course of action is selected. Such an approach enables the client and the consultant to arrive at a decision about MAPS in an open and collaborative manner (Chapters 5 and 6 will discuss further a qualitative, judical process to address such complex decisions in the face of uncertainty.)

A procedure for determining the appropriateness of applying the MAPS Design Technology in a social system is diagramed in Figure 3.1. These interactive steps are not a rigid set of requirements, but rather an attempt to provide a general structure to aid in the decision-making process. Attention is focused on the interval between entry into the client system and the decision of whether or not to continue with the MAPS Design Technology once the boundaries for the design analysis have been determined.

FIGURE 3.1   A Diagnostic Flow Chart for MAPS

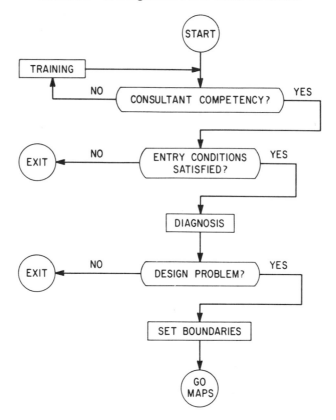

Consultant Competency

The first step in Figure 3.1 asks if the consultant possesses the ability to diagnose the client system properly. The following paragraphs will explore this question in detail, examining the skills, values, and training required to achieve entry and to perform an effective diagnosis of an organization. (See Argyris, 1962, 1970a, 1975; Bennis, 1969; Bradford, et al., 1964; Margulies and Raia, 1972; Thomas and Bennis, 1973, for a further discussion of these issues.)

The MAPS consultant is one who has developed skills and expertise in the process of mobilizing resources to more effectively define and obtain social systems objectives and the resolution of social systems problems through the normative, interdisciplinary MAPS Design Technology, and is able to transfer this knowledge to a client system. The consultant uses his expertise in both organization design and organization processes in a systems approach. This individual should be aware of the basic tenets of the theories of organization development and organization design and be able to use these skills in relating to the organization involved. (See Chapters 1 and 2 for the substantive knowledge of organization design.)

The skills required of a MAPS consultant are multidimensional and include sensing the climate and interpersonal relations of the organization, group process awareness, problem-solving skills, the ability to communicate effectively, application of organizational change and design principles, and the ability to think both conceptually and abstractly.

The sensing skill implies that the consultant is able to gather information about the organization based on personal perception, then fit this into a conceptual framework. Ideally the MAPS consultant has internalized a number of concepts and conceptual frameworks and can readily use these to diagnose an organization. Each framework provides the consultant with a different perspective by which to conceptualize and define the client's problem. He must be able to ask the right (pertinent) questions to fill in gaps in his conceptual frameworks and be aware of his own biases. The asking of questions requires special skills because individuals within the organization are often unaware of, or unwilling to offer, the information necessary for the consultant to form a proper conceptualization. Yet he must be able to gather this information. Another source of information is the consultant's observation of nonverbal cues in discussions with and interactions between members of the client system. The cues thus obtained must be verified by the consultant to help eliminate his personal biases and those of the organization.

The consultant should be experienced with and sensitive to the processes of the various groups within the organization. Much of the work that is accomplished in organizations, and an especially important part of the MAPS Design Technology, implies that people will work together in groups that have tasks to accomplish. For these groups to be effective and to learn and develop over time, they must be aware of the process ("how we do") as well as the content ("what we do") of their interactions. The consultant will play a major educational role in helping the groups develop these process skills and he must obviously possess these skills himself. At an earlier stage, these same skills will be invaluable in sensing the processes of existing groups.

Reactions to change and the causes of resistance to change should be considered by the consultant in every interaction with the organization. He should be aware of the individual and organizational needs and goals, the power relationships within the organization, and the role of the change agent, and how these foster particular reactions and resistance to change. He should try to gain information from a variety of sources within the organization about such reactions, and to consider the feelings of the organization member about the change effort. A primary goal will be to help develop within the organization the ability and skills to self-diagnose and plan for continued change, and the consultant needs skills to teach and to facilitate the organization's growth in these directions while placing fears and anxieties about change into a proper perspective.

There is an opportunity for the consultant to use his abstract ability in creative ways during the application of each portion of the MAPS Design Technology. He must have the ability to perceive the overall needs of an organization and be aware of the processes and means necesssary to achieve these needs. The MAPS consultant should possess the ability to organize and successfully execute change projects, facilitated by his conceptualization of the requirements of the system, subsystems, and individuals, and the achievement of these requirements.

Inherent in the MAPS Design Technology are certain values and basic assumptions about people and the nature of organizations. As discussed in Chapter 2, there is clearly a goal of enabling organizations to become more purposeful (Ackoff and Emery, 1972). There is an expectation that participative and collaborative processes and the utilization of valid information and free choice (Argyris, 1970a) will facilitate this development. The values and beliefs of the MAPS consultant should be congruent with those of the technology. Equally important, his behavior should manifest those values. The consultant is a model whose actions will be noted by clients. He should also be willing to accept, understand, and respect the values of the client system. Finally, in maintaining consistency among his values, those values underlying the MAPS Design Technology, and his behavior in interacting with the client system, the consultant should not lose sight of societal values. Ultimately implementation of the MAPS Design Technology should be for the benefit of society as well as for the benefit of members in the organization.

Having discussed several of the skills and relevant values necessary for the MAPS consultant, we should consider how a MAPS consultant can develop and strengthen these attributes. This might involve a training process, as indicated in Figure 3.1, but an alternative would be to consider the MAPS consultant as a team of individuals, each of whom contributes some skills and resources to the overall effort. From this perspective, the issue is to select a group that has the necessary skills or, if team members do not possess these skills or need to improve them, an appropriate training process must be arranged. In either circumstance, the values of the MAPS consultant or consultants must be contiguous with the MAPS Design Technology and its underlying values. These values, as discussed earlier (and in Chapter 9 in terms of the ethical stance to be taken), can serve as a basis for selection of new MAPS consultants as well as a unifying core for a team of consultants.

Within a team there should be a basic agreement on the process and goals of the MAPS Design Technology and the direction of change for the client. A common understanding and approach to organization design will help create a climate that encourages a sense of trust and leads to constructive confrontation of differences within the team. The team must be aware of and sensitive to its own process, and should discuss any issues that relate to either the internal matters of the team or to its effectiveness in dealing with the client system. Just as a single MAPS consultant's behavior must be consistent with his values, and just as he serves as a role model for the client system, a team or group of consultants must also foster these characteristics and behaviors. If the MAPS Design Technology is meant to foster purposeful groups in the social system, the team of MAPS consultants must also be a purposeful group and be perceived as such by members of the client system!

Training of a MAPS consultant would assume that the individual has a reasonable amount of knowledge of organization behavior, organization design, and systems change. The emphasis, in addition, would be on experiential learning and actual involvement in applications of the MAPS Design Technology. This would include workshops focusing on communications, interpersonal relations, and group process. Within these settings the individual has an opportunity to interact with others, try new forms and styles of behavior, give and receive feedback on the interactions and behavior, observe the group process, and in general learn about his own patterns of dealing with others. He will begin to develop skills to help others learn in an experiential manner. Initially, however, the individual must be in a reasonable state of psychological health (Bradford, et al., 1964).

Involvement in an application of the MAPS Design Technology as a member of the consulting team or as an assistant to the consultant will provide much of the training. It is only through seeing and actually experiencing the activities, issues, problems, conflicts, decisions, learnings, frustrations, and joys, that an individual can fully appreciate what the terms 'MAPS Consultant' encompasses. During this learning process, there must be an inclusion of the person in the planning of activities and the postsession processing sessions. As the individual develops skills, he may be given the opportunity to use them in interacting with the client system and can then receive feedback from the consultant. Over an extended period of time, an individual will gradually build his skills and be comfortable as a MAPS consultant.

Entry Considerations

Entry of the consultant into the client system usually is in two phases: (1) initial contact, and (2) sharing of expectations. The organization will contact the consultant or be contacted by the consultant through a single individual or group of individuals. At the initial meeting, and quite possibly in a number of subsequent meetings, the consultant should share his model of the MAPS Design Technology, his expectations about the organization's response and commitment, and his goals for the change process (as noted in Figure 3.1). He should try to elicit a similar sharing of expectations from the persons with whom he has contact. Often it will be necessary for the consultant to consider the question: "Who is the client?" If he feels that he is not talking to the right person or persons, he must share this feeling. It is important that the consultant establish a verbal contract with the client specifying what each expects of the other. Care should be taken to check the communications process so that both parties have a similar understanding of this contract. It may be that the consultant needs to talk to persons higher in the organization's hierarchy than his initial contact, to ensure that the process will proceed and that the answer to the question "Who is the client" can be ascertained (e.g., "the organization" or "an identified subsystem of the organization," rather than only the individual who first contacted the consultant).

This process of sharing expectations and establishing a contract will be both dynamic and continue throughout the change effort. As discussed in Chapter 2 regarding purposeful systems, Argyris has suggested that three requirements of entry must be met: (1) conditions must be present for the generation of valid information; (2) the client must have the ability to make free, informed choices; and (3) there must be an internal commitment by the organization to implement the choices (Argyris, 1970a). If the first condition is not met, the information needed in the diagnostic phase and in the development of the MAPS questionnaire will be useless at best, and at worst, harmful to the organization. The absence of the second and third conditions implies that important forces have not been considered, and possibly there is a need to redefine who the client is. The entry phase must continue until both the consultant and the client are satisfied that the three conditions can be met. Further, these issues must be continually confronted by both client and consultant as part of the verbal contract, since they serve as checkpoints during the entire change process. If these conditions are not met, the consultant has an ethical obligation to surface the issue, and if he feels that the conditions will not be met he should terminate his involvement with the client. Derr (1972) has noted the importance of entry and suggests that the consultant use this phase

> to determine the sincerity of the client, to ascertain whether or not (the consultant) has the skills and knowledge to be helpful to the client, and to make decisions about whether he will agree to act as a consultant to the organization. . . . During the entry period, the consultant and the client normally establish an open, trustful, and collaborative relationship, define the roles and expectations of both parties, define the parameters of the client system or systems on which the change will focus, discuss their motives, needs, problems, goals, and reservations, define the rules for data collection, and discuss the client's perceptions about the nature of the problem, the desirable outcomes, and the organizational constraints.

The key features of entry are therefore the sharing of expectations and the establishment of a contract between the client and consultant, which emphasizes the collaborative relationship and the three conditions specified by Argyris.

The point of entry is a critical variable. Contemporary organization designs are typically hierarchical with authority, power, and responsibility cascading downward through the formal design (Drucker, 1954; Koontz and O'Donnell, 1972; Simon, 1957). The consultant must be aware that the decision to alter the design suggested by the MAPS Design Technology requires the support of both top management and the other members in the social system. However, the literature on organizational development (OD) has made a special issue of top management support (Argyris, 1970a; Bennis, 1969; French, 1972; Greiner, 1967; Lawrence, 1973). Actually one of the major reasons cited for the failure of OD programs is a lack of support from those at the higher levels of the organization (Greiner, 1967). This is particularly crucial for the MAPS Design Technology since a consideration of a design change may affect the entire organization (e.g., a change in the organization's OPERATIONAL DESIGN) or may affect major parts throughout the organization (e.g., creating a special-purpose PROBLEM-SOLVING DESIGN with representatives from each subunit in the organization). As will be further discussed in Chapter 9, if the MAPS "contract" gets pushed too far down the levels of the organization (because top management feels that MAPS is more appropriate to their subordinates than to themselves), the resultant change program would contain more a job or work group design than organization design. The "contract" might then be quite restrictive, especially if the organization's problem is diagnosed as the latter. Consequently a Type III error is more likely to be committed if top management support is not obtained!

Diagnosis

An organizational diagnosis involves the collection of information from an organization and then conceptualization of the current system. The MAPS Design Technology is similar to organization development programs in that diagnosis takes place at two levels. First, the consultant gathers information from the client to help the consultant understand and relate to the client system. If he feels he can be of help, he suggests a method for the organization both to conduct a more systematic diagnosis (second level) and to use the results. During all aspects of diagnosis, there must be emphasis on the development of valid information (Argyris, 1970a).

Preliminary Data and Criteria for Diagnosis

The first level of diagnosis, Step 3 in Figure 3.1, seeks to ascertain the state of the client system in terms of both structural and process dimensions. These are interrelated and the effectiveness of the system is jointly determined by both. The main thrust of MAPS is organization design, which leads the social system to realize that various design problems can prevent it from reaching its full potential. It is suggested, therefore, that the organization be diagnosed in terms of its "core activities," (Argyris, 1970a) which include

1. The ability to achieve the objectives of the organization.
2. The ability of the organization to maintain its internal environment.
3. The ability of the organization to adapt to and maintain control over the relevant external environment.

These core activities in both process and structural diagnoses should be considered carefully. It should be noted that these activities to be diagnosed pertain to the criteria and interventions toward which structural interventions are directed, as defined and discussed in Chapter 2.

The preliminary diagnosis of an organization often includes a general, qualitative assessment of its "climate." Gibson and his colleagues (1973) suggest the following definition:

> Climate is a set of properties of the work environment, perceived directly or indirectly by the employees who work in this environment and is assumed to be a major force in influencing their behavior on the job.

From this definition, we see that climate is a conceptual framework within which many of the organizational characteristics, employee perceptions and feelings, group processes, and individual behaviors can be qualitatively sorted. Also implied is that climate is important to organizational performance. A MAPS consultant can consider the climate of an organization by using a classification scheme proposed by Litwin and Stringer (1968). They suggest the following eight dimensions of organization climate:

1. Structure—The level of constraints imposed by a superior or organization on an individual. The amount of conformity to rules and procedures that is required. The amount of "red tape."
2. Challenge and responsibility—The individual's perception that he is challenged and has an opportunity for achievement. A feeling of being one's own boss.
3. Warmth and support—A feeling of fellowship and being liked. A perception of helpfulness.
4. Rewards—An expectation of being rewarded for good work. An emphasis on rewards rather than punishment.
5. Performance standards—Expectations about the importance of performance. Clarity of goals.
6. Identity—A feeling of being a valued part of a group and of the organization.
7. Risk—A perception of the acceptability of taking risks in decision-making.
8. Conflict—An expectation that others are willing to listen to differing points of view. An emphasis on confronting conflict rather than avoiding it or smoothing it over.

While the climate of the organization or social system is a useful framework and concept for identifying the consequences of organizational processes and structures on the attitudes of the membership, a more direct approach is to examine the actual effectiveness of various processes. For example, how does the organization identify, define, and solve problems within the existing organization design(s)? How are decisions made and implemented? What is the type and quality of interactions between supervisors and subordinates throughout the system? How effective is the communication process? Does the right information get to the right person or subsystem at the right time? These processes (and questions) take place within the given design of the social system; some may be tapped by questions and assessments of organizational climate, others may have to be approached more directly.

A more direct structural diagnosis would have the MAPS consultant consider the impact that the organization's design has on the system's ability to perform its core activities. On a preliminary level, the consultant might simply ask the client when he last considered the effect of his design on the organization's success. The consultant will want to know how the present design was established: was it planned or did it simply emerge? To what extent is the design congruent with the unique purpose of the organization? The same general questions should be asked if the organization has more than one design (e.g., an INFORMAL DESIGN as is usual, and /or a PROBLEM-SOLVING or STRATEGIC PLANNING DESIGN).

Research suggests a relationship between environmental conditions and organization design. Dynamic environments seem to require an organic-adaptive design. Stable environments appear to require a closed, highly ordered design. If there is an incongruence between environment and design, the MAPS consultant can move toward isolating a design problem. Chapters 1 and 2 gave an extended discussion of contingency theories of organization design and several other possible mismatches among the organization's task environment, its technology, its people, and its design. Each of the possible mismatches between the design(s) and the other contingency elements, either for the entire social system or one or more subsystems, can suggest an organization design problem. Furthermore, the consultant must also ascertain the extent to which only integrative mechanisms have been applied to confront changes in the matches among the contingency elements versus whether a consideration and /or change has been shown in the actual differentiation of subsystems. As Chapter 2 proposed, organizations in general have opted for the former, which tends to be cosmetic, while avoiding the latter which tends to deal with the real source of the design problem.

The consultant will diagnose for design problems via several organizational dimensions. These dimensions, as detailed below, provide a framework to be used for diagnosis across different types of social systems. The diagnostic technique suggested is not a set of rules, but provides guidelines and parameters for the diagnostic stage (e.g., sensing and looking for potential design problems). One difficulty in effectively diagnosing an organization is that the consultant seeks flexibility and consistency simultaneously. This is evident since the consultant wants to apply consistent criteria to different types of systems, i.e., business, educational, governmental, and so on. The goals, operations, and needs of different types of social systems vary considerably and some general method of classification is required to assist the consultant in determining the effectiveness of any given system's design. Such an approach would allow for comparison of similar types of systems, and therefore the consultant could be consistent in applying diagnostic criteria.

Katz and Kahn have suggested a taxonomy of organizations that delineates four basic classes or types of systems. In each case the typology is determined by the relation of the system to society as a whole (Parsons, 1960). The four classes include: (1) productive or economic systems, (2) maintenance systems, (3) adaptive systems, and (4) political systems (Katz and Kahn, 1966).

Productive or economic systems create goods and services. They have as their primary goal the satisfaction of society's demands for basic needs. Organizations of this type are the typical profit-oriented business or corporate entity concerned with the throughput of the goods or service produced. Organizations of this type often operate under considerable pressures from similar systems that are in competition with them. The goals of such systems are the profitability and growth of the firm.

Maintenance systems perform educational and training functions. They disseminate laws, rules, and norms of behavior, and are concerned with the "socialization of people for their roles in other organizations and in the larger society" (Katz and Kahn, 1966: 112). Schools and churches are prime examples of such systems. Maintenance systems "help to keep a society from disintegrating and are responsible for the normative integration of society" (Katz and Kahn, 1966: 112).

"Adaptive structures create knowledge, develop and test theories, and, to some extent, apply information to existing problems" (Katz and Kahn, 1966: 112). The scientific institution is a prime example of an adaptive system as represented by colleges and universities. Research laboratories and government agencies that develop and test new products and technologies are also characteristic of this type. Within other types of organizations, the research and development (R & D) department would portray an adaptive subsystem to be integrated with the other organizational subsystems.

Managerial or political systems have as their primary function "the adjudication, coordination, and control of resources, people, and subsystems" (Katz and Kahn, 1966: 112). Federal, state, and municipal governmental systems are representative of this type. Some, unions and professional organizations also fall into this category. These systems are involved in policy formulation and implementation. Authority and power are concentrated within such organizations. These systems derive legitimacy from the greater society. For example, in a democracy the government derives its right to exist and function from the citizens.

Each of these four general types of social systems has very different purposes. The structural design of each is usually different, as are the rewards, values, and norms that guide them. Pure types have been described, but actually many systems are blends of several of the basic types. The MAPS consultant should apply such a typology and consider the specific nature of each system with which he comes in contact. This typology also provides a framework with which he can begin the diagnostic appraisal of different systems with some degree of consistency.

Specifically, by the use of Katz and Kahn's typology, the consultant will be able to explore the social system's design in relation to its primary purpose, namely, productive, maintenance, adaptive, or political. This step in the diagnostic process helps suggest to the consultant which specific objectives or set of objectives the system might be designed to accomplish.

Next, the existing design of the social system is further explored and more specific criteria are applied to the various designs of the system. This helps the consultant isolate specific design problem areas within the system being diagnosed. Within each of the four basic social systems the consultant will observe the interactions among and between the subsystems. Typically the system will be composed of easily identifiable groups or departments. These will be organized according to one of the following dimensions: (a) purpose (product), (b) process, (c) clientele, (d) place, and (e) time (Gulick and Urwick, 1937). For example, a manufacturing firm may be organized according to process, that is, production, finance, marketing, and so on. Again, the consultant will diagnose the appropriateness of the subsystem design according to a set of standard criteria that reflect the possibility of mismatches among contingency elements specific to the type of social system in question (i.e., primarily productive, maintenance, adaptive, or managerial, as organized via a particular set of design dimensions).

Johnson, Kast, and Rosenzweig (1973) have suggested several design criteria that further specify the focus of a structural diagnosis. Stated simply, the first criterion is: to what extent does each subsystem function under clear and understood duties, rights, and obligations? Clarity does not imply 'simple.' Rather, it connotes a clear understanding by subsystem members of what the broader system or other subsystems expects of them. If people within the subsystem are not clear about their purpose, the consultant will seek to discover the reason. A high degree of interdependence across subsystems can fragment purpose and confound the participants' understanding of their role in the system. (See Chapter 2 for a discussion of subsystem interdependencies as a major design problem. Chapter 7 considers subsystem interdependency in the framework of general systems theory.) Multiple responsibilities of members to several subsystems can cause them to be confused about what is expected of them. If a member of one subsystem is responsible to several groups, the possibility exists that his role in the organization consists of unrelated task requirements. Here a clear and easily understood purpose is lacking. Obviously if the individual does not have a clear understanding of the system's expectations it will be difficult for him to perform effectively. This does not mean that a member cannot perform effectively with responsibilities in more than one subsystem, only that it is probably a source for a design problem since special skills, norms, and climate are needed to facilitate such multisystem or multidesign membership. (Chapter 6 discusses this further.)

The second criterion is that of flexibility. To what degree is the design of subsystems and individuals within the subsystems able to respond effectively to changing circumstances? If flexibility is lacking it may be that subsystem and individual roles are incongruent with conditions and events impacting the system. The roles may be too rigidly defined. This would be especially true when rigid job descriptions and responsibilities exist in a dynamic environment. Within a changing adaptive system, such as a research organization, tight design specifications may be dysfunctional since the effectiveness of these systems frequently depends upon their ability to adapt and to explore new discoveries and research developments that do not easily fit into predetermined guidelines.

The third criterion is reliability. How consistently do the various subsystems perform their function? Here the consultant seeks to find the probability of subsystems breaking down and failing to accomplish their purpose. Subsystems may be designed to meet average or normal requirements, but may be unable to meet peak load requirements. The design may lack mechanisms for the concentration of resources to meet unusual demands. The problem often exists where work flows vary greatly according to seasonal or sporadic fluctuations. Breakdowns often occur in systems where the design has not changed in accordance with changing conditions that the firm encounters. Although most designs are never significantly altered once established, can the designs deal reliably with constant or changing task requirements over time?

The fourth criterion is acceptability. Does the design consider people's acceptance of the subsystem? Effectiveness may be impaired if members do not accept their positions within the design. Acceptance is often lacking when the design is imposed by top management or those located outside the designed subsystems. The design itself may have good potential, but the system's effectiveness is limited unless the design includes some method of gaining the participants' acceptance. Chapter 2 discussed this criterium as an instance of topdown versus participative design and described the desirability of generating internal commitment of organizational members.

To the extent that these criteria for effective design appear to be lacking, as sensed by the MAPS consultant, it may be inferred that there is at least the probability of a design problem in the social system. Basically in the diagnostic phase of the MAPS Design Technology, the consultant qualitatively examines the interactions, activities, and sentiments within and between the subsystems. He does this in accordance with the more specific criteria presented above, with the general criteria suggested by contingency theory, and with a view toward the three principles for intervention in a social system: valid information, free choice, and internal commitment (Argyris, 1970a).

Systematic Data Collection for Diagnosis

The consultant's preliminary diagnosis of the climate, processes, and designs in an organization will call upon his skills of sensing, observing interpersonal interactions and group processes, communicating and, especially, listening. As he begins to learn about these aspects of the organization, the consultant will be able to identify potential problem areas. Having developed some ideas and collected some information, the consultant will conceptualize the diagnosis to determine what additional data he will need. This second level diagnosis will generally involve the use of more structured interviews with a number of people in the organization, followed by a systematic data collection of potential design problems via formal questionnaires that include the quantitative analysis of member responses to such diagnostic questionnaires. This information and the findings that result from such second level diagnosis are the typical base upon which a decision can be made as to whether a significant design problem actually exists.

Ordinarily the MAPS consultant should interview several people throughout the organization at different functional areas and at different levels within the hierarchy. This will give him an overall view of the organization, rather than a biased view by top management, his initial contact person, or any other interest group. The typical course of events is for the consultant to interview ten to thirty people in the organization, but once a consistent, understandable set of themes or problem areas emerge, additional interviews are not necessary. This is usually evidenced when most of the information in a number of interviews becomes increasingly redundant to what has already been provided.

Following these interviews, the MAPS consultant might often proceed in a more comprehensive manner to gather and analyze data from the client system. To date, he has relied primarily on strictly qualitative assessments through observation and structured interviews. From the latter, he has obtained some basic themes and problem issues, but these may still be quite general and vague and it is difficult to suggest the relative importance of the different themes. At this point, more formal and quantitative assessments can be planned and conducted to better pinpoint and define the problems of the client system, and in particular, whether the problems stem largely from deficiencies in organization design or from other types of variables.

The survey feedback method is most suitable for this stage of data collection and problem definition (Bowers, 1973; Mann, 1957). This method can be applied in many forms, but basically it involves using structured questionnaires containing items related to organizational climate, processes, design issues, and so on, and asking all members of the organization or social system to repond to them. These questionnaires may be a set like those used extensively in other organizations, that have been pretested, validated to some extent, and generally having norms to which one can compare the given organization's responses (Bowers, 1973; French, 1972).

An alternative is to construct a questionnaire specific to the issues and concerns of the client system. While such a specially designed questionnaire would not be as reliable as existing instruments, nor would there be norms from other organizations to draw comparisons, it would be more relevant to the client system since the items on the questionnaire are directly geared to that system. Consequently, what the existing questionnaires share in reliability and normative data, the specially constructed questionnaire contains in validity and relevance (Jackson and Messick, 1967). If the basic themes and problem items elicited during the structured interviews are similar to the dimensions assessed by available questionnaires, then these can be confidently utilized. However, if the themes are unique or, as a total, are not contained in a convenient, available set of questionnaires, the MAPS consultant should seriously consider designing a special purpose questionnaire.

The first step involved in the development of a structured questionnaire for a specific client system is to enumerate the various themes or problem items that were uncovered during the observation and interview assessments. Generally the themes can be further subdivided into unidimensional items, and when the total list is combined additional items may be developed to round out the final set of questionnaire items. A typical format for this questionnaire would be a five- or seven-point Likert scale (e.g., 1 = "not at all," 7 = "extremely"), asking respondents to indicate to what extent each listed problem item or issue is of concern to them, or to what extent each item limits their potential contribution to the organization (or to their work group), including items about the actual designs of the organization. Alternatively the format might ask respondents two questions for each item: (1) where they perceive the organization to be now regarding that issue, and (2) where they would like to see the organization in the future concerning that issue. The latter format enables the calculation of "discrepancy scores," the difference between what is and what could be. The greater the discrepancy between the two perspectives on an item, the more that item represents a major problem for the organization.

Once the questionnaire has been administered to the organization and the responses have been tabulated, various calculations can be performed on the data. Means, standard deviations, ranges, discrepancy scores, and so on, can be calculated for the whole organization or by subsystem to suggest the major problem areas. If those items concerning the designs of the organization are emphasized, the MAPS consultant can be reasonably confident that the problem facing the organization can be defined as a design problem, thus minimizing the Type III error. However, if items concerning primarily process issues are most strongly endorsed, two possible explanations must be considered. One is that the problem is not mainly one of design, and therefore some other framework and a different team of consultants may be necessary to help the organization further define and address its problems. But because organizations and individuals are often insensitive to design problems and are not conscious of the impact of the design on their behavior, the results may be somewhat misleading. While the same may be true if design problems are heavily endorsed (i.e., are respondents insensitive to process variables?), our own experience in organizations suggests that people tend to recognize and attribute problems to process variables before they can articulate the consequences of ineffective designs, particularly overall organization designs rather than job designs alone.

Some of the abovementioned issues regarding the use and interpretation of survey questionnaires can be alleviated by two principal methods. The first is to provide some educational input to organizational members before they respond to the questionnaire about the various items contained in the questionnaire and their meanings. This might entail seminars on process variables, climate and organization design, and how to recognize potential problems regarding these items when they exist. The second and perhaps even more basic method, in addition to the first, is to involve all members or their representatives in the organization in developing the items for the survey questionnaire. This is consistent with the subsequent development of task items for the MAPS questionnaire discussed in Chapter 4. Starting from the basic themes and problem areas uncovered by the MAPS consultant during his initial observations and interviews, the members could add to this list, refine it, and phrase the items to fit their style of expressing issues (which is often unique to a particular organization, similar to a "culture"). In any event, the participation of members in developing the survey questionnaire and having the MAPS consultants provide educational inputs as to the meaning of process and structural variables (as well as how to calculate and interpret the results of the questionnaire) would not only facilitate the interpretation of data but would tend to assure that valid information, free choice, and commitment were actually being generated.

The MAPS Design Technology will have impact on the organization in terms of both process and structure. However, as mentioned previously, if the problem is primarily one of process, the consultant may recommend that an approach other than MAPS be used. For example, if a diagnosis concludes that there is a lack of clarity of goals, then a goal-setting or MBO (management by objectives) program might be beneficial to the organization (Hughes, 1965; Odiorne, 1965; Reddin, 1972). If the skills to teach and implement such methods were available within the MAPS consultant team, this would be initiated. If other skills were needed, another consultant would be recommended. After the organization has improved its goal clarity, there might be a new diagnosis to determine if the MAPS Design Technology would be useful to the organization.

Design Boundaries for the Design Problem

The diagnostic phase is completed when client and consultant agree on the nature of the problem facing the organization. Such agreement may not always be possible. In such cases the differing opinions will be communicated and the consulting relationship terminated, as indicated in Step 4 of Figure 3.1. Where consensus is reached on the nature of the problem, the next step is to make sure that each party understands how the problem is related to the organization's effectiveness (Chapter 6 will discuss the various components of organizational effectiveness and how MAPS affects each of these.) In those cases where the problem is determined to be one of organization design, the client and consultant must ascertain whether or not MAPS is applicable. In many organizations, prior constraints may prevent the application of MAPS. Union rules, government regulations, contracts or the like, could so severely limit MAPS that it would be impractical to attempt implementation. Enough time may not be available, or financial conditions may be so severe that the system cannot afford to proceed with MAPS. Whatever the reason, it should be made clear to both parties why MAPS would be impractical. If it is decided that MAPS is applicable, the client system or subsystem must be able to generate and respond meaningfully to the MAPS questionnaire. Before the response capabilities of the system can be known, the space within which MAPS will be applied must be determined.

It is necessary, therefore, to determine the boundaries of the design analysis, both spatial and temporal, as shown in Step 5 of Figure 3.1. If the design objective strictly concerns and is completely appropriate to one time perspective (e.g., operational purposes), then one MAPS design analysis can effectively confront the entire social systems design problem. However, to the extent that more than 100 individuals are involved (i.e. computer program limitations) and more than one time perspective needs to be handled by the social system (e.g., strategic as well as operational purposes), the social systems design problem must be decomposed into smaller and/or separate design analyses. While a representative sampling of the social system membership would often be feasible and thus would negate computer program limitations, the benefits of having most or all social system members participate would more than offset the costs of decomposing the design problem.

However, even if all the members in the organization could be included in one MAPS analysis (i.e., if there were no computer program limitations), it might still be conceptually and statistically appropriate to decompose the design problem. Basically, task items for the MAPS questionnaire that are relevant for top management may not be relevant at all for lower members of the organization, and vice versa. Responses to the MAPS questionnaire would therefore be highly skewed on some items, which may violate some of the statistical assumptions to be discussed in Chapter 4. But conceptually, and perhaps realistically, there are some differences in ability and perceptions of tasks throughout the hierarchy, which suggests that separate MAPS analyses are relevant to different portions of the organization. This latter course might lead to a more optimal solution rather than simply combining all "natural" differences in one analysis. Chapters 8 and 9 will touch upon this decomposition issue again, and it will probably seem more pertinent after the reader has comprehended the entire MAPS Design Technology.

We now consider additional decomposition issues. For example, an organization might apply the MAPS Design Technology by identifying several autonomous divisions and then investigating the redesign of these divisions by separate MAPS analyses. This entails a horizontal decomposition of the design problem. Alternatively the design of one or more divisions could be managed by a vertical decomposition. This would be accomplished by distinguishing natural "breaks" in the organization's hierarchy, such as the institutional, managerial, and technical levels (Katz and Kahn, 1966; Parsons, 1960), and then performing a MAPS analysis for each of these hierarchical spaces. In some cases it may be desirable to decompose the design problem by some combination of horizontal and vertical boundaries, although each design case would have to be determined by a careful analysis of the intra- and interboundary interdependencies. Significant suboptimizations would certainly result if the design problem were decomposed in a manner whereby considerable interdependencies existed across the design boundaries and if these were not taken into account in the design analysis. Such suboptimization would be manifested even further if these cross-boundary interdependencies were rooted in the given structures within the design boundary; consequently a change in design would either be constrained by these interdependencies or would require a particular change in the design of other subsystems (where the interdependencies are "connected") for each to operate effectively. However, if the interdependencies across the design boundary were largely rooted at the boundary and not within it, the structures within the boundary could be redesigned with greater freedom and with less likelihood of suboptimization.

A second major issue of determining the design boundary is temporal as opposed to spatial whether the objectives of the design are primarily for short-range or long-range purposes, or the translation of long-range into short-range activities. Short-range purposes are generally addressed by OPERATIONAL DESIGN, long-range by STRATEGIC PLANNING DESIGN, and the translation purposes by PROBLEM-SOLVING DESIGN. While these distinctions might be manifested in the vertical decomposition of hierarchical levels (i.e., institutional levels are designed for strategic planning, while technical levels are designed for operational purposes), this is not automatically the case. The highest levels of the organization (or social system) may have been designed via operational criteria explicitly (because we know most about these and therefore can be most explicit), or long-range activities and planning may become dominated by short-range pressures.

The important point, however, is that an OPERATIONAL DESIGN may need to be quite different from a STRATEGIC PLANNING DE-SIGN (i.e., human, technological, information, etc., resources may need to be mobilized and structured differently for these different designs), and therefore it is essential to be explicit concerning the time frame of the design objectives. If the purpose of the design is strictly operational, this provides a boundary on the design analysis (i.e., to consider the mobilization of resources for short-run purposes). The design of a social system for strategic planning purposes also imposes a time boundary on the design analysis.

Just as issues of suboptimizaton had to be considered for the horizontal and /or vertical decomposition of the design problem, the same issues are relevant for decomposing the design problem into OPERATIONAL, STRATEGIC, and PROBLEM-SOLVING DESIGNS. In the latter case, however, suboptimization results if the social system is given only one design and all activities are expected to be performed within that one design. This often occurs when the organization is designed for operational purposes and when strategic or problem-solving purposes are confronted only by an INFORMAL DESIGN. Alternatively, the social system may have its resources mobilized in more than one design, for a social system is analogous to differentiating a given system to match different resources more effectively with different environmental problems (Lawrence and Lorsch, 1967a).

Given the complexity of the issues involved in identifying, defining, and then decomposing the design problem, it should not be surprising that the process to decide on these issues is also quite complex and dynamic. The foregoing has mainly outlined some of the steps in the process as well as some of the general criteria involved in making the various decisions. Both the MAPS consulting team and members (or representatives) of the organization must go through the decision process together, sharing values, expectations, information, and perceptions. While it is difficult to indicate a specific set of steps from identifying a design problem to precisely defining the design boundaries for the MAPS analysis (because each situation would contain its own organic evolution of decisions between consultant and client), a general approach can be suggested. This approach, the judicial process, is described in detail in Chapters 5 and 6 (Implementation and Evaluation) where the complexities of the decisions also require a qualitative, organic, and flexible decision process (Kilmann and Mitroff, 1975, 1977; Mitroff and Kilmann, 1975a; Wirt, 1973).

Briefly, once the organization's problem has been defined as a design problem via the various diagnostic assessments, members of the organization (or their representatives) individually prepare short statements as to the nature of the design problem, the important issues involved, and how the problem would be resolved ideally. These statements might also include a recommendation (though tentative) of the design boundaries for a MAPS analysis (i.e., vertical, horizontal, and temporal considerations, including whether more than one design is necessary for organizational effectiveness). The members would then be divided into groups by the MAPS consulting team according to similarity of perspectives and recommendations. In these groups, the members would prepare a group statement that would be more comprehensive than the individual statements, with supporting arguments for their particular views. When the group statements are completed, representatives from each group would meet to debate their differences and to examine critically the underlying values, assumptions, and arguments for each proposal.

In essence, the same data sources (i.e., data from observation, interviews, and survey questionnaires, as discussed earlier), can suggest alternative views of the design problem depending on the assumptions that are made, the values underlying the assumptions, and the implicit design concepts that different individuals will perceive as relevant. However, through an active debate of these differences, a synthesis can be developed that creatively combines the advantages of the different approaches and positions, and minimizes the disadvantages or weaknesses. The synthesis that emerges as a result of the debate not only tends to minimize the Type III error (i.e., that the wrong problem was solved), but because the judicial process involves both the MAPS consulting team and members of the client system, greater acceptance and commitment to whatever decisions are made is usually evident. Further, because the expertise, perspectives, and resources from the consulting team and the organization were applied, the decisions themselves are expected to be better as well as being the 'right' decisions.

The resulting synthesis or decision that would evolve from the above judicial process, would specify the intended design boundaries for the social system for a MAPS analysis. For example, MAPS would be recommended to analyze the functionality of the organization's OPERATIONAL DESIGN for the existing X, Y, and Z divisions, involving all top, middle, and lower management personnel. Or MAPS would be recommended to create a separate PROBLEM-SOLVING DESIGN to exist approximately five hours per week, and twenty members from each A, B, C, and D department would be nominated to be involved in this design. Alternatively MAPS would be recommended to create a temporary STRATEGIC PLANNING DESIGN that would involve thirty middle managers from M and N product groups, and ten top managers at corporate headquarters to work 10 hours per week for approximately three months to develop a 25-year planning horizon for the organization. Chapter 4 will discuss how the MAPS Design Technology can actually create these bounded designs for a social system, and why more than one design may be necessary to improve organizational effectiveness (e.g., an OPERATIONAL and a STRATEGIC PLAN-NING DESIGN).

Certainly further research is needed to develop a reliable and efficient means of assessing the relative advantages and disadvantages of defining different design boundaries for the MAPS Design Technology (different ways of horizontally and vertically decomposing social systems design problems), so that the MAPS analyses would minimize the suboptimization of dealing with less than the total system.

Go MAPS?

Looking back at Figure 3.1, once the design boundaries are established (although this decision should not be considered fixed), the next steps of the MAPS Design Technology are set in motion. This involves generating the task items for the MAPS questionnaire, specifying the people items (those included within the design boundaries), and having members respond to this MAPS questionnaire (assuming a particular scientific model of MAPS, as will be discussed in Chapter 4). However, the decision to "go MAPS" and to begin the MAPS questionnaire process assumes that the members to be involved in the design analysis are willing and able to participate in the process. Even though various commitments and psychological contracts may have been established during the diagnostic and problem identification stages, new issues of commitment, motivation, and knowledge always arise. Therefore the process of climate assessment, climate building, educational inputs, judicial decision processes, and so on, may be instituted at numerous points throughout the MAPS design process. While the reader will recognize this in the discussions in Chapters 4, 5, and 6, where these issues and processes are continually raised, it should be emphasized that the qualitative aspects of the MAPS Design Technology (including the organic, flexible, and evolutionary aspects of its steps) require such frequent assessments and process interventions.

For example, in the decision to go MAPS, are the members sufficiently aware of the MAPS Design Technology to participate in developing a useful and relevant MAPS questionnaire? Perhaps various educational inputs are required to help members conceptualize their task objectives, task activities, and so on, in order to write "good" task items for the questionnaire. This process is somewhat analogous to management by objectives (MBO), but it has become evident that individuals cannot automatically write good objectives (Reddin, 1972). Usually members require not only an educational input but also actual experience in writing objectives, obtaining feedback, practicing further, and so forth. The same holds true for MAPS. In some cases (see Chapter 8) members design the MAPS questionnaire, respond to it, see the results from the MAPS Computer Program, and then the membership decides that following this experience they want to redesign their MAPS questionnaire since they now understand it better.

The major point is that various educational, climate building, and practice sessions (and "dry runs" of the MAPS design analysis) may be necessary to assure that the "final" task items on the MAPS questionnaire and the responses to it foster valid information, free choice, and commitment (Argyris, 1970a). These criteria are central to all steps of the MAPS Design Technology. Thus when the decision is made to go MAPS, it is made with the understanding that these criteria will continually guide the interactions between the MAPS consulting team and members of the client system throughout the entire MAPS process.

CONCLUSIONS

With the boundaries set, the initial entry and diagnostic phase of MAPS is completed. If the diagnosis is incorrect the problem will be misstated, and the consultant will have failed to formulate the problem correctly. If the wrong problem is isolated, the solution will be ineffective while the original problem remains. For example, if an organization's difficulties are centered in process issues, a change in the design of the organization may be completely useless. The converse, of course, is also true: if an organization is incorrectly designed, no amount of process intervention will resolve the problem. The method of entry and diagnosis suggested in this chapter is intended to minimize the probability of solving the wrong problem, that which Mitroff has called the Type III error (Mitroff and Featheringham, 1974). When both consultant and client agree that the problem is one of design and that it can be solved by implementation of MAPS, the next steps in the technology can be undertaken. Chapters 4, 5, and 6 will discuss these steps in detail but, as Chapter 6 (Evaluation) will emphasize, the steps of MAPS are cyclical. If for a variety of reasons the initial design problem is not solved or if new design problems emerge, the entry and diagnostic steps are again set in motion and the MAPS design process continues.

Chapter 4
Input, Analysis, and Output

In collaboration with Robert T. Keim and Walter P. McGhee*

The MAPS Design Technology is proposed as a systematic set of methods and procedures to actually design an effective social system. The core of the MAPS design process uses questionnaire data on members' task and /or people preferences (via the MAPS questionnaire), to group tasks into task clusters and people into people clusters, and can then assign each people cluster to a task cluster (via the MAPS Computer Program), which results in alternative organization designs (via the MAPS output formats). MAPS is intended for a wide variety of design objectives, such as forming OPERATIONAL, PROBLEM-SOLVING, STRATEGIC PLANNING, and INFORMAL DESIGNS, as well as certain combinations and variations of these "pure" designs; and the creation of these designs is centered mainly around this core of the technology.

While Chapter 3 introduced and discussed entry and diagnosis, MAPS consists formally of as many as twelve distinct steps starting from this entry and diagnosis (including the identification of a problem that can be confidently conceptualized as one of organization design), and progressing to the evaluation of whether a newly implemented design actually improved organizational effectiveness (i.e. that the design change actually solved or managed the initial problem). Specifically, the steps include the following:

1. Entering and diagnosing the organization or social system.
2. Conceptualizing the design problem and determining the boundaries of the analysis (e.g., who is to be included, which departments, divisions, etc.).
3. Specifying the design objectives (e.g., designing for operational purposes, for strategic planning, etc.).
4. Choosing one of the scientific models of MAPS (i.e., different combinations of input variables, computer analyses, and output formats in relation to design objectives or conceptual models of the problem).
5. Developing the task and /or people items for the MAPS questionnaire (i.e., tasks to accomplish, people to work with on the tasks).

*This chapter also benefited from the contribution of Samandar N. Hai.

103

6. Responding to the MAPS questionnaire (e.g., the extent to which each respondent would like to work on each task and with each other respondent).

7. Analyzing the design data from Step 6 via the MAPS Computer Program (i.e., using multivariate statistics to generate alternative organization designs by showing which groups of people should work on which clusters of tasks).

8. Selecting a MAPS design (i.e., choosing one of several designs that can be generated in Step 7 via a dialectic debate).

9. Implementing the selected design (i.e., providing resources, authority, policies, responsibility, etc., for members to actually work in the new design; team building and support to help them learn to work effectively in the new design).

10. Monitoring the implementation process (e.g., assessing resistances to change, emerging problems, etc., and then utilizing strategies to best manage the process).

11. Evaluating the results of the design change (i.e., does the new design solve or manage the initial problem? Does the new design improve organizational effectiveness?).

12. Rediagnosing the organization or social system (i.e. reinstating the problem-solving process as described by the Diamond Model in the introductory chapter).

Regarding these twelve distinct steps, it should be evident that the core of the MAPS Design Technology is repesented in Steps 5, 6, and 7—the input, analysis, and output of the computerized design analyses. This core is what makes MAPS concrete and operational, and around which the prior and later steps have been developed. Without this core, MAPS would be strictly a qualitative, or "soft," technology and therefore would not have the advantages of precise quantitative formulations. It is important to point out, however, that although the core of MAPS is the concrete and computerized aspect of the technology, it is in a broader sense the smallest aspect of the whole technology. Figure 4.1 attempts to illustrate the relative proportion of MAPS that is the core versus the other more qualitative aspects. In particular, the steps of the technology prior to the core are primarily system entry and diagnosis (Chapter 3) while the steps following the core are primarily concerned with implementation and evaluation (Chapters 5 and 6). The basic reasons why the prior and latter steps are so important relative to the core (even though the former are qualitative), is that the prior steps determine the validity of the data gathered

FIGURE 4.1   The Relative Importance of the Core of MAPS versus the Other Steps of the Technology (ST,NT,SF, and NF are the Jungian types illustrated and defined in Fig. 1.3)

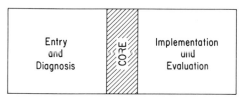

The Whole MAPS Design Technology

Entry and Diagnosis	CORE	Implementation und Evaluation

= quantitative portion (ST)

= qualitative portion (NT, SF, NF)

in the core and the steps following the core, determine if the potential of the MAPS output will actually be manifested.

Figure 4.2 provides a similar view of the twelve steps of MAPS by suggesting where these steps fall on the Diamond Model of problem solving discussed in the Introduction. The core of MAPS is thus the scientific model, collecting data to solve the model (responses to the MAPS questionnaire) and deriving design solutions. While these steps are certainly important, the discussion on the Diamond Model emphasized the overriding importance of appropriately conceptualizing the problem and later effectively implementing a solution. All the stages of the Diamond Model are interdependent, as are the steps of the MAPS Design Technology, but too often academicians (those who develop technologies) concentrate on the quantitative and rigorous aspects of the technology (i.e., the core) and either ignore or treat lightly the relevance of the technology to particular social and organizational problems, and its actual implementation (Kilmann and Mitroff, 1977). The latter is the main concern of practitioners.

In this chapter special attention is given to provide the reader with a thorough understanding of the core of MAPS (input, analysis, and output). Included are the derivation and characteristics of the six

FIGURE 4.2 The MAPS Design Technology vis à vis the Diamond Model of Problem Solving Developed by Segasti and Mitroff, 1973 (The numbers refer in the figure to the 12 formal steps of the MAPS Design Technology; numbers 5,6, and 7 are the core steps of MAPS)

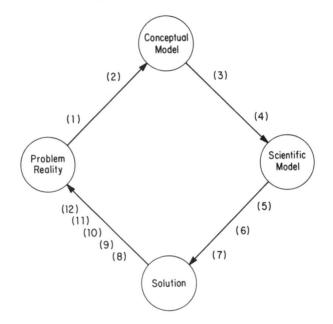

scientific models of MAPS and how these pertain to the creation of fundamentally different organization and social systems designs. However, as we present and discuss these aspects of MAPS, we cannot emphasize enough that these quantitative steps are only valid to the extent that the qualitative steps are performed appropriately and effectively. The core of MAPS is thus a necessary, but not sufficient, condition for designing effective social systems.

INPUT: THE MAPS QUESTIONNAIRE

The MAPS Design Technology requires the members of the social system to respond to two types of questionnaire items: (1) to indicate on a scale the extent to which the member views particular tasks as important now or in the future to accomplish social system objectives, according to how the member believes he can best contribute to these objectives, and (2) to indicate on a scale the extent to which the member can interact well with each of his social system colleagues in the process of performing social system tasks.

Task Items

Once the design boundaries have been defined, it is desirable to have all members within these boundaries involved in the development of the task items for two reasons: (1) their inputs (information, perspectives, interests, task abilities, etc.) are probably the most relevant concerning the possibilities for attaining social system objectives, and (2) their commitment to any new design is essential for that design to be successfully implemented in the social system (Argyris, 1970a). This process of developing task items for the MAPS questionnaire is paramont to the design of purposeful social systems (as discussed in Chapter 2), and assumes that the entry, diagnosis, and boundary decisions (discussed in Chapter 3) were appropriately addressed by the MAPS consultant and the social system so that meaningful and valid information will actually be generated.

If the design objective is strictly for operational purposes, only the members within the design boundaries need participate. However, if the design objective involves strategic purposes and the social system's adaptability to its environment (i.e., an open system), then it is also necessary for identified members of this environment to participate in the development of the MAPS questionnaire. In essence, any individual or group of individuals whose present or future behavior impinges on the social system in question may have a relevant input to make regarding the design of the social system, because they represent the environmental changes to which the system will need to adapt. This participation of individuals in the environment is not essential if the design objective is mainly operational since the latter reflects internal, day-to-day activities that are not directly affected by environmental changes. Also, since the environment of the social system has potentially a much larger membership than that within the social system, it will generally be necessary to provide participation for the MAPS questionnaire through stratified random sampling (i.e., stratified via major environmental segments) (Kish, 1961). A later section in this chapter (The Six Scientific Models of MAPS) will further discuss the differences between designing for operational versus strategic purposes, as well as other design objectives.

A general procedure for developing the task items for an organization division being designed for operational purposes is as follows: Top management first outlines some broad categories of either organizational objectives or basic functions to which the division is committed. Then the members are asked to generate specific task items that describe the activities they currently perform, activities they feel should be performed, and/or activities they would like to perform that fall into the categories outlined by top management. This process attempts to integrate individual and organizational objectives in a manner analogous to management by objectives (Argyris, 1964; Odiorne, 1965; Reddin, 1972). If a large number of task items are generated (greater than 100), it will usually be necessary for a representative group to look over the list and eliminate or combine redundant or ambiguous items. The final list should consist of approximately 40–100 items that are agreeable to both top management and the members involved, where each item is concise (one or two phrases) and each meaning entirely clear to all members in the design analysis.

Figure 4.3 illustrates how a final list of task items is developed into the first portion of the MAPS questionnaire. The items in the figure were developed by fifty members of a division from a major U.S. corporation comprising five levels of management (from first-line supervisors to the vice-president of the division) across three functional areas. It should be noted that the design objective of this list of task items was for operational purposes, therefore individuals external to the division were not involved.

People Items

The second type of item appearing on the MAPS questionnaire is termed "people" items. These are simply a listing of all the members involved in the design analysis. As illustrated in Figure 4.4, each member is asked to indicate how much he would like to interact with each other member in the pursuit of social systems objectives. These items attempt to summarize the interpersonal factors, shared interests, and political or personal reasons for desired interactions among members. Naturally, because of the general style in which the questionnaire is phrased, each member may apply his own criteria. This also affords the possibility of members' choosing one another based on congruency (i.e., compatible differences) as well as on similarity. Basically, if various groups are composed of individuals with too diverse interpersonal styles, attitudes, and values they

FIGURE 4.3 An Illustration of Section I from the MAPS Questionnaire

Please indicate how much you would be interested in participating in either all or a portion of each of the following organizational tasks.

	NOT AT ALL	MUCH BELOW AVERAGE	BELOW AVERAGE	AVERAGE	ABOVE AVERAGE	MUCH ABOVE AVERAGE	OF PRIME INTEREST
Acquaint or sell customer on proposed system job	——	——	——	——	——	——	——
Furnish technical support in meetings with customer	——	——	——	——	——	——	——
Attempt to influence customer specifications	——	——	——	——	——	——	——
Participate in specification review with customer	——	——	——	——	——	——	——
Prepare detailed system description	——	——	——	——	——	——	——
Determine if all customer obligations have been met	——	——	——	——	——	——	——
Recommend design changes to simplify, reduce cost, and standardize	——	——	——	——	——	——	——
Coordinate new assemblies to utilize standard parts	——	——	——	——	——	——	——
Identify new product opportunities	——	——	——	——	——	——	——
Develop new product sales promotion and literature	——	——	——	——	——	——	——
Introduce new products to the customer	——	——	——	——	——	——	——
AND SO FORTH. . . .							

109

FIGURE 4.4 An Illustration of Section II from the MAPS Questionnaire

Listed below are all the participants in this analysis. With regard to the task items that you endorsed in Section I, please indicate *how much you would like to work with each individual listed.*

For those individuals with whom you are not familiar, mark the category designated 'don't know the person'. Such a response is better than a guess. When your name appears please mark your response toward the 'none I'd like more' category for statistical purposes and to preserve your anonymity.

	DON'T KNOW THE PERSON	NOT AT ALL	MUCH BELOW AVERAGE	BELOW AVERAGE	AVERAGE	ABOVE AVERAGE	MUCH ABOVE AVERAGE	NONE I'D LIKE MORE
John Doe	——	——	——	——	——	——	——	——
Bill Green	——	——	——	——	——	——	——	——
Sam Jones	——	——	——	——	——	——	——	——
Jim Smith	——	——	——	——	——	——	——	——

AND SO FORTH. . . .

will have a difficult time in fully utilizing their technical resources in a task environment that requires much interaction among members. Consequently most designs must be formally based on some interpersonal and social compatibility within social systems subunits (Argyris, 1962).

Questionnaire Instructions

The instructions for Sections I and II of the MAPS questionnaire, shown in Figures 4.3 and 4.4, are only one way of approaching task and people items. Using the Jungian framework we can suggest four perspectives for a respondent endorsing task items and people items, which results in four different types of information to be used in designing an organization. Figures 4.5 and 4.6 summarize these four Jungian phrasings and perspectives for the MAPS questionnaire. Thus the ST approach (Sensation-Thinking) emphasizes expertise vis à vis task items and specific, detailed resume information regarding people items. The SF approach (Sensation-Feeling) considers specific personal and subject reasons for endorsing task items and social motivational reasons for choosing people. The NT approach (Intuition-Thinking) is future oriented with regard to expertise that might be appropriate to specified tasks and also has a future orientation in the anticipation of working with people, but the NT only "needs" a broad, impersonal summary of the people issues as shown by the person's name. Finally, the NF approach (Intuition-Feeling) responds to a future orientation vis à vis the subjective aspects of task items and tends to respond best to people information in the form of a picture, a summarized statement of an individual's subjective qualities. The reader is referred back to Chapter 1, and specifically to Figure 1.3, for a discussion and summary of the four Jungian types and how these are germane to organization design issues.

Each of the foregoing Jungian phrasings are alternative sources of, and /or perspectives on, information for creating various organization designs. The choice of which phrasings to use in a particular application of MAPS (or some combination of the "pure" phrasings) will generally be determined by discussions between the MAPS consultant and members of the organization in early steps of the technology. As we will see shortly, the steps in the core of MAPS (as well as other steps) present several alternatives to those deciding on the design process, but it is beyond the scope of this book to detail each decision process. Suffice it to say that the judicial decision process introduced in Chapter 3 and discussed in the following chapters is often used to

FIGURE 4.5   Sample Instructions for Section I of the MAPS Questionnaire on Task Items on a 7-Point Likert Scale

---

ST   Please indicate the extent of your expertise in pursuing the following task issues and activities, by grading your expertise for each task in the space provided.

SF   In the space provided, please indicate the extent to which you would enjoy pursuing the following task issues and activities.

NT   How much do you anticipate that your expertise could contribute to the successful accomplishment of the following task issues and activities?

NF   How much of a rewarding and pleasant experience do you anticipate by being involved in the following task items and activities?

NOTE. See Figure 1.3 for illustrations of the four Jungian Types.

FIGURE 4.6   Sample Instructions for Section II of the MAPS Questionnaire on People Items on a 7-Point Likert Scale

---

PURE TYPE

ST   Please evaluate the following individuals as to the extent of their expertise in relation to the tasks you most strongly endorsed. (Résumé of each individual may also be shown.)

SF   Please indicate to what extent you would enjoy interacting with the following individuals. (Interests, likes, and values of individuals may also be shown.)

NT   How supportive and complementary do you anticipate the expertise of the following individuals would be for the successful accomplishment of those tasks you most strongly endorsed?

NF   How much of a rewarding and pleasant experience do you anticipate by being involved with the following individuals? (A picture of each individual may also be shown.)

NOTE. See Fig. 1.3 for illustrations of the four Jungian Types.

facilitate the decisions made in the context of the MAPS Design Technology, and to ensure that members will respond to the MAPS questionnaire (and to the other steps of the technology) in a thoughtful, forthright, and meaningful manner.

The Validity of the MAPS Questionnaire

Because of the importance of the input to the MAPS anlysis, It should be mentioned that the use of self-report questionnaires has received considerable concern and attention by psychologists in general and psychometricians in particular (Jackson and Messick, 1967). The issue focuses on whether individuals can validly report their perceptions, attitudes, behavior, values, interests, needs, and so forth, on a five- or seven-point Likert scale, which is the format of many self-report instruments (and of the MAPS questionnaire). Naturally if one adopts a Theory X posture on this matter, the assumption would be that individuals are not aware of their attitudes and other subtle aspects of their personality (or that these are not even conceptualized to exist), or that they cannot be trusted to meaningfully and honestly endorse a questionnaire. In a sense one must assume Theory Y if any reliance is to be placed on responses to questionnaires, or if the use of questionnaires is to be considered in the first place.

The issue, however, is much more complicated than this Theory X-Theory Y distinction concerning whether individuals can report on their own perceptions, experiences, task abilities, and so on. Specifically, a number of reliability and validity issues must be considered (Jackson and Messick, 1967). For example, self-report questionnaires are subject to various response distortions including "social desirability." Thus individuals may respond to a questionnaire more in terms of what they see as desirable responses or what they expect the administrator of the questionnaire is "looking for" rather than how they really feel about the items on the questionnaire and this social desirability bias may occur in an unconscious manner. In a methodological study, for instance, Thomas and Kilmann found that this response bias could explain as much as 90 percent in the variance of individual responses to questionnaires measuring conflict-handling behavior (Thomas and Kilmann, 1975), and these authors strongly recommend that researchers pay more attention to this social desirability variable, attempt to control it in the construction of new instruments, and to consider the response bias as an alternative explanation for interpreting the responses to self-report questionnaires.

Other methodological issues include reliability (e.g., that responses to the questionnaire are stable over time if stability is expected, given what is being measured) and construct validity (i.e., that the questionnaire assesses what it purports to assess and not some other construct, trait, or variable). Loevinger (1967) presents a comprehensive classification of reliability and validity issues as follows: (a) substantive validity (defining the pool of relevant items for the instrument and the selection of items, factor-analyzing items to investigate the underlying dimensions of the concept being assessed, and testing the internal consistency of items identified with each dimension); (b) structural validity (that the format of the instrument or questionnaire and the calculation of individual and organizational scores is consistent with the intended concept being assessed); and (c) external validity (investigating the expected relationships between the responses or scores of the instrument and other measures or manifestations of actual behavior). This classification incorporates the notions of reliability and validity discussed by Peak, Cronbach and Meehl, and Campbell, as reported in Jackson and Messick (1967).

While it would take a lengthy discussion to systematically evaluate the nature and use of the MAPS questionnaire on each and every aspect of reliability and validity, it does seem appropriate to consider briefly some of these issues since much reliance is placed on member responses to the MAPS questionnaire (i.e., the resulting social systems designs suggested by the MAPS analysis dependent completely on the validity of the input).

First, consider the social desirability response bias presented above. The extent to which individuals (1) feel they are being evaluated, (2) do not trust the use to which their responses will be applied, and (3) are unsure about their own abilities and worth all tend to foster this response bias. Many of the diagnostic and educational steps discussed in Chapter 3, and the climate building and participation of members in developing and responding to the MAPS questionnaire are expected to minimize social desirability as a motivation for responses to the MAPS questionnaire. This is particularly true for individuals described in (1) and (2) but may not have much effect on (3). Nevertheless, while the steps leading to the input may not altogether eliminate this response bias, its effects at least should be minimal. On the other hand, the extent to which the prior diagnostic, educational, and climate building steps are not performed well will tend to intensify social desirability responses.

Second, the issue of reliability is not as relevant to the MAPS questionnaire as it is to the instruments attempting consistently to assess fairly stable personality dispositions in individuals. Each application of MAPS utilizes a different MAPS questionnaire for somewhat different and/or unique purposes. Furthermore, because member interests and abilities change, because the task environments of organizations change, and since the objectives of the organization itself can be altered abruptly, one should be slightly suspicious if responses even to the same MAPS questionnaire did not change over time. However, if responses changed on a daily or weekly basis, this might suggest that the questionnaire is "unstable" or not especially reliable, particularly if the social system in question existed in a fairly stable environment. Clearly the issue of reliability for the MAPS questionnaire is highly contingent on the design objectives (operational vs. strategic), and the legitimate expectation that some amount and frequency of change will be shown. In other words, to investigate the "reliability" of the MAPS questionnaire is not an either/or question but depends instead on many situational factors. While some organizations have completed the same questionnaire more than once (see Chapter 8), this was done because a change was expected and was demonstrated in fact. To date, a MAPS questionnaire has not been administered twice if no change was expected, but this needs to be done to achieve an important test of reliability.

To support the basic reliability of the MAPS questionnaire it should be stated that test-retest reliability is not the only criterion. Other criteria include the following: equivalent forms, split-half, and internal consistency reliability (Jackson and Messick, 1967). The last mentioned standard, while emphasizing concurrent versus longitudinal reliability, is shown by the frequently high internal consistency of task items within task clusters and of people items within people clusters, to be discussed further on (Cronback, 1951). Nevertheless, the issue of reliability will be researched further.

Finally we consider the three forms of validity summarized by Loevinger (1967). Substantive validity for the MAPS questionnaire is suggested by the careful process involved in defining the pool of items to appear on the questionnaire that provide considerable content or face validity. Very few other social science instruments can claim such a detailed and systematic process of determining the final list of questionnaire items. However, the issue being considered is whether other types of variables or items should be included on the MAPS questionnaire as additional sources of information for designing social systems. (This will be discussed further in Chapter 9 in relation to the future of MAPS.) Naturally the choice of people items is self-evident, assuming that the design boundaries have been appropriately established. The issue of internal consistency has already been mentioned, and the use of factor analysis to uncover the underlying dimensions of the many task (and people) items is "coincidentally" considered by the factor analysis procedures of the MAPS Computer Program to be discussed subsequently.

Structural validity, following Loevinger's framework, is suggested for the MAPS questionnaire by the seven-point Likert scale, which is suitable for the calculation of Pearson correlations, the statistic assumed by the factor analytic procedures of the MAPS analysis (Harman, 1967). The responses to the MAPS questionnaires thus provide the appropriate format for deriving clusters of task and people variables (and their assignment) as intended by the MAPS analysis. Although the actual statistical distribution of responses to MAPS questionnaires may be skewed away from the assumptions of a normal distribution, various calculations and transformations of raw data are conducted to minimize the effect of these skews. While one might argue that Pearson correlations and factor analysis assume interval scaling and that a seven-point Likert scale is closer to being ordinal, the distribution and scaling of questionnaire responses must generally be considerably different from a normal, interval distribution before nonparametric statistics would yield significantly different results (Nunnally, 1967). Currently research is under way to examine the differential effects of parametric versus nonparametric correlation and clustering procedures on MAPS analyses (e.g., do such different statistical assumptions and procedures lead to significantly different organization designs of both practical and statistical significance?).

External validity is perhaps the most difficult aspect of validity to demonstrate since it is analogous to the process of theory construction, empirical testing, theory reconstruction, and so on, which is necessarily a major longitudinal undertaking. To date the evidence of external validity for the MAPS questionnaire (and the entire MAPS Design Technology) comes from the various applications of MAPS to actual organizational and social systems as well as from several strictly research investigations. Chapter 8 summarizes aspects of these "external validity" studies, although specific studies attempting to isolate the effect of the MAPS questionnaire alone have not been conducted. This should certainly be a focus for further research.

Although a number of research studies investigating the reliability and validity of the MAPS questionnaire are either in progress or are planned, it seems appropriate to place these issues in perspective with other research instruments and questionnaires in the field. In essence, if one rejects the use of self-report questionnaires for the MAPS Design Technology, one must also reject the great majority of empirical research studies that have relied on self-report assessments. We do not intend this comparison to serve as an excuse or rationale for using the MAPS questionnaire (i.e., if others can do it, so can we), but only to appreciate the state of the art of questionnaire development. Although they have a number of pitfalls, such questionnaires are still a very efficient means of data collection and will undoubtedly continue to be used as the major source of assessment. Until there is a viable alternative means of assessment that can gather large quantities of diverse information quickly, efficiently, and at relatively low cost, we will have to rely on questionnaires while attempting to appreciate, manage, and minimize the methodological problems as best we can.

THE MAPS ANALYSIS

While a great variety of statistical analyses are possible from member responses to the MAPS questionnaire, the following multivariate analyses are most significant for the evaluation and possible change of a social system's design: (1) separating the list of task items into distinct clusters representing various task structures of the social system, (2) separating respondents to the MAPS questionnaire (i.e., the members directly involved within the boundaries of the design, in contrast to individuals who may have generated task items via environmental memberships) into people clusters to confront the various task structures of the social system, and (3) assigning clusters of tasks to clusters of people (respondents), which results in possible subsystem designs for the organization. This section not only describes the essential steps and features of the MAPS analysis (including the MAPS Computer Program which performs the various analyses), but it also considers some key issues and concerns regarding the use of multivariate statistics, namely, whether sampling or population statistics are appropriate and whether task and people clusters should be of homogeneous or heterogeneous composition.

It should be emphasized that only through the use of multivariate analyses can all the relevant information needed to design a complex social system be processed and utilized, since no group in top management could possibly comprehend and process all the task preferences and abilities, interpersonal preferences, task interdependencies, and so on, of twenty or more members to designate an effective organization. Briefly described, multivariate analyses, such as factor analysis (Harman, 1967), are ways of reducing the apparent complexity of large amounts of information to a number of separate clusters via the elimination of redundancy and overlap (Simon, 1962). Items of informaton are grouped together because they overlap (i.e., are similar and covary), while separate clusters or groupings themselves are unique (i.e., are dissimilar and independent). Perhaps a major reason that organizations have been designed by the dictates of top management is because technologies such as MAPS have not been available to allow the many lower members of the organization to have their preferences efficiently processed via multivariate programs.

Raw Data Transformations

Since MAPS relies on the multivariate procedure of factor analysis, a number of transformations of the raw data from member responses to the MAPS questionnaire are required to improve the data's suitability for this type of analysis. Specifically, the formal factor analytic method requires input data to be multivariate normal and homocedastic (Harman, 1967). Responses to the MAPS questionnaire are generally subject to the following three types of skewing (McKelvey and Kilmann, 1975).

One skew results because respondents unfamiliar with various task items simply endorse the "not at all" category. Consequently the distribution of responses on the task items are usually normal except for a large skew at that point. If this bias (skew) were not altered slightly, the "not at all" responses would have much more influence in the solution than the "of prime interest" responses. In order to alleviate this bias, all the task items are standardized around the same mean and standard deviation.

A second skew in the input data comes from the high number of "don't know the person" responses on the people items, especially when the MAPS analysis cuts across traditional design boundaries; consequently, members have not had the opportunity to interact with other members listed on the MAPS questionnaire. Furthermore, aside from this type of skew for the response distribution on people items, there are likely to be differences in the variance of responses across the people items. This latter bias would give some names more influence in the design solution than others. The solution to the people item skews is to compute standardized item distributions using "valid" responses for each people item, and then to insert the calculated mean whenever the "don't know the person" responses appear. Not only does this procedure equalize the effect of the separate people items, but the "don't know the person" responses have no effect on the intercorrelations.

The third source of skewing results from different responses to the seven-point Likert scaling system on the MAPS questionnaire. For example, some individuals respond primarily by using the end points of the scale. Since factor analysis relies on product moment correlations, it is clear that a person who uses primarily "ones" and "sevens" would have much more of an effect upon the design solution than a person who perhaps made the same kind of discrimination but happened to use "threes" and "fives." This skew can generally be eliminated by standardizing the input data by response style; that is, each individual's responses across the task and people items are standardized to the same mean and standard deviation.

Forming Task Clusters

Once the raw data has been transformed to alleviate the various skews, a factor analytic technique is applied to separate the MAPS task items into clusters representing various social systems task structures. The factor analysis procedure consists of an interactive process for estimating communalities (starting with the highest correlation in row estimate), producing the initial eigenvectors by the principal factor method, and using Kaiser's Varimax formula for orthogonal rotation (Harman, 1967).

The design objective manifested in this procedure closely approximates what is referred to as a unifactor solution (Harman, 1967), an ideal solution in which each variable loads extremely high on one factor and has zero loadings on all other factors. The properties of this procedure that are most useful for organization design include: (1) high interrelationships of task items within the same cluster, and (2) low interrelationships across different clusters. A desirable feature of high interrelationships of task items in a cluster is that all the task items placed in the same cluster are seen by organization members as belonging together for one reason or another, which suggests that those task items should be handled together (i.e., in one subsystem of the organization or social system). Furthermore, the low interrelationships across the task clusters suggest that the different clusters of tasks can be performed relatively independent of one another by different subsystems with minimum needs for coordinating activities across the subsystems.

The basic property of the MAPS analysis that suggests minimum coordination across the separate clusters of task items is that all the important task interdependencies are contained within the clusters; therefore these interdependencies can be managed explicitly and not left to develop into significant interface conflicts among subsystems (as discussed in Chapters 1, 2, and 3). For example, given the current design of the social system, a task activity in one subsystem may need to be directly linked with tasks from other subsystems in order for the entire system to accomplish its objectives. The MAPS Design Technology is designed to draw out these interrelationships of tasks into a separate task cluster. Without this procedure, the single task items might remain uncoordinated or simply not be linked together appropriately. The phenomenon just described is termed a "latent task structure," because without such an analysis of task items these interrelationships would remain obscure and hidden.

Using a factor analytic procedure to form task structures creates a particular problem for social systems design in that both positive and negative loadings can and generally do appear on the separate task clusters. If, for the sake of argument, the positive loadings represent the central thrust of the task cluster, then the negative loadings represent tasks that social systems members see as not belonging to the central thrust; and perhaps these negative loaded items represent a direct "opposition" to this thrust (versus being simply independent of the thrust, in which case the items would appear on other task clusters). However, for the objective of designing a purposeful social system, it is not enough to indicate that a particular task cluster "rejects" one or more task items. Instead, the question arises as to which task clusters would have items congruent with the central thrust of the clusters? The solution to this question requires that each task item generated and responded to by the social system be placed on a congruent task cluster, in fact, on its most congruent task cluster. In other words, each task cluster would have the same signed loadings of task items comprising the cluster, and those task items that had to be reassigned to other clusters because their signed loadings were opposite to the sign of the central thrust of the cluster would be placed on the task cluster with the highest appropriate loading. If a task item was not congruent with the central thrust of any task cluster in the factor analytic solution, the item would be placed on its least incongruent task cluster. An algorithm has been added to the factor analytic procedure described earlier to allocate task items to task clusters in a manner consistent with the design objectives of purposeful systems.

The factor analytic procedure used for MAPS allows the list of task items to be separated into different numbers of clusters. This follows from the property of this procedure that the solution is indeterminate, since it is rather arbitrary in regard to how many factors or clusters to rotate (Harman, 1067). Thus seventy task items might be distributed into two, three, or perhaps as many as twenty clusters (i.e., until negative roots are encountered). These different task clusters represent different task structures for the social system, while each task structure attempts to contain the important task interdependencies within the clusters (i.e., to maximize the internal consistency of task items within a cluster and to minimize the average intercorrelations between clusters, subject to the reallocation procedure discussed above).

Forming People Clusters

The second type of MAPS analysis concerns the creation of new clusters of social systems members that can be utilized to address specified task clusters. In essence, this is the core of the MAPS method in that clusters of people are actually identified as being able to pursue social systems tasks with the greatest potential for developing effective social systems. MAPS thus sets the stage for a mechanism to implement new social systems design if this is desired. Lacking this latter mechanism, the analysis thus far has only indicated possible new task structures within preexisting subsystems. Unless a new design of subsystems can be provided that reflects such new task structures, it is unlikely that any systematic design changes will occur (i.e., subsystem designs heavily control task-oriented behavior in social systems).

The basis of this analysis involves separating the respondents of the MAPS questionnaire into people clusters according to their similarity in endorsing task items and in indicating which of the listed members as people items they can best interact with in the pursuit of social systems tasks. In essence it is expected that if respondents are placed in the same people cluster as a result of congruencies on task and people variables, the resulting subsystem is more likely to marshal its problem-solving abilities and resources toward agreed-upon objectives.

With the intention of designing purposeful social systems, the factor analysis on respondents creates the same type of problem noted earlier in regard to the analysis on task items. In particular, both positive and negative loading respondents appear on a given people cluster. If the positive loadings represent the central core of the people cluster, the negative loadings represent individuals not wanted in the people cluster by the core members. Purposeful subsystems should evolve from people who want to get together for positive reasons and not because they all have a common dislike for one or more other individuals. The solution to this problem is identical to that for the task clusters in that noncore members can be reallocated to other people clusters, specifically, to their most congruent people cluster or to their least incompatible people cluster. An algorithm has been added to the factor analytic procedure to perform this reallocation of respondents appropriately in line with the design objectives of purposeful systems.

The MAPS analysis of respondents, like the analysis of the task items, permits different solutions. For example, a given number of respondents may be divided into different numbers of people clusters, starting with two people clusters, until the roots become negative (Harman, 1967). Each solution represents a slightly different way of decomposing the membership, and each solution attempts to bring together into people clusters members who have interpersonal and task congruency.

Figure 4.7 illustrates the form of a data matrix resulting from responses to the MAPS questionnaire, and shows the distinctions between the MAPS analysis on task items versus the MAPS analysis on respondents. The latter is based on correlations between respondents, while the former is based on correlations between task items. The columns thus show task and people variables (i.e., columns on computer keypunch cards), while the rows of the matrix represent each member responding to each task and people item (variable) on the MAPS questionnaire (on a seven-point Likert scale; see Figures 4.3 and 4.4).

Selecting a Social Systems Design

The foregoing MAPS analyses can be combined specifically to match each people cluster with a task cluster for each possible design solution (i.e., the number of clusters that are extracted for both tasks

FIGURE 4.7 The MAPS Data Matrix (Arrows indicate variables included in the MAPS analysis of task items (top) and of respondents (right). The lines in the data matrix following the arrows indicate the cases included in the analyses)

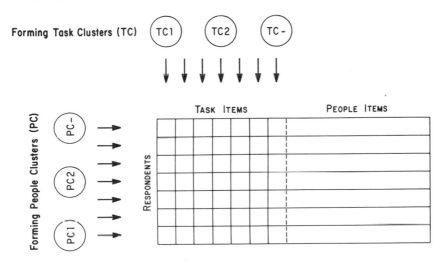

and respondents). For example, the "five cluster" solution would separate seventy task items into five task clusters and fifty respondents into five people clusters. Figure 4.8 illustrates the MAPS Design Matrix for this hypothetical situation. Then an operations research method is used to assign each people cluster one of the task clusters, with the objective of maximizing the overall "fit" between the two (King, 1965). In other words, each people cluster would be matched as much as possible with a task cluster that represents the members' first choice. The same match-ups can be determined for a two-cluster solution, a three-cluster solution, and so on, until either the task clusters or the people clusters have reached their statistical limits (i.e., the next highest solution encounters negative roots). At this time an index is computed that describes the "goodness of fit" between each people cluster and its assigned task cluster for each of the cluster solutions. For the sake of clarity, we shall now explicitly define a people cluster as a grouping of organizational or social system members via the MAPS analysis, and a task cluster as a grouping of organizational or social system tasks also via the MAPS analysis. A subsystem, however, is specifically the match-up of a people cluster with a task cluster (i.e., a subsystem is a task-oriented group).

FIGURE 4.8   An Illustration of the MAPS Design Matrix for a Five Cluster
Solution: 50 Members and 70 Task Items

DISTRIBUTION OF 50 MEMBERS	DISTRIBUTION OF 70 TASK ITEMS				
	TC1	TC2	TC3	TC4	TC5
People Cluster 1 (10 members)	.95	1.54*	.06	− .32	.76
People Cluster 2 (5 members)	2.07*	− .15	.67	.98	−1.32
People Cluster 3 (8 members)	− .51	1.02	1.27*	−1.05	.29
People Cluster 4 (12 members)	1.20	− .86	−1.20	− .21	3.05*
People Cluster 5 (15 members)	.42	1.06	− .29	1.14*	.94

NOTE. TC1 = Task Cluster 1 with specified task items, etc.; Members of each people
cluster are listed in alphabetical order.
* The most efficient matches between people clusters and task clusters. With the
standardized means as elements in the matrix (based on member responses to the
MAPS questionnaire), a goodness of fit index can be computed to compare the
efficiency of several design solutions that can be derived from the same MAPS data
source (i.e., comparing the five cluster solution with the six cluster solution, etc.).

The MAPS Computer Program

A FORTRAN program has been developed to combine all the
foregoing analyses and indices into one computer run. This program
begins with the raw data from member responses to the MAPS questionnaire and first performs the various transformations (standardiza-
tions) to remove the several skews so that the data is appropriate to the
assumptions of factor analysis. Then factor analyses are applied to the
transformed data via the extraction of two clusters of task items, two
clusters of respondents, and so forth until either reaches its limits.
Next the reallocation of tasks and respondents to their most appropriate clusters is performed so that all clusters contain the same signed
loadings in a manner that reflects the objectives of purposeful systems. Indices are then calculated (and standardized) that make up the
elements of each MAPS Design Matrix (Figure 4.8). Following that an
operations research algorithm is applied to assign each people cluster
a task cluster in the most optimal manner, for each design solution
(i.e., for each MAPS Design Matrix that can be formed). This algorithm also calculates the goodness of fit index for each of these
solutions: a coefficient of purposefulness.

Currently the MAPS analysis is performed using factor analysis, specifically an orthogonal varimax rotation that computes independent factors. However, one could argue whether some other multivariate clustering technique should be used. Presently MAPS researchers are considering oblique as opposed to orthogonal rotation (Nunnally, 1967). Another method under consideration to serve as the core of the MAPS analysis is a nonparametric technique that could make use of ordinal data, hierarchical clustering (Nunnally, 1967). This technique is becoming more widely used in the social sciences and computer programs are available to perform the analysis. Thus the next step in the evolution of the MAPS analysis is to evaluate the alternate solutions (i.e., organization designs) produced by these various multivariate techniques to ensure the best use and interpretation of the information on the MAPS questionnaire. However, the goals of the MAPS researchers are oriented toward effecting social systems change and, statistical arguments aside, MAPS can and will be applied to organization design and redesign. If better statistics and multivariate procedures can be used, they will be examined in order to improve the MAPS design solutions.

As an example of how important the MAPS Computer Program is, consider the following comparison. Around 1955, before a factor analysis program was readily available on the computer, it would take approximately ten people working forty hours a week for one year to compute a single factor analysis on twenty variables. About 1965 the same factor analysis could be performed on the computer in approximately four hours. In 1975 the same factor analysis computation could take as little as five seconds. The MAPS analysis, however, entails as many as twenty factor analyses as well as other data transformation and operations research algorithms in the complete program. Most MAPS analyses can now be performed from raw data to printouts of alternative organization designs in less than five minutes, which may involve as many as 200 variables (task and people items). Clearly, this is much beyond the capabilities of managers to comprehend and duplicate without the use of the computer and the MAPS Computer Program.

Sampling versus Population Statistics
for the MAPS Analysis

Because of the complexities of the MAPS analysis, in particular the use of many multivariate statistics, an issue arises as to the appropriateness of these various statistical calculations given "sample size" considerations. Specifically, a key issue in utilizing various statistics (e.g., means, correlations, multivariate analyses) is the ratio of variables to respondents. Psychometricians generally recommend that a sample contain at least five to ten times as many respondents as variables (Nunnally, 1967). Otherwise it is expected that any inferences drawn from the statistics will be unstable, and therefore not generalizable to other research samples. In the extreme, if there are fewer respondents than variables, the inferential statistics are expected to be either indeterminate or totally misleading (Nunnally, 1967). Clearly the MAPS analysis has varying ratios of respondents (members included in the design analysis) to variables (task and people items on the MAPS questionnaire). Further, since the analysis to form people clusters is a transposition of the traditional data matrix (i.e., "respondents" are variables and "variables" are respondents, see Figure 4.7), and since the analysis to form task clusters entails using only the task items as variables (see Figure 4.7), either or both of these analyses may have the same number of respondents as variables, or one of the analyses may even have fewer respondents than variables (depending on the relative number of task items vs. task and people items vs. respondents).

While these various ratios of number of respondents to number of variables would be a major problem for inferential statistics, as noted above (i.e., drawing inferences to other samples), this is not a problem for the MAPS analysis for two reasons.

First, the results of any MAPS analysis are intended solely for the use of the organization or social system in question and are not meant to be applicable or generalizable to any other organization or social system. In each application the task items are unique, the people items are unique, and the respondents are unique. Thus each MAPS analysis is for all practical purposes dealing with a defined population and not a sample. Only when stratified sampling is to be used to represent environmental segments in developing task items for the MAPS questionnaire (as discussed earlier) are sampling procedures appropriate.

Even if the MAPS questionnaire (task items) were partially developed by the inputs of sampled environmental segments, only the designated organizational members included in the design boundaries respond to the questionnaire, and this set represents the population of the design analysis and not a sample. Only if representation within the design boundaries were included in the MAPS analysis would sampling statistics be in operation and the ratio of respondents to variables be of importance. In such a case the design analysis would be expected to generalize to all members contained in the design boundaries, whether or not they responded to the MAPS question-naire. Not only has this type of application not been attempted, it is also not recommended, since commitment to the resulting design might be sacrificed as mentioned earlier. In other words, since the principles of valid information, free choice, and internal commitment (Argyris, 1970a) are emphasized throughout the design process, all members within the design boundaries are expected to develop and respond to the MAPS questionnaire even if the MAPS analysis has to be decomposed to several analyses (as discussed in Chapter 3 on decomposing the design problem). Each MAPS analysis would there-fore entail a population and not a sample.

Second, it is also important to recognize the distinction between sampling versus population statistics as it applies to research studies with the MAPS Design Technology. One might initially expect that sampling statistics are appropriate for research studies when some statements or hypotheses are tested on a number of organizational samples to draw conclusions about organization design theory or the MAPS Design Technology in general. Even here, however, one can argue that the various respondents to variable ratios shown in MAPS analyses are not crucial since each bounded system is a separate data point; that is, each MAPS analysis on some organization constitutes a single response, just as an individual (however internally designed) is utilized as a single respondent in a research study that seeks to make inferences about a broader population of individuals. Stated differently, the sample size for a research study using the MAPS analysis is not the number of respondents within design boundaries but the number of organizations or social systems designed by MAPS. Therefore, if we are concerned about respondent-to-variable ratios for drawing conclusions from inferential statistics in MAPS research studies, the "respondents" are the number of organizational units designed by MAPS and the "variables" are the various independent and dependent measures used to assess various design relationships (e.g., the relationship between a design change via MAPS and organi-zations' responsiveness to environmental changes). Only if research studies are conducted within some design boundary may the re-searcher have to consider the number of respondents to variables within the MAPS analysis, if the researcher wants to draw inferences for other MAPS applications.

In summary, the MAPS analysis is based on population statistics and not on sampling statistics, so that the various ratios of respon-dents to variables are irrelevant except for some special research foci as noted above. It should also be stated that due to the manner in which communalities are estimated (Harman, 1967), an analysis in which the number of respondents (cases) are fewer than the number of variables, an indeterminate solution cannot result.

Homogeneous Versus Heterogeneous Composition of Subsystems

As discussed in Chapter 1, a number of studies in the field of organization design have described a variety of approaches to make organizations more effective (Kilmann, et al., 1976; Lorsch and Lawrence, 1970). A central theme in all these approaches is that organizational subsystems should be designed so that each has homogeneous attributes and characteristics (as well as process specialization) in order to address its objectives most effectively and /or to best "fit" with the nature and characteristics of a homogeneous segment of the organization's task environment (Thompson, 1967). Such a design of homogeneous subsystems is expected to facilitate the management of the organization's complex and differentiated environment, where some environmental segments are very dynamic and others are very stable, but where homogeneity is designed within subsystems to effectively manage overall environmental uncertainty (Lawrence and Lorsch, 1967a).

The extensive literature on group dynamics and small-group decision making and problem solving, however, raises potential inconsistencies and important reservations in regard to the central theme of homogeneity that underlies the literature on organization design. In particular, a major issue or theme considered by the small-group literature is whether heterogeneity of group composition is best for solving complex problems whereas homogeneity is best mainly for solving simple and routine problems (Hoffman and Maier, 1964, as summarized by Shaw, 1971). While the combined results from this series of research studies are by no means conclusive, the main argument that heterogeneity of members' personalities, skills, and perspectives would facilitate the solution of a complex task (because a variety of approaches and perspectives require utilization on a complex task or problem), is naturally a compelling and logical explanation.

The inconsistency between the two literatures stems from the general experience and acknowledgment that organizations, as whole systems, are attempting to confront and solve complex problems, and since organizational environments are becoming increasingly dynamic and complex (Bennis, 1966a; Duncan, 1972; Emery and

Trist, 1971), it is important for those who are designing or redesigning organizations to know whether organizational subsystems should be homogeneous or heterogeneous (or some combination) with regard to various design dimensions. It is evident that the MAPS Design Technology is heavily rooted in the assumptions and findings of the organization design literature and, as a result of the factor analytic procedures, MAPS does group tasks into homogeneous task clusters and people into homogeneous people clusters. Consequently it is of crucial importance to recognize that the MAPS analysis is explicitly creating homogeneity within the newly designed subsystems; therefore no matter how well or effectively the other steps of the technology are performed, if homogeneity is an inappropriate design assumption, the resulting designed subsystems via MAPS are likely to be ineffective.

It is therefore essential for the development of organization design theory as well as for the further development and application of the MAPS Design Technology, that the design assumption of homogeneity is explicitly examined and tested. In view of this, Kilmann and Seltzer (1975) performed an experimental study to investigate whether homogeneous or heterogeneous group composition would lead to better subsystem outcomes (quality and acceptance), including the effectiveness of the process by which these outcomes are achieved. An experimental design was chosen to maximize "internal validity" of whatever results would be forthcoming, and the MAPS Design Technology was applied similar to the method used in an organizational setting to maximize "external validity" (generalizability) to such settings (Campbell and Stanley, 1963). Furthermore, to foster the validity of the experiment, two tasks were utilized (each to assess a different aspect of outcomes), management students were the subjects, and the MAPS analysis was modified so that heterogeneous subsystems could be designed. Finally, it should be apparent that MAPS can deal with the issue of homogeneity versus heterogeneity on the two design dimensions: task composition and people composition.

The results of the experimental study provided evidence that homogeneous people composition augments acceptance, but heterogeneous people composition enhances the quality of the decision. The opposite effect seems apparent for task composition; that is, heterogeneous task composition augments acceptance of the group's decision by its members, while homogeneous task composition enhances the actual quality of the decision. As explicated by Likert (1961), the overall effectiveness of an organizational decision is a multiplicative product of both quality and acceptance. Consequently both forms of composition may need to be considered further in regard to the design of organizations.

In terms of the group process that occurred as the groups were attempting to accomplish the objectives of the two tasks, there were substantial differences that related to the type of task being performed. On a values type task the task composition was an overriding factor, as compared to people composition which had a greater impact on a technical type task. Specifically, group process was fostered by homogeneous task composition on the values task, while group process was fostered by homogeneous people composition on the technical task. In either case homogeneity was conducive to better group process as perceived by the members in the experimental groups.

At this point it is necessary to return to the organization design issues raised earlier and attempt to provide some synthesis of the various findings. In particular, the two outcome assessments (quality and acceptance of decisions) as they pertain to organizational effectiveness need to be balanced with a consideration of group process. While it can be argued that the outcome variables are of prime importance, real organizational settings do not always have or are amenable to precise outcome measures, and therefore reliance must be placed on process variables (presumably, better process leads to better outcomes). A synthesis of these different perspectives is also meant to help resolve the indicated discrepancies between the organization design and the small-group literature in regard to homogeneous versus heterogeneous subsystem (group) composition.

Consider the objective of designing effective subsystems for the successful accomplishment of value type tasks (analogous to strategic planning). The results of the study indicated that subsystems would gain both quality and acceptance by either homogeneous task and people composition or by heterogeneous task and people composition, but not by mixed conditions (i.e., homogeneous task and heterogeneous people composition, or heterogeneous task and homogeneous people composition), since the latter designs would emphasize quality or acceptance but not both. However, since value type tasks do not have "objectively correct" answers, designers might decide to choose the homogeneous task and people composition because it facilitates group process via homogeneous task composition. Similarly, with the objective of designing effective subsystems for technical type tasks (analogous to operational activities), the same two design combinations are suggested (both homogeneous and both heterogeneous) because they tend to generate both the quality and acceptance necessary for overall effectiveness. However, if the outcomes of the technical tasks are not clearly or easily measurable, design of homogeneous task and people compositions is desirable since group process is facilitated by people composition on technical type tasks.

The overall results of the study thus seemed to indicate that the combined homogeneous designs would be the most generally appropriate for a variety of design objectives unless group process was not important (hence the combined heterogeneous designs), or unique design objectives were being pursued that emphasized either quality or acceptance but not both (hence the mixed designs).

As a result of the Kilmann and Seltzer study, some general support is given to the use of factor analytic and clustering procedures that explicitly create homogeneous task and/or homogeneous people compositions of organizational subsystems. Additional research on this topic is currently under way and if the heterogeneous compositions receive more support there are plans to formalize the design of heterogeneous subsystems into the MAPS Computer Program. Perhaps such additional research may suggest a contingency approach to the use of MAPS that would indicate for which design objectives or social systems tasks, homogeneous versus heterogeneous subsystem compositions should be designed. In the meantime homogeneity will be utilized as the underlying design criterion since it is still supported mainly by the organization design literature and by the specific experimental study just presented.

How can the apparent discrepancies in organization design and small-group literatures be synthesized? Consider an analogy of organization to small group, where the unit of analysis for the organization is the subsystem while the unit of analysis for the small group is the individual. By designing subsystems that attempt to contain the important interdependencies, the organization is creating greater homogeneity within the subsystems; simultaneously, however, there is greater heterogeneity between subsystems. In retrospect, this situation is analogous to that of the small-group literature since each individual in a group can be considered homogeneous within himself, while for complex tasks the literature emphasizes the need for heterogeneity across individuals, which is analogous to heterogeneity across subsystems (but homogeneity within) for the organization. Perhaps the apparent inconsistency is not so much a difference in substance but a variation in the level of analysis: the individual for the group and the subsystem for the organization.

Meanwhile the Kilmann and Seltzer study has benefited from the motivation to experimentally test the apparent inconsistency that led to further understanding of both areas of investigation.

THE MAPS OUTPUT

Currently the output of the MAPS analyses (via the MAPS Computer Program) is a printout for each design solution (e.g., two clusters, three clusters, etc.) that shows an alphabetical listing of the members in each people cluster along with an itemized listing of the tasks composing the task cluster assigned to each people cluster. These lists of task and people assignments portray the various MAPS designed subsystems for the organization or social system. Figure 4.9 shows an example of a MAPS output, although the actual output would include the MAPS Design Matrix (as illustrated in Figure 4.8) as well as the calculated "coefficient of purposefulness" for each design solution. The issue arises, however, as to the most meaningful and useful form that this output could take to facilitate the following: (1) an understanding of social systems design in general and the MAPS designs in particular, and (2) what it means to choose one design over another, and the consequences to the social system of a different design.

The traditional approach to this problem of representing the design of the social system or organization is the organization chart. As described in most organization theory and management texts (Gibson, et al., 1973), the organization chart presents the basic design categories (i.e., how the subsystems are defined), the position of the manager who is primarily responsible for the activities and performance of each subsystem, and the formal lines of authority (and communication) that define the relationships of one subsystem to another. The organization chart is often elaborated to include the positions, functions, and authority relationships among organizational members (and not just subsystems), and some organizations further develop their representation of organization design to specify members' job designs by means of a job description: a fairly detailed accounting of the objectives and/or activities that concern the member.

The organization theory literature appears to lack alternative ways of representing an organization's design (the organization chart is only one alternative) and methods by which these different representations tend to facilitate decisions, based presumably on the informa-

FIGURE 4.9   An Example of Output From the MAPS Computer Program:
A Strategic Planning Design for a Multinational Corporation

People Cluster 1 Assigned to Task Cluster 4

Person 8
Person 12
Person 21
Person 23
Person 28
Capital Availability
Acquisition and Merger Possibilities
Projection of Cash Flows
Return on Investment
Monetary Exchange
Insurance Against Risks

People Cluster 2 Assigned to Task Cluster 1

Person 1
Person 6
Person 14
Person 31
Person 35
Legal System of Host Country
Host Government Attitudes Toward Foreign Investment
GNP /Per Capita Income
Market Potential
Distribution Channel Systems
Production Costs
Social /Cultural Factors Impacting Upon Products

People Cluster 3 Assigned to Task Cluster 6

Person 2
Person 3
Person 18
Person 29
Restrictions on Ownership
Level of Industrialization
Raw Materials Availability
Availability of Cheap Labor and Trained Management

AND SO FORTH. . . .

tion portrayed in such representations. This problem is analogous to that of representing cash and material flows in the organization via the various summarized accounting reports (Gordon and Shillinglaw, 1964). Since decisons that must be based on an assessment of cost, revenue, cash, and related kinds of tangible assets are constantly required, accountants and economists have designed summarizing indices (i.e., ratios, tables, figures, etc.) so managers can more easily comprehend and respond to complex decision problems in their organization. The argument here is the need for representations of organization design that would summarize the more intangible yet equally important aspects of organizational behavior which have been discussed as social systems design issues.

Specifically, we have viewed design as the differentiation of subsystems within the social system or organization and the subsequent integration of subsystem behavior into a functioning whole. As Lawrence and Lorsch (1967b) emphasize, however, differentiation and integration occur in other dimensions besides product, function, and authority patterns. They found differentiation with regard to behavioral attributes such as leadership style, personality type, and different cognitive, emotional, and structural orientations. Yet these differentiations have not to our knowledge been represented as summarized information for decision makers. Also, the different mechanisms and /or requirements for integration have not been a part of representations of organization designs (e.g., extent of interdependencies among subsystems, committees created to foster intersystem coordination, etc.). The point we wish to emphasize, however, is that these additional kinds of differentiations and integration aspects undoubtedly have an important bearing on how work gets done in the social system; consequently, since many decisions will have to be made that are based upon or affect these issues, it seems necessary to represent organization and social systems design to facilitate such decision making.

As indicated, the current MAPS output represents the social systems design in a fairly limited manner: the listing of task clusters assigned to people clusters including the MAPS Design Matrix. Research is currently under way, however, to explore alternative representations of organization design: (1) the kinds of information that should be included in the design representation, and (2) the form in which this information should be displayed.

In regard to the first point, the MAPS analyses not only design people clusters, task clusters, and their match-ups (i.e., subsystems), but they can also provide information on the internal consistency of either via an alpha coefficient of internal consistency (Cronback, 1951), and the extent of interrelationships among the various people clusters and task clusters (via intercorrelation coefficients). This information might be useful in suggesting the potential and need for team building within subsystems and for inter-team building because of intergroup interdependencies and conflicts. Further, the MAPS Design Matrix provides information not only on the optimal match-ups between people clusters and task clusters, but also on the extent to which each people cluster prefers and is able to perform both unassigned (via the calculated indices of all elements in the matrix) and assigned task clusters (see Figure 4.8). This information might be exceedingly useful when the social system needs to reallocate some task activities across subsystems because of slack in one subsystem or because of an "overdemand" for services or products in one or more subsystems. In particular, such information would help the social system to transfer members or task responsibilities in the most optimal manner.

The second issue concerns the form that this information would take; that is, how is the information to be represented to managers who will be making decisions related to the organization's design? Different form possibilities include: (1) tabular charts, (2) flow charts, (3) diagrams, and (4) matrices. Research studies will investigate the effect of these different forms on the quality of decisions, based on the information displayed by these varied representations of social systems design. In addition it is probable that one single form will not emerge that is best in all decision situations. Instead a contingency framework would be developed to suggest which type of representation provides the most useful display of information for which kinds of decisions.

THE SIX SCIENTIFIC MODELS OF MAPS

Thus far, we have presented the standard model of MAPS: an integration of task and people items in forming subsystems of organizational members. Generally, however, this standard model is only applied to a subset of design problems (e.g., designing for operational activities). A greater variety of organization designs is needed to cope with a broad range of social system purposes and objectives. The basic assumption is that unless the organization explicitly designs or mobilizes resources with definite responsibility, authority, and policies to actually pursue various objectives, the objectives are not likely to be accomplished. Stated differently, the foundation of organizational behavior as we conceive it is the design process and the resulting organization designs.

Most organizations generally have one formal design represented as the organization chart. This design usually specifies the major design categories (e.g. marketing, finance, production, etc.) and the various positions utilized to coordinate these functions into total organizational behavior. From our experience in organizations and from the abundant literature in the field, it seems safe to argue that the formal designs of most organizations are for performing day-to-day activities and effectively producing well-defined products and services rather than for solving complex and changing problems. Thus the basic design of most organizations is ST, precise, well-defined and oriented toward specific short-range tasks and goals. The NT, SF, and NF Jungian types, however, portray organization designs that are characteristically different from the predominant ST design. Briefly, the NT design is more open and flexible and emphasizes planned interactions with the environment. The NF design, also open and flexible (less rigidly structured), has less of the traditional hierarchy than the NT design. The SF design, which contains the specificity of the ST design, focuses on interpersonal interactions and communication and also has less of the traditional hierarchy (due to the F). (See Chapter 1 and Figure 1.3 for a discussion and illustration of Jungian psychological types applied to organization design.)

From various studies of managers and their concepts of organization design, these four different designs have consistently emerged from the four Jungian types (Kilmann and Mitroff, 1977). Figure 4.10 shows how each of the four types of managers actually draws or represents the organization design via an organization chart. It is interesting to note that only the ST design "looks" like the typical organization chart, which is consistent with the above arguments. It is also interesting that the ST chart usually lists specific tasks in each box while the SF chart lists the names of specific people. Generally both the NT and NF charts are vague and do not get down to detail. These charts often show the boxes (fewer than the ST and SF charts) without anything written inside them. Also the NT and NF designs, particularly the latter, generally show more flexibility and freedom for organizational members, which is necessary for dynamic environments, complex problem solving, and strategic planning.

Figure 4.10 provides labels for each of the four organization designs. Thus the ST is labeled the OPERATIONAL DESIGN, the NT is termed the PROBLEM-SOLVING DESIGN, the ST is called the INFORMAL DESIGN, and the NF is entitled the STRATEGIC PLAN-

FIGURE 4.10   Organization Designs for the Four Jungian Types (See Fig. 1.3)

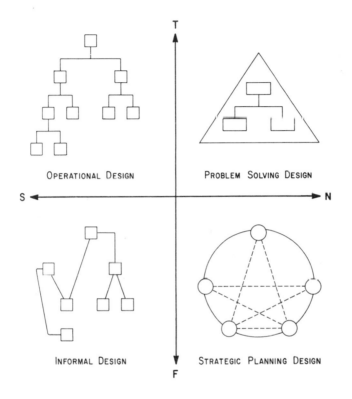

NING DESIGN. Chapter 6 will describe in detail how these different designs deal with the different components of organizational effectiveness and how an organization may need to have more than one design to be truly effective. Briefly, the organization can obtain (1) internal efficiency, by designing a viable OPERATIONAL DESIGN (one that emphasizes specificity, control, optimal work flow, etc.); (2) internal effectiveness, by designing a viable INFORMAL DESIGN (allowing members to communicate across formal channels to satisfy social and informational needs); (3) external efficiency, by designing a viable PROBLEM-SOLVING DESIGN (to confront the problems posed by the organization's environment); and (4) external effectiveness, by designing a viable STRATEGIC PLANNING DESIGN (to define the problems posed by the environment).

One might argue that organizations should develop these designs in a particular order. There appears to be some logic or sense in first defining the problems (STRATEGIC PLANNING DESIGN), coping with or attempting to solve the problems (PROBLEM-SOLVING DESIGN), then engaging in particular tasks and activities to implement the solution (OPERATIONAL DESIGN) and then allowing for some deviation or discretion from formally prescribed behaviors to foster member motivation and commitment (INFORMAL DESIGN). At this point, however, the organization would need to reexamine its concrete day-to-day designs (the OPERATIONAL and INFORMAL) to determine whether they were in fact appropriate to the problems and objectives suggested by the long-range planning designs (PROBLEM-SOLVING and STRATEGIC PLANNING).

The cycle of designs and designing would therefore continue from NF to NT to ST to SF to NF to NT, etc., where, at each stage, the organization would mobilize its resources in a particular manner to approach or strive for particular forms of organizational effectiveness. The reader should recognize that this sequence of organization designs is quite analogous to the steps in the Diamond Model of problem solving shown in Figure 1, Introduction and Overview. The difference is that rather than simply suggesting the processes that must occur (i.e., defining the problem, developing a scientific model, deriving a solution, implementing the solution, etc.), we are suggesting that the organization must design resources explicitly to create organization designs to guide, foster, and reward people to actually pursue these processes.

We do not mean to suggest, however, that organizations should change their designs in sequence over time or that organizations should have all four designs. If either were the case, the organization might spend all its energy and time designing for something rather than doing something. Consequently, only in some very unique situations (perhaps extremely dynamic and changing environments) would organizations be shifting designs frequently and have four such different designs. Actually it might be more appropriate to have the "cost" of designing as part of the resources absorbed in converting various inputs to outputs, motivating members, satisfying the community, and interacting with the environment; that is, the cost of designing should be subtracted from overall organizational effectiveness. In this way one could better recommend how much of the organization's resources should be devoted to designing versus doing.

In most cases the organization will find it appropriate to have two formal designs, one that guides the day-to-day activities (ST and SF) and one that defines and deals with long-range problems (NF and

NT). These two designs would coexist but each would have a very different purpose. Often these designs will ensure that the four components of effectiveness are being explicitly approached while not absorbing the large amount of resources that would be involved by having as many as four distinct designs. However, two designs are already much better than one because the one design is usually the OPERATIONAL DESIGN, which is ineffective for dealing with complex problems and contemporary organizations are facing increasingly dynamic and changing environments that pose more complex and ill-defined problems than they encountered in the past. Thus two formal designs distinguished on the S-N dimension will generally foster organizational effectiveness if the design process itself is effective (not too costly) and the resulting designs are appropriate for attaining their effectiveness objectives.

Derivation of the Six Models

The MAPS Design Technology can be applied to design many types of organizations for a variety of design objectives. In particular, MAPS can be used to create each of the designs shown in Figure 4.10 as well as integrated combinations of these designs (i.e., an integrated ST and SF design and an integrated NT and NF design).

As was discussed earlier in this chapter, the analysis performed by the MAPS Computer Program groups respondents to the MAPS questionnaire into people clusters. These people clusters, however, may be formed by different input data. They may result strictly from task items by respondents being placed in the same cluster if they have similar perceptions about the task items they wish to perform. Alternatively, people clusters can result from people items, where respondents are grouped together if they have similar perceptions of with whom they can interact with best. And thirdly, people clusters may be formed by combining or integrating perceptions of tasks and people. This last analysis groups respondents together if they have similar perceptions regarding the tasks and people in the organization.

The analysis performed by the MAPS Computer Program is also capable of forming task clusters for the organization that represent a focus of activities, objectives, and issues for the people clusters (i.e., each people cluster can be assigned a task cluster for each n by n MAPS design solution). Unlike the formation of people clusters, however, only task items are utilized to develop task clusters. In other words, task items tend to be grouped together if respondents (as a whole) see them as belonging together (i.e., as correlating highly with one another). Thus the choice is not which input to use to form task clusters, but whether or not task clusters should be shown as output from the MAPS Computer Program and if the output should specifically assign each people cluster a task cluster. Two alternatives for the output of MAPS are the following: (a) show both people clusters and task clusters, and their assignments; (b) show only the set of people clusters for each design solution. Incidentally, although a third alternative is to show only the task clusters, the MAPS Design Technology was developed to design or redesign people into organization subsystems so, minimally, the technology requires the formation of explicit people clusters.

Figure 4.11 shows the full array of different designs (genotypes) that are possible with MAPS: the six scientific models. The various models result from the different combinations of choices for the designers (i.e., representatives of the client system in interaction with the MAPS consultants). The three rows of Figure 4.11 indicate the particular input and analysis utilized to form people clusters: task items, or task and people items, or just people items as input to computing various multivariate statistics. The two columns in Figure 4.11 show whether both people clusters and task clusters (and their assignments) are described as output from the MAPS analysis or if only people clusters are shown. The combinations result in the six models each of which, as has been suggested, also contains a series of social systems designs. For each model the MAPS Computer Program generates a two-cluster solution, a three-cluster solution, etc., until certain statistical limits are reached (i.e., when computed eigenvalues are no longer positive numbers).

Characteristics of the Six Models

Sketched on Figure 4.11 are the two Jungian dimensions that define and give substance to the six models. The S-N dimension defines the horizontal characteristics, namely, should the output of the MAPS analysis be so specific as to indicate not only people clusters and task clusters but also the particular assignments between the two (Models I, III, and V)? Or should the output only present the people clusters so that the various subsystems developed would not get "locked" into a specified set of tasks and issues, but would remain free to create, elaborate, imagine, and experiment with different and changing task definitions (i.e., such people clusters derive their own task clusters), even if people clusters were partially or totally formed by member responses to a defined set of task items (Models II, IV, and VI). In other

FIGURE 4.11   A Schematic Representation of the Scientific Models

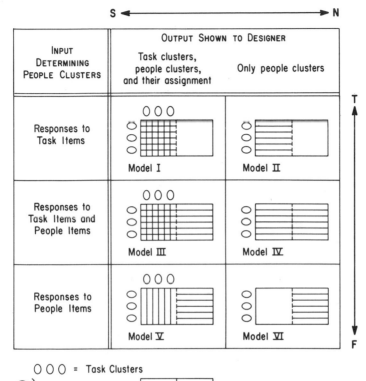

O O O = Task Clusters

O
O } = People Clusters
O

| Task | People |
| Items | Items | = MAPS Data Matrix (Figure 4.7)

O O O
O
O } = Task Clusters Assigned to People Clusters
O   (for a number of design solutions: 2 clusters,
       3 clusters, etc., see the MAPS Design Matrix in
       Figure 4.8)

words, the defining characteristic of models relevant to the two columns is the specificity versus the implied openness (intuition) expected to result from the output that is actually shown to the social system.

As can be seen in Figure 4.11, the T-F dimension is used to define the distinguishing characteristics of the models categorized by the rows. Thus the extreme Thinking (T) orientation emphasizes that only responses to impersonal tasks are to be used in forming people clusters (Models I and II), whereas the extreme Feeling (F) orientation utilizes only member responses to people in forming people clusters (Models V and VI). Since both task and people items can be combined (integrated) in the analysis to form people clusters, the middle row of Figure 4.11 integrates the Thinking and Feeling orientations, i.e., Models III and IV simultaneously consider impersonal tasks and interpersonal interactions as determining subsystems of organizational members.

Model I: The OPERATIONAL DESIGN

Outstanding examples of Model I have traditionally been bureaucracies (Weber, 1947) whose primary emphasis is on the day-to-day, routine task activities of the organization. People are relevant and important only to the extent that they possess the necessary skills and job qualifications to carry out the specified, preassigned tasks. Whether the individuals like one another or can interact well is not only incidental but irrelevant to the goals of the design. Because of their emphasis on tasks and work roles instead of on people, and on specificity and control instead of on interpersonal relations, such organization designs are most suitable to ST type individuals (see Chapter 1).

Model II: The PROBLEM-SOLVING DESIGN

Like Model I, Model II also uses only task input data, but unlike Model I the output of Model II presents only people clusters. Thus Model II is also defined by a lack of concern or relevancy for interpersonal and interaction qualities, but since it does not present task clusters and their assignments, this model is more flexible in adapting to changing environments and not being "locked" into a given task definition. For this reason Model II is known as the PROBLEM-SOLVING DESIGN, which is still dominated by task items but has degrees of freedom in generating and acting upon new ideas and perspectives.

Model III: The INTEGRATED OPERATIONAL–INFORMAL DESIGN

Model III makes equal (simultaneous) use of both task and people items to form people clusters. Since task clusters and their assignments to people clusters are shown explicitly in the MAPS output, Model III is best suited for fairly well-defined environments in which task items and task clusters are expected to be appropriate for a reasonable period. This model, unlike both Models I and II, does consider members' perceptions of interpersonal relations and interaction desires so that the Feeling component is represented in Model III designs.

Model IV: The INTEGRATED PROBLEM-SOLVING–STRATEGIC PLANNING DESIGN

Model IV, like Model III, simultaneously combines member responses to task and people items in forming people clusters. However, because Model IV presents only people clusters as the output, this design model is expected to be flexible and adaptive to new ideas and new task dimensions. In fact, since Model IV takes into account members' interpersonal perceptions (and hence the Feeling component), designs from this model are expected to be more adaptive than those of Model II (PROBLEM-SOLVING DESIGN). In essence, by making explicit use of people perceptions in forming people clusters, the generation of new ideas will be fostered by more cohesive and supportive people clusters; that is, interpersonal compatibility, if used properly, is conducive to idea testing and is supportive of the deviation necessary for creativity.

Model V: The INFORMAL DESIGN

In Model V, only member responses to people items are utilized in forming the people clusters while, as always, responses to the task items are utilized to form task clusters. The MAPS output, just as in Models I and II, shows the assignments of people clusters to task clusters. This parallel or independent use of task and people items results in a genotypic design which is often seen in the "informal" organization. Thus people are grouped totally on interpersonal perceptions (the Feeling component) even though the various people clusters are still expected to perform the required and predetermined tasks. The INFORMAL DESIGN is often a response to the formal OPERATIONAL DESIGN, in which interpersonal needs are either denied or repressed but where there may still be a need for such interpersonal interactions. If this is the case, members will generally get together to interact and may actually perform their tasks in these informal or parallel people clusters rather than in their formal OPERATIONAL DESIGN people clusters. However, instead of having Model V develop informally and even haphazardly, this genotypic design can explicitly and perhaps more effectively be created by MAPS and be used for other identified design objectives as well.

Model VI: The STRATEGIC PLANNING DESIGN

In the sixth genotype only responses to people items are used to form people clusters and only the latter is shown in the MAPS output. For this genotype the environment of the organization may be so complex and ill-defined that task items cannot be usefully generated. The most that can be done, perhaps, is to bring people together into people clusters that have some interpersonal compatibility. These subsystems can then be used to better appreciate and define important environmental objectives for the organization. At a later time these identified objectives or task items may become inputs to other genotypic designs that the organization may need to create to actually accomplish these objectives. Thus the purpose of the STRATEGIC PLANNING DESIGN is to conceptualize and identify objectives for the organization by designing people clusters that bring together the appropriate set of people who have the requisite psychological and substantive skills for engaging in planning (Mason, 1969; Mason and Mitroff, 1973).

The Core of MAPS: A Summary

The diagrams in each cell of Figure 4.11 summarize the core of MAPS: various inputs, analyses, and outputs of the six scientific models of MAPS. The reader is referred back to Figure 4.7 of this chapter, which illustrates the basic MAPS Data Matrix of the technology. The basic matrix was shown as Model III (the INTEGRATED OPERATIONAL–INFORMAL DESIGN), the first model developed for the MAPS Design Technology (Kilmann, 1974d). The other models of MAPS, as can be seen in Figure 4.11, are simply variations of this basic data matrix. They are different combinations of the following: (a) whether the MAPS input for determining people clusters is responses to task items, people items, or both task and people items; (b) whether or not the MAPS analysis includes task clusters assigned to people clusters via the assignment algorithm; and (c) whether the MAPS output shows the assignment of task clusters to people clusters, or only people clusters. Seeing how the data matrix changes from one model to another gives a pictorial view of how each model is actually related to the other, how each confronts task and people items similarly in some ways and differently in others.

Figure 4.11 thus portrays the most basic level of different models that MAPS is now capable of generating. It does not, as has been mentioned, exhaust all of the possible designs. Each of the six models in Figure 4.11 defines a genotype; that is, each defines and gives rise to a whole family of designs. Thus for each model there is a two-cluster solution, a three-cluster solution, and so on, until negative eigenvalues are encountered. It should be emphasized that in discussing the scientific models we are clearly assuming that the steps of the MAPS Design Technology prior to, including, and following the selection of a model (and a design from that model) are appropriately enacted so that the design actually manifests the characteristics we have described. Alterations in these other steps of MAPS would even further compound the complexity of a design choice.

It should also be mentioned that for the two integrated genotypes (Models III and IV) it is not simply a matter of integration or lack of it (in comparison with the other models.) There can be variable weighting of task and people items either by weighting the existing items or by varying the relative number of task items to people items. For example, instead of fifty task items and fifty people items (an equal integration), we could have ninety task items and ten people items, or ten task items and ninety people items, or any other combination. Furthermore, the responses to task and people items that are utilized in forming various designs would generally be guided by the appropriate (corresponding) instructions to the task and people portion of the MAPS questionnaire shown in Figures 4.5 and 4.6. For example, in creating an OPERATIONAL DESIGN, the list of task items would be preceded by the ST instructions shown in Figure 4.5, to be consistent with the nature of the design being developed. The instructions on the MAPS questionnaire for the integrated designs, however, would be an integration of the relevant "pure" instructions, as shown in Figures 4.3 and 4.4 (forming an INTEGRATED OPER-ATIONAL–INFORMAL DESIGN).

A Variant to the Six Models

There is an additional variant to Figure 4.11 that gives MAPS further flexibility. Rather than showing either task cluster assignments or no task clusters as a basis for the different models in Figure 4.11 (i.e., Models I, III vs Models II, IV, VI), two different types of task items can be distinguished that tend to serve the same purpose.

The two columns shown in Figure 4.12 delineate whether the task items on the MAPS questionnaire specify operational activities, or problems, and strategic issues. These combinations also result in six genotypic models—each assuming a different design objective and consequently different combinations and sources of information are needed to create different designs.

FIGURE 4.12   The Scientific Models of MAPS: Varying the Nature
of Task Items

INPUT DATA UTILIZED TO DETERMINE PEOPLE CLUSTERS	NATURE OF TASK ITEMS	
	Task items specify operational activities	Task items specify problems and strategic issues
Responses to Task Items	Pure OPERATIONAL DESIGN	Pure PROBLEM-SOLVING DESIGN
Responses to Task Items and People Items	INTEGRATED OPERATIONAL-INFORMAL DESIGN	INTEGRATED PROBLEM-SOLVING STRATEGIC PLANNING DESIGN
Responses to People Items	Pure INFORMAL DESIGN	Pure STRATEGIC PLANNING DESIGN

T
∧
|
|
∨
F

S ⟵——————————————⟶ N

Sketched on Figure 4.12 are the same two Jungian dimensions shown in Figure 4.11. The S-N dimension defines the horizontal characteristic of the designs: the Sensation (S) focus on short-term operational activities, or the Intuition (N) concern with problem formulation and strategic issues. The T-F dimension defines the same characteristics as the Figure 4.11 models. In other words, instead of viewing the N dimension as not showing specific task clusters, an alternative is to describe broad, general issues as task items and thus to allow the MAPS analysis to portray broad, general task clusters in the N models (the PROBLEM-SOLVING DESIGN, the STRATEGIC PLANNING DESIGN, and the INTEGRATED PROBLEM-SOLVING-STRATEGIC PLANNING DESIGN). In creating these latter designs one must decide whether to show broad, general task clusters to the social system (as based on N type task items) or not to show task clusters at all, especially if the task items tend to be specific and narrow so that the resulting task clusters might "lock" the social system into a rather narrow focus. Chapters 7 and 8 will provide hypothetical and actual examples of these different possibilities for using MAPS for N social systems designs.

It should be evident now that the four "pure" designs shown in Figures 4.11 and 4.12 (as designed by the MAPS Design Technology) are the same basic Jungian designs indicated in Figure 4.10, and that these four designs have as their objective the attainment of their corresponding component of organizational effectiveness (i.e., the ST component is Internal Efficiency, the NT is External Efficiency, the SF is Internal Effectiveness, and the NF is External Effectiveness to be discussed in detail in Chapter 6). For example, in order to attain Internal Efficiency, the organization needs an OPERATIONAL DESIGN. Such can be created with the MAPS Design Technology by forming people clusters based on members' responses to operational task items and assigning each people cluster a specific task cluster. Similarly, in order to obtain External Effectiveness, the organization may need a STRATEGIC PLANNING DESIGN that can be created with MAPS by forming people clusters based on members' responses to people items and assigning each people cluster a task cluster consisting of strategic task items (see Figure 4.12), or by not assigning any task clusters at all (see Figure 4.11).

Of special interest are the two integrated designs for, as we have suggested, it is not usually feasible or necessary for the social system to have all four designs to deal directly with all four components of organizational effectiveness. Usually the social system can best approach effectiveness by having two explicit designs: one for operational and informal purposes and the other for problem-solving and strategic planning purposes. The two integrated designs thus portray the ingredients of two designs that seek to cope feasibly with all four components of organizational effectiveness.

CONCLUSIONS

This chapter has discussed the core of the MAPS Design Technology: input, analysis, and output. While the basic computer technology involves the clustering of people and tasks, and the assignment of task clusters to people clusters, several alternatives are available to the designers in the scientific models of MAPS. These different models in turn reflect the variety of designs discussed by the contingency theories presented in Chapter 1, which are defined by the more basic Jungian dimensions of Sensation-Intuition and Thinking-Feeling. In addition, the process of developing task items for the MAPS questionnaire is meant to facilitate the designing of purposeful social systems discussed in Chapter 2. In this chapter it was assumed that the entry, diagnosis, and boundary decisions discussed in Chapter 3 were appropriately handled by the MAPS consultant and the social system in question so that the system would meaningfully develop and respond to the MAPS questionnaire (i.e., generate valid information) to achieve a meaningful and valid output of the MAPS analysis.

Earlier in the chapter mention was made of the MAPS Computer Program which performs all the necessary analyses. The actual program allows the user to specify which one (or several) of the six models of MAPS is to be computed. However, for reasons which will be discussed further in Chapter 9, this program is only available to a trained MAPS consultant. The prime reason for this is ethical control of the technology and to ensure that MAPS will be used for the intended purposes: to foster purposeful social systems. The MAPS Computer Program is continually being expanded and tested so that it does in fact design effective social systems. For example, several empirical studies are currently in progress that test different aspects of the computer program (and the resulting designs) in controlled laboratory settings as well as in actual field studies (see Chapter 8). A forthcoming book will report on these experimental studies so that more information and knowledge will be available concerning the validity of the MAPS Computer Program.

Now we turn to the next step of the technology following the core: the implementation stage. As shown in Figure 4.1, this step and the succeeding one (evaluation) are mainly qualitative as opposed to quantitative and rely heavily on the clinical, intuition, and behavioral skills of the MAPS consultant. Although the core of MAPS provides the technology with its framework and focus, we must reemphasize that its qualitative aspects greatly determine whether the core's potential is actually realized. This includes the steps prior to the core (entry and diagnosis) as well as implementation and evaluation.

Chapter 5
Implementation

In collaboration with Richard P. Herden*

The preceding chapters have taken us through three stages of the Diamond Model of problem solving (Sagasti and Mitroff, 1973). Stage one, conceptualization, concerns the formulation of the problem into a conceptual model. This stage was discussed in Chapter 3, where organizational diagnosis determines whether the problem can be conceptualized as one of design and goes on to establish the boundaries for change. Stages two and three, scientific modeling and solution generation, were discussed in Chapter 4. Here the MAPS Design Technology serves as a metamodel from which the appropriate genotype (scientific model) is chosen. The chapter went on to discuss solution generation through the development and processing of people and /or task items via the MAPS Computer Program, resulting in a set of alternative designs. Chapter 5 will focus on the fourth stage of the Diamond Model, implementation. We will begin with the design decision, suggesting approaches to choosing the appropriate design. Next we will discuss the implementation of the chosen design through a collateral phasing methodology that involves process interventions designed to produce a viable social system. We will then describe the special implementation issues inherent in particular design objectives (e.g., implementing an OPERATIONAL DESIGN vs. implementing a STRATEGIC PLANNING DESIGN). Finally we will discuss the topic of monitoring the entire implementation process, which includes the identification and assessment of resistances to change and the planning and implementation of strategies to effectively manage these resistances.

It is important to note that while implementation completes the four stages of the Diamond Model, the problem-solving process is continuous (Sagasti and Mitroff, 1973). The four stages are interdependent and no one stage can be identified as the beginning or ending point in the process. Chapter 6 will deal with this issue by extending the monitoring process discussed in this chapter to the evaluation of the total intervention and to organizational effectiveness.

---

*This chapter also benefited from the contributions of Rajaram B. Baliga, Shankar R. Kapanipathi, and Vadake K. Narayanan.

THE DESIGN DECISION

The design decision of concern here focuses on a choice from among the several alternative designs within a given scientific model of MAPS. In statistical terms this decision attempts to minimize Type I and II errors (rejecting an appropriate design alternative and accepting an inappropriate design alternative, respectively), while the decision to select one of the six models (and to define the organization's original problem as one of design) attempts to minimize the Type III error (selecting the "wrong" definition of the problem and the "wrong" model). For the present we will assume that the "right" MAPS model has already been selected and will focus our attention on the general process of choosing from among the resulting alternative designs. In a later section we will return to the genotype decision and address the special issues that arise from the selection of a particular scientific model, which are necessarily interrelated with the more micro design decision as well as the implementation of the chosen design.

The reader may recall from Chapter 4 that the multivariate procedures of the MAPS analysis permit several alternative designs from the same data source. Basically the respondents to the MAPS questionnaire can be designed into two clusters, three clusters, and so on, until certain statistical limits are reached. Similarly the task items can be designed into two task clusters, three, and so on. The people clusters are then assigned to the task clusters for each solution resulting in a 2 × 2 alternative, a 3 × 3 alternative, and so on. Each of these solutions is a different way of decomposing the members and tasks of the social system into a different subsystem design, while each solution is based on the same design criteria: to form groups that are task and interpersonally congruent, to form task clusters that clearly separate similar task items (those within the same cluster) from dissimilar task items (those contained in different task clusters), and to optimize the "goodness of fit" between task clusters assigned to people clusters.

The Existing Design versus the MAPS Design

The design decision requires that the social system engage in a decision-making process that clarifies the distinguishing features of the alternative designs (including the current design) and will allow the social system to make a valid and well-informed choice of which design to implement (or retain). Before such a decision process is suggested, however, it is worthwhile to consider several reasons why the MAPS designs may be quite different from the existing design.

First, the existing design is based typically on a decision by present or past top management, while the MAPS designs are based on the perspectives of all participants who will be affected by the design. If there is a large discrepancy between these two points of view as reflected in the designs, it may indicate a lack of full utilization of the resources, skills, and motivation of the system's members.

Second, the current design was often developed to reflect stereotyped notions of skill specialization (i.e., individuals are hired into predetermined "slots") or the traditional notion of functional departmentation (e.g., marketing, production, finance, etc.). The MAPS Design Technology, on the other hand, is not biased by these notions; it does not "see" these categorizations, but simply develops subsystems by containing the important task and member inter-dependencies. The latter, because of changes in the organization's environment and /or changes in the nature of member's skills, may be quite different from traditional expectations; consequently the MAPS designs would be different from the current social system design.

Third, the current design is likely to have been based upon the implicit acceptance of technological and physical constraints (e.g., man-machine interfaces and architectural arrangements). MAPS, on the other hand, is largely "blind" to such limitations, given an intervention boundary. Thus the MAPS designs may differ from the current design and may also point out a unique combination of tasks that was hidden by an assumed technological constraint or may suggest the need to shift individuals' locations, which was not evident because of an assumed physical limitation.

Fourth, it is possible that the actual activities occurring in the social system resemble the MAPS designs more than is implied in the formal organization chart. Thus the MAPS design may highlight the "informal" organization (i.e., how the work actually gets done), while the current formal design is misleading and out of date.

Fifth, it is possible that certain task items generated by individuals other than members of the immediate social system (e.g., consumers, community representatives, etc.) resulted in one or more task clusters that are not currently being performed by the organization. If the organization's objectives include responsiveness to environmental needs and adaptation to a changing environment, the MAPS design may suggest the mobilization of additional or different resources to deal with these new task clusters effectively.

Finally, one or more task clusters that were previously latent or hidden may emerge in MAPS designs. Although many members may have felt that the task items are important and perhaps performed aspects of these items in their current subsystems, they have not identified these task items as a separate focus for the system. The MAPS analysis, however, not only reveals the separate task cluster but may also reveal its high endorsement by the members. Often such a task cluster represents an important set of task interdependencies that members endorse as especially relevant to organizational objectives. Thus the MAPS design may suggest the creation of one or more additional subsystems to facilitate the integration of the existing subsystems in the organization.

The extent to which the MAPS designs differ from the existing design of the organization or social system renders comparison quite important to the future of the system. For example, given the above general reasons for why the several designs might be different, what are the advantages and disadvantages of each design from a number of perspectives, including Internal Efficiency and Effectiveness and External Efficiency and Effectiveness (to be discussed in Chapter 6). Not until the members of the social system develop a good appreciation of the relative trade-offs of the designs can they be expected to make an actual selection.

It should be evident that evaluating the relative worth of different designs, one that is currently operating and a set that is only pictured, is not a simple matter. Evaluating an organization design involves many subjective factors (e.g., implications for members' motivation) and uncertainties (e.g., expectations of goal attainment and adaptability). Consequently a decision process is required that can account systematically for the subjective and uncertain aspects in evaluating so complex a problem as social systems design. One approach to this problem is analytical, and utilizes subjective probabilities and value estimates to assess statistical errors (Type I, II, and III) and to arrive at the relative values of design alternatives. This judicial, participative approach was suggested in Chapter 3 as an important procedure for making many of the complex, qualitative decisions at various steps of the MAPS Design Technology. We will now suggest how this judicial process can be utilized for helping a social system, with the aid of MAPS consultants, to choose a new design. As will be seen, this design may simply be one of the several MAPS designs generated by the MAPS Computer Program, or it may be a modification and /or synthesis of alternative MAPS Designs and the current social systems design. What is important, however, is that the chosen (or synthesized) design is based on valid information and free choice, and will therefore tend to generate internal commitment by social system members to have their behavior guided by that design.

The Judicial Process for Design Selection

The first step in the judicial process for the design decision is the creation of individual perspectives. Each individual affected by the design decision (or representatives, if more than fifty individuals are involved) is asked to select the design (from the set of MAPS designs and the current design) that he or she most highly endorses. These individuals are further asked to describe why they endorse that particular design and to indicate its advantages and disadvantages. It should be noted that although a typical MAPS analysis produces eight or more alternative designs, system members tend to endorse only three or four of the alternatives. Thus while the decision involves complex issues, the number of alternatives endorsed is usually quite manageable.

Group perspectives are then developed by bringing together the individuals who endorsed the same design and asking them to develop a group description of the advantages and disadvantages of the particular design. This second step serves to highlight the differences among alternative designs, to reinforce individual perspectives, and to provide a foundation for a meaningful confrontation—the groups provide a support base for individuals to strongly examine and present their viewpoints on the different designs.

The third step is a dialectical debate. One or two representatives from each group of the preceding step meet in an integrated group. They are encouraged to discuss their perspectives and values as well as the perceived advantages and disadvantages of their endorsed design. The representatives, reinforced by their group meetings, tend to exaggerate their design's advantages and to diminish its disadvantages. This stage is important since it serves further to highlight the differences among designs. As the debate progresses, the MAPS consultant encourages individuals to critically question and discuss the strengths and weaknesses of their own perspectives as well as the perspectives of the other representatives. Once each individual in the integrated group has achieved this objective, the process moves toward a synthesis.

The synthesis step begins with a change of atmosphere. The members of the integrated group initiate a collaborative effort to identify the points of difference that emerged during previous steps and to use those differences to define the most appropriate design. The group may choose one of the alternative designs or they may utilize several alternatives, thus formulating a new design that capitalizes on the strengths of the several designs while minimizing their weaknesses. Whether the final decision is a single alternative or a synthesis of alternatives, the value of that decision rests upon free and informed choice (Argyris, 1970a). A methodology such as the judicial process provides the greatest possibility for such a choice by involving representatives of the social system and by utilizing those most committed to discuss the different designs (i.e., those who originally endorsed the designs).

In the foregoing discussion it was assumed that the MAPS output produced design alternatives that were different from the existing social systems design. For completeness, however, it must be stated that the MAPS designs may be essentially congruent with the existing one. If this is the case, there may be two primary explanations.

First, the current groupings of tasks and people may be perceived by the social system as appropriate for interfacing with the existing environments and for mobilizing resources to meet the needs of social system objectives. Although the value of the effort expended in going through the MAPS analysis may not be obvious in this case, in reality it may actually have been highly beneficial. The social system, in assessing its tasks, responsibilities, and resources, has gained a better insight into organizational objectives and the contribution of each member to those objectives. Through participation, the social system's climate may have been improved by giving each member a sense of involvement and by further opening up two-way communication. Also, the social sytem may have reaffirmed its purpose and have generated a feeling of "oneness," an emphasis on organizational rather than subsystem objectives.

Second, the congruence of designs (the existing design vs. the MAPS designs) may be the result of member concern with vested interests and the status quo. Basically if no new tasks were identified, and if each individual in the social system endorses only those tasks he is currently performing and only those people with whom he is currently working, the designs will certainly show no differences. This outcome is not very likely, however, since the MAPS analysis forms clusters based upon total endorsement. Thus if only some of the members follow such a pattern, the endorsements of the majority of members will mediate the effects of the few. Nevertheless, if few differences are found between the existing design and the MAPS designs, the system should be aware that this outcome may be a result of a system-wide resistance to change. The MAPS consultants should explore this possibility when designs are essentially congruent. Factors contributing to such an outcome could be lack of trust, win /lose attitudes by system members, poor individual self-concepts, and so on, which result in a self-sealing, static system. In such cases the system's climate is not conducive to change, and process interventions would be necessary before design changes could be considered again. If, however, an effective diagnosis had been applied prior to the MAPS core, such factors would probably not have been overlooked. Usually the MAPS consultants, by use of valid observations, interviews, and survey questionnaires, would have ascertained if the climate in the social system were not conducive to structural interventions.

IMPLEMENTATION OF THE CHOSEN DESIGN

If the social system decides that the current design is most appropriate (either by means of the above judicial process or via congruency of current and MAPS designs), then no further design action is necessary at this time. The social system may still decide to further evaluate the functionality of the present design by continuing the measurement and analysis suggested in the evaluation step of the MAPS Design Technology (see Chapter 6). Where a new design is desired, various implementation actions are required to create an effective social systems design.

Referring again to the Diamond Model, the implementation steps in the MAPS Design Technology can be thought of as a problem situation in itself. Thus the first concern in the implementation of the chosen design is the development of a conceptual model for effecting a design change. In this stage the new design is studied and compared with the existing design to conceptualize the nature of the desired change. The many possible factors that impinge on the organization, both in the current and in future periods must be identified. Perhaps the most important factor that determines the social system's design objectives is the genotype decision discussed in Chapters 3 and 4. The choice among the alternative scientific models of MAPS (genotypes) is in essence a choice among design objectives. Thus the objectives of a pure OPERATIONAL DESIGN differ significantly from those of a pure STRATEGIC PLANNING DESIGN and these differences greatly affect the development of a conceptual model of implementation. Furthermore, defining and conceptualizing the implementation process is also significantly affected by whether a new organization or a continuing organization is being designed or redesigned and by the degree of congruity between the existing design (and its objectives) and the chosen MAPS design.

Once a conceptual model of implementation is derived (via the MAPS consultants in interaction with the client system), then specific strategies for actually implementing the chosen design may be considered (analogous to developing or choosing a scientific model). A specific implementation strategy is chosen by matching design objectives with the strategy most likely to implement such a design (analogous to solving the scientific model). Finally the chosen implementation strategy is set in motion and applied (i.e., implementing the solution). This brings us back to the problem definition stage of the Diamond Model, where the questions are whether the chosen design was actually implemented as had been anticipated and whether new problems arose as a consequence of implementing a new design. One such problem that frequently emerges is the resistance to change which requires the social system members and the MAPS consultants to conceptualize the nature of these resistances, to consider models to solve or at least manage the problem, to engage in process interventions to implement some strategy to manage resistances to change, and so forth.

In other words, the implementation process may require several cycles through the Diamond Model where, at each completed cycle, new problems may emerge as the design is being implemented. These problems must be confronted appropriately if the potential benefits to be derived from the new design are to be realized. Some of these problems can be readily foreseen (e.g., resistance to change) while others must be searched for and assessed via a monitoring system for the entire implementation process. Once the various problems are managed and the new design can be viewed as actually implemented, then the issue (or problem) emerges as to whether the new design did appropriately manage (or solve) the initial social system problem that was conceptualized to be one of organization design. This issue of evaluation and organizational effectiveness will be discussed in Chapter 6.

The remainder of this chapter presents a specific approach to the implementation problem: an outline of a methodology for implementing a chosen (or synthesized) social system design that is referred to as "collateral phasing." Variations of this methodology are also considered in order to address different design objectives (i.e., different conceptual models of implementation). Finally, a methodology for monitoring the entire implementation process is suggested to help identify and manage the various implementation problems that may emerge.

Collateral Phasing

The selection of a design from the alternatives produced by the MAPS analysis cannot guarantee that each identified subsystem will fully develop its potential and be able to coordinate its activities effectively with the other subsystems. Therefore an implementation program is necessary to develop the potential represented by the chosen design into effective social system behavior. In most cases the MAPS Design Technology will be applied to existing social systems as opposed to newly forming systems. The former situation poses a complex problem that requires a carefully managed transition period during which the new design is phased in and the old design is phased out or modified to accept the additional design. This transition period may vary from a month to a few years depending upon the number of individuals and subsystems involved and upon the nature and complexity of the social system's tasks. Also bearing on the time of the transition period is the extent to which the new design is different from the existing design (as discussed earlier).

The term "collateral phasing" refers to the period during which the social system is involved in two (or more) designs staffed by the same individuals, which phase into each other over time (i.e., time, energy, and resources move from one design to the other). This concept builds upon the notion of collateral organization suggested by Zand (1974), although the objective may not be to have the two designs coexist indefinitely (e.g., an existing OPERATIONAL DESIGN replaced by a new OPERATIONAL DESIGN). Naturally, if the MAPS Design Technology is being used to form a new social system, collateral phasing may be unnecessary. However, the same types of interventions suggested within the collateral phasing process to develop the new design would still be necessary for development of a new social system.

The collateral phasing process may generally be described as a series of steps intended to phase in a new design and to realize the potential of that new design as an effective social system.

Step 1: Identity Formulation

The first step can be identified as one of identity formulation, in which each subsystem meets to determine its central thrust or identity. Subsystems are asked to prepare a detailed statement concerning the title, objectives, scope, organization, and so on, of their assigned task cluster with information regarding the resources, skills, technology, and so forth, that will be necessary to implement the task cluster successfully. Some of the guidelines provided for developing a management by objectives system (MBO) would be helpful at this stage (Odiorne, 1965; Reddin, 1972).

In carrying out this step the subsystem members are instructed to assess critically each of their assigned tasks and to give consideration to each of their anticipated roles vis à vis the tasks. In this regard, consideration should be given to the "leadership structure" within the subsystem (i.e., how each member can influence the management and operation of the subsystem) and whether a further subdivision of members within the subsystem would facilitate the efficient performance of the task cluster. Regarding the latter, if a subsystem has twenty or more members and /or tasks, it might be useful to apply the MAPS analysis to further specify the design of the subsystem. The resulting subsystem design, whether MAPS produced or not, may identify a task or small subset of tasks that do not seem to be central to the thrust of the subsystem. These tasks may then take on new meaning that would make them central, or they may be transferred to another subsystem following a sharing of subsystem identities.

Step 2: Information Sharing

The second step in the process would have each subsystem share its identity statement with the other subsystems. While maximum participation is desirable, it will often be necessary to choose representatives of each subsystem to carry out this step. In cases where membership size requires such representation, a series of meetings is suggested to allow maximum feedback to the remaining subsystem membership. Such feedback to, as well as input from, the total system is important since each member has an important stake in the outcome of the process.

This step serves to better define the identity of each subsystem in light of total system objectives and to clarify the purpose of individual subsystem tasks. Further, it tends to foster an awareness of potential interface conflicts among the subsystems and to make each subsystem realize that it cannot operate entirely independent of the others. Included in this interunit sharing would be a consideration of how the several subsystems could best coordinate their efforts into a functioning whole (i.e., integration).

Integration may be accomplished in several ways. A traditional management hierarchy might be contemplated that has a separate group of managers responsible for coordination via formal authority relationships among those managers and the subsystems. Such an approach implies an existing hierarchical system of authority to choose the new supervisory strata and may limit the benefits of the highly participatory process carried on to date. Approaches that may be more supportive of a purposeful social systems design would include nonhierarchical coordinating groups and Likert's "linking-pin" concept (Likert, 1961).

The former approach may be appropriate where the MAPS analysis has identified a task cluster composed of coordination tasks and where a cluster of members has highly endorsed that task cluster. In such a case the total system has indicated that the coordination tasks should be undertaken as a unit and a subgroup of the total system has indicated an interest and commitment to carry out those tasks. With such total system support and with participative definition of coordination responsibilities, the nonhierarchical coordination subsystem should function effectively.

The latter approach of the linking-pin function would be appropriate where the MAPS questionnaire did not include coordination items or where the MAPS analysis resulted in a design that spread the coordination tasks among the subsystems. In either case the total system has not identified the need for a unified coordination effort, but may have differentiated the coordination function by assigning coordination tasks to the most crucial subsystems. The linking-pin coordination mechanism requires each subsystem to nominate a "leader" who would represent the subsystem to other such leaders whenever a need should arise for coordinating and negotiating interface issues among the subsystems. Otherwise, the leaders would be active members of their subsystems just like any other member.

Step 3: Negotiation and Bargaining

The third step in the collateral phasing process involves a reassessment of subsystem identities. During the information-sharing step above, subsystems may be expected to gain a better insight and appreciation of their individual tasks and central thrust as well as the interpersonal compatibility and skill congruence of their members. As a result individual tasks, or possibly individual members, of a particular subsystem may be viewed as being more appropriate to another subsystem. Although such occurrences will be reduced by the judicial process of design selection where an integrated solution could have been chosen, the organization should be aware that such tradeoffs may be desirable at this stage and must provide a means for allowing them. In the case of task items a continuation of the mechanism employed during the information-sharing step (representation or total system participation) can be utilized, in which subsystems bargain and negotiate over such tasks, transferring them to some other, more appropriate subsystem. Similarly, individuals must be given freedom to negotiate their own transfer to more appropriate subsystems, particularly where their skills could be better utilized with a different task cluster. For member transfer it is recommended that the individual be responsible for negotiating such transfers by taking the initiative to discuss the situation with both his assigned subsystem and his desired one. In some cases the organizational climate may not yet be conducive to such open, two-way communication. Thus it is important that the freedom to make member transfers be left open during the following step in which much of the climate building may occur. Ordinarily, in applications of MAPS, less than five percent of individuals or tasks are actually transferred. However, since some tasks and people may be placed in clusters because of small numerical differences, actual preferences (following the identity statements) should not be sacrificed to statistical calculations prior to the implementation process.

Step 4: Team Building

The fourth step of the collateral phasing process involves the various methods of team and interteam building over an extended period of time to help members learn a new kind of management and social systems behavior (i.e., purposeful behavior) within a new social systems design. This step is aimed at improving the interpersonal skills of the system as differentiated from technical skills, which will be discussed in the following step. Generally most individuals have not experienced what it is like to work in a truly purposeful system in terms of the different forms of decision making, communication, and leadership that should be shown within and across subsystems.

Team building, primarily by use of the laboratory method (Argyris, 1962; Bradford, et al., 1964), is an educational process that not only gives members the opportunity to experience purposeful designs but also helps them to increase their effectiveness in such a social system. The process of team building, and of process intervention in general may have a number of objectives which, in practice, may not be clearly specified. During the implementation phase, perhaps one of the most critical objectives of team building is to prepare the social system to manage conflict effectively.

Kilmann and Thomas (1974) have proposed a model of conflict that combines two dimensions to describe four perspectives of conflict, as shown in Figure 5.1. The first dimension, process versus structure, differentiates between the temporal series of events (process) and the conditions existing at a point in time (structure) that influence behavior. The process model emphasizes the influence of preceding events and the anticipation of succeeding events on individual behavior, and recognizes that such events may be perceived as incongruent. The structure model emphasizes the influence of conditions at a point in time that produce both positive and negative forces which act on the individual and thus influence his behavior. (See Chapter 1 for a further discussion of process versus structure.) The second dimension, internal versus external, differentiates between the events and conditions within an individual (internal) and the events and conditions outside the individual (external) that shape his behavior. The internal model thus focuses on phenomena that occur within an individual, such as his assumptions, perceptions, motives,

FIGURE 5.1 A Model of Conflict For MAPS Implementation
(Adapted from Kilmann and Thomas, 1974)

	Process (events)	Structure (conditions)

External (Outside the Individual)	EXTERNAL PROCESS
	
	Perspective: behavior is shaped by events outside the individual
	
	Role requirements:
	    conflict /ambiguity
	
	Intervention:
	    Interaction Management
		EXTERNAL STRUCTURE
		
		Perspective: behavior is shaped by conditions outside the individual
		
		Task relationship:
		    differentiation /integration
		
		Intervention:
		    Contextual Modification

Internal (Inside the Individual)	INTERNAL PROCESS
	
	Perspective: behavior is shaped by events inside the individual
	
	Theories of action:
	    espoused /practiced incongruity
	
	Intervention:
	    Consciousness Raising
		INTERNAL STRUCTURE
		
		Perspective: behavior is shaped by conditions inside the individual
		
		Individual satisfaction:
		    need /reward conflicts
		
		Intervention:
		    Selection, Evaluation, and Training

insights, decision-making style, and anticipation of others' responses. The external model focuses on phenomena that occur outside the individual, such as conflicts of interest, norms, another's threats and concessions, and third-party interventions. Combining the two dimensions results in the following four perspectives on conflict and conflict management: (1) External-Process, (2) Internal-Process, (3) External-Structure, and (4) Internal-Structure. Thus conflicts can exist within any one of the four quadrants representing the two dimensions and, more importantly, conflicts can be conceptualized to stem from one or more of the four perspectives.

In paper by Kilmann and Rahim (1975), it was shown that neither structural intervention (organizational redesign) nor process intervention (organizational development) alone could influence all four perspectives of conflict. Traditional OD approaches have had major impact on the External- and Internal-Process quadrants, while traditional organization design approaches have had major impact on the External-Structure quadrant. It is clear that neither approach effectively confronts all sources of conflict. The MAPS Design Technology directly address the External-Structure source of conflict and, by involving the total system in generating task items, choosing the appropriate scientific model of MAPS, and making the design decision, the technology sets in motion participative processes that deal with the remaining three quadrants. During the team building step of implementation such processes can reach their potential for handling conflict management from all four perspectives. While the specific intervention situation will determine the appropriate thrust of team building, a number of general subjects may be identified. From the external process perspective, role conflict and role ambiguity issues may surface. From the internal process perspective, individuals' theories of action may be incongruent with their espoused theories (Argyris and Schon, 1975). From an internal structure perspective, individual needs and social systems rewards may be in conflict. Generally it seems appropriate to initiate emphasis on the internal process perspective through "consciousness raising" (Bucklow, 1966) with intrateam-building processes, and then to expand to role conflicts and to need/reward conflicts through interteam-building processes.

The need for trained process consultants becomes most evident at this stage, although process isssues must be examined and managed throughout the MAPS Design Technology. Depending upon the size of the social system in question, it may be appropriate to train in-house process facilitators who would work with the MAPS consultant(s) in team-building efforts throughout the system. Such a resource would prove beneficial to the system in continued organizational development efforts after successful design implementation.

Step 5: Technical Skills Development

The fifth step in the collateral phasing process is for the subsystem designed by MAPS and developed by various OD methods, to begin performing the tasks that the subsystems have defined and adopted. While this step may often be taken along with the preceding one, it is generally useful to distinguish team development from strictly task behavior. The latter involves the subsystem members in learning new ways of performing tasks, utilizing their skills, and interfacing their task outputs. Thus, besides the need for developing cohesive, motivated, and committed subsystems, these subsystems have to learn to perform effectively vis à vis the technological requirements and challenges of their system. This stage may require technical specialists to advise the subsystem on how to best utilize their skills as a new team, or it may require simulations of hypothetical projects, or perhaps some trial and error learning on real social system tasks. Naturally, this step in the implementation process is highly dependent upon the substantive nature of the social system in question. In general however, it is important that the system identify substantive educational needs and develop training programs to meet those needs. As discussed previously, it is also important that the system continue to support the transfer of human resources to their most appropriate subsystems.

Step 6: Independence and Purposefulness

The sixth step in the collateral phasing process occurs when the new subsystems are given responsibility for performing the required social systems tasks. While the learning of new task behavior may still be proceeding actively, each subsystem will gradually command more of its intended resources and will perform more of its complete task cluster. Eventually the initial social systems design will have its resources transferred to the MAPS design, completing the collateral phasing process. The processes initiated during Steps 4 and 5, which involve the behavioral and technical learning of the social system, may be continued in some form and enhanced by periodic team-building and task skills sessions.

DESIGN OBJECTIVES AND IMPLEMENTATION

It will be recalled from Chapter 4 that the major design objectives are determined in large part by the genotype decision. To briefly review the alternative models, there are at least six different scientific models of MAPS (see Figures 4.11 and 4.12): OPERATIONAL DESIGN, PROBLEM-SOLVING DESIGN, INFORMAL DESIGN, STRATEGIC PLANNING DESIGN, INTEGRATED OPERATIONAL–INFORMAL DESIGN, and INTEGRATED PROBLEM-SOLVING–STRATEGIC PLANNING DESIGN. These models are formed by different combinations of input data used to determine the people clusters, whether task assignments are shown, and /or by the nature of the task items. For example, the input of responses to task items that specify operational activities results in design alternatives within the OPERATIONAL DESIGN genotype. Similarly the input of responses to people items and task items, where the task items specify problems and strategic issues, can be used to generate design alternatives within a STRATEGIC PLANNING DESIGN genotype.

It should be clear that the choice between such extreme models is based upon quite different design objectives. In the former case emphasis is on operational tasks and on respondents' perceptions of the interdependencies of those tasks. Thus the design objective of the OPERATIONAL DESIGN is to develop subsystems of highly interdependent, operational tasks staffed by individuals who have the expertise to work effectively on the resultant task clusters. In the latter case emphasis is on general problems and strategic issues and on respondents' perceptions of individuals who could work well together on those items. Thus the objective of the STRATEGIC PLANNING DESIGN is to develop subsystems of compatible people who can interact creatively in managing problems and strategic issues. The preceding example of divergent design objectives could be extended to the other four models, which also would have significant implications for implementing the chosen design alternative. Rather than examine all six models, we will utilize the two mentioned models to provide examples of the effect of design objectives on implementation.

Operational Design

In the OPERATIONAL DESIGN the success of the resulting subsystems rests heavily on individual ability to perform specific tasks and to interface task outputs with other subsystem outputs effectively. This task emphasis requires critical assessment of required expertise and resources to perform the task cluster. The identity formulation and information-sharing steps of the collateral phasing process must ensure that such resources (both technical and human) are identified and that the requirements of each subsystem are met in the most efficient manner.

The integrative mechanisms developed during implementation will be instrumental in assuring that technical resource requirements are met and that future allocations are made in the most effective manner. The form of such mechanisms depends upon the nature of the environment being faced by the OPERATIONAL DESIGN and on the technology employed. Where the environment is highly stable and the technology routine, hierarchical coordinating groups and standard operating procedures may be appropriate. To the degree that the environment is a bit more dynamic, nonhierarchical coordinating groups or "linking-pin" mechanisms with flexible policies would be more appropriate. Presumably, however, the OPERATIONAL DESIGN was chosen (Model I) because the environment was assessed to be fairly stable; otherwise the designed activities are not expected to be affected by environment, technology, or membership changes (or even the interactions of present members, since this design aspect is not considered in the OPERATIONAL DESIGN).

Just as integrative mechanisms are instrumental to technical resource allocation, human resource requirements must also be met. During the negotiating and bargaining and the team-building steps of the collateral phasing process, the degree of skill congruence will be more clearly defined. During these steps, individuals whose skills may be more relevant to other subsystems should be aided in seeking their own transfer to the more appropriate subsystem. Also, during Step 5 of experiencing the new system, it is important to design and initiate training programs that will provide the skills necessary to accomplish the subsystem task clusters. Such programs should be designed with full participation of the integrating mechanism to avoid unnecessary duplication of effort. Attention should then be directed toward institutionalizing the training effort to facilitate the entry of new personnel into the system during future periods. This does not necessarily imply that a traditional training subsystem needs to be created, but it does mean that a process of technical training needs to be established which will continue to assess skill needs and to meet those needs after the new design is implemented.

While the emphasis on task performance and task skill is extreme in a pure OPERATIONAL DESIGN, the need for interpersonal skills may become evident. During the team-building step of collateral phasing, some intrateam-building efforts can be provided. In other words, while the building of task-effective work groups is the first priority for an OPERATIONAL DESIGN, the possibility that interpersonal and intergroup conflicts might emerge should not be overlooked. In regard to the latter, the management of conflict among subsystems will be influenced significantly by the level of interpersonal relations existing in the integrating mechanism (e.g., the leadership structure). As the intrateam-building process proceeds, learning experiences should be expanded to include situations in which subsystems must share resources and coordinate outputs. Thus the process moves from team building to system building.

Intrapersonal conflicts may emerge as a result of Internal–Structural incongruities (see Figure 5.1). If the new design differs radically from the old, necessary role changes may be relatively significant. In addition, if individuals have occupied the old roles for a considerable time, role transfer may be more difficult. To complicate matters the existing reward system may be incompatible with the new design. The reward system must be tailored to the design objectives. In an OPERATIONAL DESIGN the need to reward productivity is obvious. Where skill transfer is difficult, reward systems should recognize transition periods and should not penalize individuals for lower productivity during this period. Perhaps less obvious is the need to reward behavior which facilitates design implementation and interpersonal functioning. It may be necessary to reward individuals explicitly for successful role transfer to offset perceived losses in status, power, and so on. In this regard financial incentives alone may be inadequate. Individuals who might be expected to have difficulty in role transfer should be identified and the forces inhibiting transfer should also be isolated and reduced. The fact that MAPS utilizes real participation and fosters commitment will help to overcome such resistance to change. However, some individuals because of long role incumbency and /or dramatic role transfer requirements may be expected to have difficulty, and should therefore be identified early in the implementation process and special efforts made to aid them in role transfer.

Strategic Planning Design

The STRATEGIC PLANNING DESIGN emphasis differs significantly from that of the OPERATIONAL DESIGN. The latter design emphasizes specific, operational task performance, while the former emphasizes broad, systemic issue and problem conceptualization. In essence the success of the strategic planning subsystems rests heavily on individuals' ability to identify major issues and problems from a systemic viewpoint, to work closely with other members of the subsystem in conceptualizing such issues and formulating policies to manage them, and to integrate such policies among strategic planning subsystems and between the strategic planning and operational subsystems.

The very nature of a strategic planning system is one of adaptability to changing environments. Consequently the identity formulation step of the collateral phasing process must serve to define the major thrust of each subsystem and the environmental segments to be addressed, and also to identify necessary interfaces between the organization and these segments. The information-sharing step serves to highlight subsystem differences, to better identify necessary environmental interfaces, and to provide integrating mechanisms among subsystems as well as between the strategic planning and operational subsystems. The integrating mechanisms for the STRATEGIC PLANNING DESIGN must be flexible to support the adaptive nature of the design. In this regard the "linking pin" concept seems to be optimal. Interactions among subsystems can be anticipated to take many forms and to require differing integration skills. Utilizing the linking pin concept, an individual member of a subsystem may be selected to provide the integrating mechanism depending upon the nature of the required interface among subsystems. Thus one linking pin will serve the integration function for a particular interface requirement, then return to his subsystem role upon completion of his integrative duties, and another "linking pin" may be selected for the next interface requirement.

Such an adaptive process requires interpersonal relations that are free from vested interests and power issues. Individuals must be accepted as "equals" and be oriented toward the best interest of the total social system. The team-building step of the collateral phasing process is instrumental in creating such a climate. Intrateam-building processes should concentrate on consciousness raising and Model Two behavior (Argyris and Schon, 1975) to deal effectively with issues of power equalization, role conflict, and conflicts in conceptualization. In regard to the latter the nebulous, systemic nature of the issues confronting the STRATEGIC PLANNING DESIGN will undoubtedly produce competing conceptualizations of particular problems and issues within subsystems. Each subsystem must be capable of accepting such competing models and of utilizing the differences to formulate the most complete conceptualization. The dialectic inquirer is suggested as an appropriate philosophical approach to such situations, and will be discussed further in Chapter 7. The reader is also referred to Kilmann and Mitroff (1977), who present several methodologies and technologies for handling complex, ill-defined problems that are particularly germane to strategic planning objectives. The problem-solving exercises and skills development that Kilmann and Mitroff discuss would therefore be most appropriate for the implementation process of the STRATEGIC PLANNING DESIGN.

Conflicting conceptualizations may also be anticipated among subsystems, particularly where major policy issues are involved. Interteam-building processes should concentrate on utilizing such differences constructively. Interteam-building processes must also manage power equalization and role conflicts that may emerge at the system-wide level for a number of reasons. Some of these causes may be a function of the design change itself.

First, the organization may or may not have had an explicitly designed strategic planning system in the past. In cases where there was such a system, it might have been functioning in a bureaucratic, hierarchical manner. The fact that the organization is committed to a fully participatory change process reduces the chance of conflicts involving power equalization. It is still possible, however, that interpersonal conflict could emerge based upon perceived power differentials. The team-building step must confront such issues and provide for acceptance and evaluation of individuals based upon professional contribution rather than traditional authority status.

Second, the STRATEGIC PLANNING DESIGN may be staffed by individuals who have full-time responsibility to it, or who may also have responsibilities in the OPERATIONAL DESIGN. Where individuals have only strategic planning assignments and there was no prior strategic planning system, role ambiguity may exist following a transfer from operational to strategic tasks. The team-building process should aid individuals in adjusting their viewpoint from a narrow, functional perspective to a broad, systems perspective. Experiential learning processes such as simulation or case analysis may be instrumental in such an adjustment. Where individuals' responsibilities are split between strategic and operational tasks, role conflict issues may emerge. Individuals may exhibit difficulty in moving effectively from one role to the other. The team-building process should aid individuals in differentiating such roles and in identifying effective behavior appropriate to each role. Team building can also be effective in reducing role conflict by helping to create cohesive groups that support appropriate role behavior. This may require team-building efforts in the operational subsystem even if that system is not undergoing design changes. (Chapter 7 will provide a more elaborate discussion of multisystem designs, in which a member is involved in more than one design and needs to switch back and forth between them.)

During the collateral phasing step of experiencing the new system, team-building efforts can continue while subsystems begin to function within the new design. As strategic issues and problems are identified and conceptualized, subsystems will begin to formulate tentative policies to resolve them. At this step the need for integration between the STRATEGIC PLANNING and OPERATIONAL DESIGNS may become most evident. Where individuals have both strategic planning and operational roles, a natural "linking pin" system exists to facilitate the integration necessary to assure that policy formulation is implemented effectively. Where strategic and operational responsibilities do not coincide, additional integrative mechanisms will be necessary. In cases where the environment is relatively stable and the operational technology fixed, policies may be promulgated via specific plans and procedures. Traditional control systems may be adequate in such situations to assure proper implementation. Where the environment is dynamic or when the operational technology is changing, more adaptive mechanisms may be required. While the linking pin concept may be appropriate in some cases, a more formal process may be desirable in others. For example, a system of committees may provide a mechanism for implementation and control, as well as two-way information links. Elected representation may be appropriate when few committees are needed. When many committees are contemplated, a MAPS intervention might be considered to aid in designing the actual committees used for integration purposes (as discussed in Chapter 7). The SF INFORMAL DESIGN might be the appropriate design in such cases, to integrate the pure OPERATIONAL and STRATEGIC PLANNING DESIGNS.

The foregoing discussion of the effects of a particular scientific model of MAPS on the implementation of a chosen design could be extended to the remaining alternative models. Although the discussion was necessarily general, it is hoped that the issues raised show the need for careful planning of design implementation. All too often theoreticians seem to emphasize the conceptualization and scientific modeling phases of the problem-solving process while underemphasizing the solution generation and implementation phases. At the same time practitioners tend to reverse the above emphasis. The MAPS Design Technology helps to avoid such neglect by systematically considering each phase and recognizing the interdependencies among them.

MONITORING IMPLEMENTATION

The design decision and the collateral phasing process take us through the general Diamond Model of problem solving, but the need to explicitly identify resistances to change poses another problem that may be approached through the model. While such a problem can be discussed as a separate cycle of the model, it is important to recognize that the problem is not distinct temporally. Resistances to change can and must be identified at every stage of the MAPS intervention. In this section, we will concentrate on those resistances that occur during implementation of the chosen design. Chapter 6 will place such a monitoring process in perspective, showing that it actually constitutes one aspect of the entire evaluation process.

Since the redesign of a social system represents major change (innovation), forces tend to develop, both within and outside the boundaries of the system, to resist change, maintain the status quo, or actually to obstruct change (Coch and French, 1948). Rather than ignore these forces, many of which are "natural" and serve to provide the system with stability, it is deemed necessary to assess and explore them to foster design change. Because the social system can control the forces developing within its boundaries better than forces from the external environment, attention is focused on the former (Kilmann and Mitroff, 1977).

Referring again to the Diamond Model of problem solving, the problem of resistance to change must first be conceptualized. Just what is resistance to change, and how may we identify it? The process of adopting an innovation entails going from a state of relative certainty to one of uncertainty, and the latter state arouses anxieties, threats, fantasies, and fears. For example: Will I still have a job after the system is redesigned? Will I still be considered competent? Will my new subsystem really develop into a better one than my present subsystem? Will my salary be affected by the design change? At the individual level such questions may be conceptualized as the result of conflicting forces at the system level. In Lewinian (1947) terms, the interaction of driving and restraining forces produces a force field that determines the state of the system. A useful conceptualization of resistance to change, therefore, is a state in which the forces for change are at least offset by forces against change. Such a conceptualization focuses attention on the assessment of important forces that are active during the intervention.

While such forces can be identified theoretically from a broad conceptual viewpoint, it is necessary to move to the scientific modeling phase of the Diamond Model to develop a methodology that will identify the specific forces acting in a unique intervention. In this way certain action steps can be planned and implemented to resolve or at least manage the resistance problem. Several organizational development models have been formulated to deal specifically with resistance to change (Bennis, et al., 1969). Before these methods can be applied, however, the resistances must be identified and assessed.

The literature on organizational innovation has recently provided a model of the innovation process consistent with our normative approach to change. Slevin (1973) presents a model and methodology for measuring the key variables determining whether an individual, group, or organization is likely to adopt a specified innovation. The model has been shown to be a better predictor of innovation than other models of the innovation process (Dickson and Slevin, 1973).

The Slevin model includes the following variables: (1) the new or target level of performance of the system considering an innovation, (2) the system's current level of performance, (3) the costs of adopting the innovation, (4) the rewards associated with adoption of the innovation, (5) the probability that the adoption of the innovation will lead to the achievement of the target level of performance, (6) the probability that the target level of performance can be achieved without the innovation, and (7) the dependent variable, the probability of adopting the innovation. Using Likert-type attitude scaling or semantic differential scales, a linear regression equation can be utilized to estimate the effect of each variable for a population considering an innovation (i.e., a social system adopting a new design via the MAPS Design Technology).

Various combinations or comparisons of these variables can highlight different types of constraining forces. Comparing the target level of performance with the current level indicates the "aspiration level" of the members; for example, how much better should the design be? The cost relative to the rewards of engaging in the change process is an important indicator of the incentives operating in the situation (e.g., incentives that motivate or demotivate member participation). Also, differences in the probabilities of achieving the target level of performance with or without the innovation suggest members' expectations concerning the possible impact of the new social system design.

In addition, the essence of the model can be extended to include more specific costs and rewards associated with the innovation. These can be listed by representatives from the social system, then included as items in the innovation questionnaire along with the other variables. Alternatively, instead of a questionnaire designed by the social system itself to monitor the implementation process, Schultz and Slevin (1975) have developed an extensive questionnaire based on the variety of variables proposed in the implementation literature (March and Simon, 1958; Schultz and Slevin, 1975). Specifically, the 56 Likert-type statements cluster on seven factors related to implementation: (1) effect of innovation on manager's job performance, (2) interpersonal relations, (3) changes resulting from the innovation, (4) goal achievement and congruence, (5) support for the innovation/lack of resistance, (6) client-researcher interface, and (7) urgency for results. Thus this implementation questionnaire can be used for any social system engaged in adopting an innovation. The uniqueness of the social system under consideration and the desirability of having a pretested instrument versus a specially tailored one will generally determine which of these alternatives is chosen. (See Chapter 3 for a discussion on using a pretested questionnaire versus a specially designed one for the diagnostic phase of the MAPS intervention.)

Utilizing the linear regression analysis to determine the relative effect of the variables and /or the various comparisons, as based on the data from the implementation questionnaires, will provide inputs to planning action steps to facilitate the implementation process. A force-field analysis may be performed by representatives from the social system to isolate the important driving and restraining forces operating in the situation. This type of analysis may also be made through survey feedback procedures (Bowers, 1973; Katz and Kahn, 1966). The data collected via the implementation questionnaire can be categorized and fed back to the organizational subsystems, where the results can be compared to other subsystems and to the individual subsystem's expectations. Then representives, with the aid of internal or external change agents, can develop intervention strategies to increase the driving forces and to reduce the restraining forces. This might involve interventions such as seminars to help members better understand organization design issues and the MAPS Design Technology which would provide an opportunity for members to share their anxieties, concerns, needs, and so on, so that they can better manage the uncertainties they experience. Such interventions would then be incorporated during the team-building step of the collateral phasing process. Data analysis and action planning may also require top management to agree with and commit itself to certain actions; for example, all members involved in the design analysis will be utilized in the new design, salaries will not be changed because of the new design, and so forth.

It should be emphasized that the process of monitoring implementation is not meant to be just a one time assessment, since there may be several questionnaires, data analyses, and action steps. Thus assessment and action may occur at the start of collateral phasing (just after a given MAPS design is selected) and again at one or more time intervals during collateral phasing. (See Keim and Kilmann (1975) for a longitudinal study of monitoring the implementation process for two organizations implementing the MAPS Design Technology.) However, it may also be desirable to monitor the entire process of a social system applying the MAPS Design Technology from the definition of the boundaries of the analysis and the design of the MAPS questionnaire through the implementation of a new design. Certainly members' attitudes and perceptions throughout the process are a major determinant of successful use of the MAPS Design Technology. And while having members respond to questionnaires frequently may not be feasible because of an "overtesting" reaction, careful observation and interviews by the change agent are necessary and appropriate to any change process (Margulies and Raia, 1972). Thus many of the issues raised in this section are relevant to the earlier steps of MAPS as well as to the actual implementation of the MAPS design, although the latter is perhaps the most rigorous test of the technology.

CONCLUSIONS

As we have seen, design poses a complex, ill-structured problem for social systems. The MAPS Design Technology provides a systematic methodology for explicitly confronting the major issues of design and for analyzing the massive information generated through participative processes. The technology guides the system toward a complete conceptualization of the problem and provides for the free and informed choice of the scientific model appropriate to the solution of that problem. Such a process serves to enhance the potential effectiveness of social systems design. The implementation phase is intended to guide the social system toward reaching that potential.

The implementation phase begins with the design decision, which is made from among alternative designs produced by the MAPS Computer Program and based upon the chosen scientific model. We have suggested a methodology by which the system can assess the alternatives and arrive at a free and informed choice. The judicial process serves to involve the total system in highlighting the differences among design alternatives (within a particular model of MAPS) and then arriving at a decision that includes individual needs as well as system objectives.

The implementation of the chosen design is accomplished via a process of collateral phasing that proceeds, through a series of six steps, to develop individual and subsystem potential and to integrate those subsystems into an effective social system. During this process, resource requirements (both technical and human) are identified and processes are initiated to provide for them. Personal and interpersonal needs are assessed and team-building procedures are instituted to provide for effective and supportive subsystem performance. Finally, a system for monitoring the progress of the implementation was discussed. While such a monitoring system was suggested in a separate section of this chapter, it should be clear that monitoring is an activity which must occur thoughout the implementation phase to identify resistances to change and other emerging problems that require effective management. Actually, the concept of monitoring may be expanded to include the total intervention and may thus become one aspect of evaluation, discussed in the next chapter.

Chapter 6
Evaluation

In collaboration with Richard P. Herden

This chapter concludes Part II on the MAPS Design Technology with a systematic consideration of the evaluation problem: evaluating the impact of a MAPS intervention on organizational effectiveness. It should be stated at the outset, however, that this chapter, perhaps even more than the earlier ones, demonstrates how the material covered in this book is designed as much for the social sciences in general as it is for the particular MAPS Design Technology. Therefore, although the various discussions presented in this chapter are related to MAPS, and while this book on MAPS motivated the writing of this chapter, most of the discussion is directed to the general problem of evaluating social science interventions.

Further, although the evaluation process is discussed as the last part of the MAPS Design Technology, it will be apparent that evaluation can actually occur at any point in time and at any stage of the MAPS intervention. Referring to the Diamond Model of problem solving, the step-by-step process can begin at any stage and proceed in any sequence (Sagasti and Mitroff, 1973). This reflects the cyclical and dynamic nature of the problem-solving process. Consequently, it is only for a particular logic in presenting the material (Kaplan, 1964) that evaluation is discussed last. The reader will notice at several points in this chapter, however, that various aspects of the evaluation process will usually be enacted prior to and also during each step of the MAPS Design Technology.

The need for the evaluation of organizational interventions is obvious. The organization is reluctant to allocate resources to programs unless they can be justified in some way. Practicing managers are interested in information, especially cost-benefit data to justify expenditures both before and after the fact. Academicians are also in need of information to develop theories of and methods for organizational development. Although the needs are apparent, evaluation results are sparse. Evans (1974) has estimated that evaluation results are available for fewer than 10 percent of all OD programs.

The reason for the lack of evaluation can be traced mainly to the kinds of organizations and to the interventions themselves. Since organizations are complex systems, a change in one component of the system will have a series of effects on other components. It is difficult to predict the sequence and nature of these changes, and therefore it is difficult to establish a means of monitoring the change. Since organizations are open systems, they are constantly being affected by internal and external factors. It is difficult to separate the effects of intended, internal interventions from those of uncontrollable environmental factors. The intervention itself presents a problem for evaluation. Many organizational change processes are essentially reactive in nature. An initial stimulus produces reactions that cannot be completely predicted, so subsequent stimuli must be tailored to prior reactions. Even when the intervention is proactive, the pattern of change is not completely predictable. It is difficult to design an evaluation process capable of adjusting to the unanticipated results of a change program. Much of the literature dealing with the evaluation of social change addresses itself to such problems (Abert and Kamrass, 1974; Weiss and Rein, 1970). There are, however, additional problems that must be confronted in designing effective evaluation programs. These problems involve the less obvious interactions among the organization, the intervention, and the evaluation program. Furthermore, evaluation designs that have been formulated as experimental and quasi-experimental research designs generally assume the statistical conditions of stable agricultural fields rather than the conditions of dynamic and turbulent organizational phenomena.

This chapter will attempt first to make explicit the relevant interactions among the stages of an evaluation program by presenting a general model of the evaluation process. Since the ultimate goal of any organizational intervention should be to increase effectiveness, a model of organizational effectiveness is presented that facilitates the evaluation of interventions. Then the participative, judicial process is proposed to operationalize the evaluation process for an organization concerned with evaluating the impact of a MAPS intervention (as well as other interventions) on the various components of organizational effectiveness.

A MODEL OF THE EVALUATION PROCESS

The process of evaluation can be thought of as what Mitroff and Sagasti (1973) refer to as an ill-structured problem. We will utilize their Diamond Model to examine this problem and to identify the stages through which the problem is resolved or managed (Sagasti and Mitroff, 1973). Figure 6.1 represents the Diamond Model applied to the evaluation problem.

FIGURE 6.1   A Model of the Evaluation Process

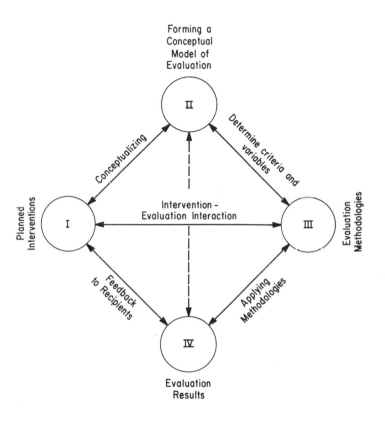

Conceptualization

The first stage in the evaluation process is that of conceptualization. The evaluator (or group of evaluators) formulates a conceptual
model for evaluating the intervention. This model will be determined
by his perspective of the intervention goals, the process of change,
and the needs of recipients for evaluation results. The way in which
the evaluator perceives these variables and formulates the model is in
part determined by his personality. The Jungian typology (Jung,
1923) discussed previously could again be utilized to suggest that the
individual evaluator will process information about the intervention

goals, the process of change, and the needs of recipients for evaluation results in a manner congruent with the perception component of his personality, Sensing (S) or Intuition (N). He will formulate a conceptual model for the evaluation that is based upon his perceptions and is congruent with the judgment component of his personality, Thinking (T) or Feeling (F).

It is important to note that various evaluators of the same intervention, utilizing the same apparent information base, may arrive at different conceptual models. The conceptualization stage might result in a more effective model if several personalities were purposefully brought to bear on the problem. Ideally each of the four Jungian personality types (ST, NT, NF, SF) would be utilized. Kilmann and Mitroff (1975, 1976, 1977) have consistently found that individuals of these four types define, conceptualize, and solve complex problems quite differently. In addition representatives of the various potential recipients of evaluation results would also be beneficial to the process. At least two basic groups of recipients can be identified: the client and the academic audiences. In some cases the community or other environmental sectors may be relevant audiences. The evaluator and the change agent may be different individuals in some interventions and the change agent would thus represent another input in these cases. Each of these sources could be expected to be represented by slightly different personalities having different needs for evaluation results and different perceptions of the process of change. During this stage the different needs must be identified and any need conflicts recognized. The judicial process utilized specifically by Mitroff and Kilmann (1975a) for the evaluation of scientific research, and discussed in prior chapters, would seem appropriate for such a multidimensional conceptualization and will be discussed shortly.

Basically the conceptualization stage defines the evaluation problem and establishes a general framework to confront it. This stage is critical to the success of the evaluation since it establishes limits within which the evaluation will be conducted. To avoid limits that would restrict the usefulness of the evaluation, it is necessary to perceive the problem within its broadest practical realm. If the evaluation problem is conceptualized incorrectly, narrowly, or simplistically, the remaining stages of the evaluation process will be adversely affected or, in the extreme, will be entirely irrelevant. Thus conceptualizing the evaluation problem accurately may be the most critical stage of the entire process. Explicit formulation of the evaluation problem by the different Jungian psychological types, debate about the different conceptualizations, and derivation of a synthesis is expected to minimize the Type III error, defined as the probability of solving the wrong problem when one should have solved the right one (Mitroff and Featheringham, 1974).

Evaluation Methodologies

The second stage of the evaluation process consists of selecting specific evaluation methodologies. This stage begins with the conceptual model and develops a scientific or operational model for the evaluation. Personality is a factor in determining the influence of the conceptual model on the methodology, and it could again be argued that more than one perspective would be appropriate at this stage with representation from the different recipient groups. Perhaps a more crucial factor that must be confronted is the influence of the evaluation methodology on the outcome of the intervention.

Methodologies such as experimental designs are desirable because they control extraneous variables. However, these techniques may be counterproductive for the intervention itself. An obvious disruptive influence of experimental design would be the requirement of random assignment of subjects to test and control groups. This would be particularly disruptive in the case of structural interventions. Quasi-experimental designs that do not generally require random assignment may still raise issues surrounding the existence of control groups (Campbell and Stanley, 1963). The effects of an intervention on the behavior of one organizational segment may be influenced by the behavior of unaffected segments. Evidence of such influences exist in the OD literature. House (1968), for example, found that the effects of sensitivity training on individual behavior were strongly influenced by the behavior of individuals not subjected to such training. The effects of structural interventions may be similarly modified by interaction between affected and control groups. Quasi-experimental designs such as time series, multiple time series, institutional cycle, or nonequivalent control groups avoid the disruptive problems of randomized assignment to treatment groups but often require repeated measures or observations (Campbell and Stanley, 1963). Care must be taken in such instances to assess the potential effect of measures or observations on the intervention. When instruments such as questionnaires are utilized repeatedly for measurement in such analyses, the instruments themselves may influence the intervention.

The choice of evaluation methodology, therefore, should be made by several individuals with differing perspectives and only after a careful assessment of the possible influences of methodology on the intervention. This decision presupposes a consideration of the relative values attached to the intervention and to the evaluation of the intervention (e.g., Which is more important, the intervention or the evaluation?). The consideration of such values is highly individualistic and largely dependent upon personal needs. The organizational member could be expected to place considerably different values on intervention and evaluation than the change agent and the evaluator. Individual change agents or evaluators could also be expected to differ on value emphasis. The change agent and the evaluator, in their roles as consultants, possess great potential influence on the decision of methodology. Thus it is important that they make their values explicit. This involves a clear recognition of their individual needs as well as their ethics. A recognition of individual needs provides a basis for assessing individual preferences among competing methodologies; an explicit statement of ethical position provides a basis for choice among competing methodologies. For example, our ethical position is to allow individuals greater choice and control over their behavior as it affects their involvement and meaningfulness in personal and organizational life. (For a more detailed discussion of ethics, see Chapter 9). Given this clearly stated ethical position, we would exclude methodologies that are expected to reduce individual choice or control although they might provide information that would best meet our personal academic needs.

Regardless of the evaluation methodology chosen, it is desirable to have some basis of comparison for the results of the evaluation. In cases where design (intervention) boundaries have been set that include only a segment of a total organization (or social system), it may be possible to use another segment as a nonequivalent control group or comparable time series (Campbell and Stanley, 1963). In many cases, especially where boundaries include the total organization, a suitable control group will not be available. (See Chapter 3 for a discussion of the formation of design boundaries.) In these cases it is necessary to establish a normative model as a basis for comparison. One approach to the development of such a model would utilize scenarios as a basis of comparison for evaluating the impact of the intervention. As will be seen, the judicial process can be designed to include the use of such scenarios to help operationalize the evaluation process.

Results of Evaluation and Feedback

The third and fourth stages in the evaluation process consist of applying (implementing) the chosen methodologies and feeding the results back to the identified recipients who are involved or are affected by the intervention and its evaluation. The most critical factor in these stages is the assurance that the evaluation techniques will remain flexible and adaptable. As the intervention progresses, change will be manifested in increasing segments of the organization and in different forms. The evaluator must be alert for unanticipated consequences and adapt the evaluation process to assess them.

Up to this point we have treated evaluation as if it consisted of four distinct stages, the completion of which resolved the problem of evaluation. It is important to emphasize that the stages are interdependent and cyclical in nature. The completion of one full cycle of the evaluation process does not necessarily solve the problem. The feedback of results to the identified recipients may suggest new problems, and a new cycle of planned interventions and evaluation then begins.

Furthermore it is important to recognize that the form in which the evaluation results are presented should depend upon the recipient of the results. As stated earlier, four recipients of evaluation results are readily identifiable: the client representative, the change agent, the evaluator, and the organizational member. The client representative and the change agent have similar needs for data to evaluate the intervention and plan future action. The form of presentation may differ, however, depending upon the individual's personality and technical knowledge. The evaluator has an additional need for data to assess the evaluation process itself. Many interventions also require evaluation feedback to organization members. Primarily this group needs data to guide future individual and organizational behavior. In recognition of these differences in evaluation needs and in personality, the data should be presented in different forms. The total evaluation results shown to the different recipients provide the information to plan future interventions, new conceptual models of evaluation, modifications in subsequent evaluation methodologies, and so forth.

A MODEL OF ORGANIZATIONAL EFFECTIVENESS

A conceptual model for evaluating an intervention must include an assessment of organizational effectiveness. The improvement of the latter is the presumed objective of any organizational intervention.

We have found that the Jungian framework also provides a useful description of organizational effectiveness: the ST, NT, NF, and SF psychological functions. (See Chapter 1 for a discussion of these four types, especially Figure 1.3.) Actually it should not be surprising that conceptualizing organizational (evaluation) problems and components of organizational effectiveness are greatly influenced by the same basic psychological functions. The ST (sensation-thinking) type would approach effectiveness through detailed impersonal facts and impersonal analytical reasoning. We label the ST component Internal Efficiency. The goal of this component would be to maximize the ratio of outputs to inputs. The NT (intuition-thinking) type would approach effectiveness through the whole or gestalt by synthesis and impersonal analytical reasoning. The NT component is termed External Efficiency. The goal of this component would be to maximize the bargaining position of the organization in environmental exchanges. The SF (sensation-feeling) type would approach effectiveness through detailed facts and personalistic value judgments. We have labeled the SF component Internal Effectiveness. The goal of this component would be to maximize member motivation. The NF (intuition-feeling) type would approach effectiveness through the gestalt by synthesis and personalistic value judgments and will be referred to as External Effectiveness. The goal of this component would be to maximize societal satisfaction.

Figure 6.2 presents the general framework of the model of organizational effectiveness. The major dimensions of efficiency and effectiveness are similar to the components of organizational effectiveness identified by Katz and Kahn (1966). They defined organizational effectiveness as the maximization of return to the organization by economic and technical means, and by political means. A major difference in the two models evolves from their internal and external dimensions. Katz and Kahn perceived economic and technical means as being essentially internal to the organization and political means as essentially external. We have clearly recognized internal and external components of each.

To give additional substance to the model of organizational effectiveness, we will elaborate further on each of the four components in the model vis à vis the organizational behavior literature, since various theories and frameworks of organizational effectiveness have dealt with one or more of the Jungian components. Also, since the major focus of this book is on the MAPS Design Technology, each effectiveness component will be briefly considered in relation to how it may be affected by a MAPS intervention.

FIGURE 6.2   A Model of Organizational Effectiveness
(See Fig. 1.3 for Illustrations of the four Jungian types)

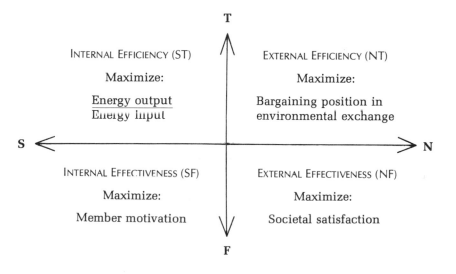

Internal Efficiency

The ST, or Internal Efficiency, component is equivalent to the traditional notion of productivity included in several discussions of organizational effectiveness. Mott (1972), for example, calls this the production criteria and identifies three variables: quantity, quality, and efficiency. Internal Efficiency is the traditional subject of industrial engineering, concentrating on work flows and controls to optimize quantity, quality, and efficiency. This component is also the subject of microeconomic analysis, particularly in regard to marginal productivity of variable resources as a function of costs. Briefly, the Internal Efficiency component focuses on the conversion of inputs to outputs and the minimization of the conversion costs via the efficient allocation of tasks and division of labor. MAPS directly addresses this component through the formulation and clustering of task items. The resulting task structures and their influence on work flows are important determinants of the production criteria. The combination of task and people clusters will influence the utilization of resources, which helps to further satisfy the stated criteria.

External Efficiency

The NT, or External Efficiency, component deals with the acquisition of resources and the distribution of products and services. Yuchtman and Seashore (1967) have utilized a system resource approach to organizational effectiveness. They define the effectiveness of an organization "in terms of its bargaining position, as reflected in the ability of the organization, in either absolute or relative terms, to exploit its environment in the acquisition of scarce and valued resources" (Yuchtman and Seashore, 1967: 898). This notion is similar to that of Lawrence and Lorsch (1967a), in that the bargaining position of an organization depends upon its ability to interface successfully with its environment. The concept of differentiation is central to this interface and constitutes one of the goals of a MAPS analysis. The formulation of task and people clusters reflects in part the way individuals perceive relevant environmental segments. To the degree that these resultant subsystems facilitate acquisition of resources, External Efficiency will be improved.

External efficiency is also involved with micro- and macroeconomic issues concerning markets for resources and final products. Plant location, pricing, market segmentation, and make or buy decisions are examples of issues requiring accurate and timely environmental information. Thus External Efficiency focuses on the efficient transfer of technical and informational resources between the organization and its environment, emphasizing that the organization is very dependent on its environment for such exchanges. MAPS may be utilized to confront these issues directly by the design of strategic information systems, particularly when relevant environmental segments are involved in the formulation of task items (Ghymn, 1974; Kilmann and Ghymn, in press).

External Effectiveness

Yuchtman and Seashore (1967) recognized the dangers of maximizing the exploitation of the organization's environment but gave few clues as to what constitutes optimal exploitation. The NF, or External Effectiveness, component addresses this problem by assessing environmental or social satisfaction. Pickle and Friedlander (1967) approached this component through what they called organizational success. They identified seven "parties-at-interest" who determine organizational success: owners, customers, suppliers, employees, community members, creditors, and local, state, and federal governments. They argue that the criterion by which to measure organizational effectiveness is the success in fulfilling societal needs. They measured each of the seven societal parties in terms of their satisfaction relative to the ninety-seven small businesses included in the study. Their findings show that the satisfaction of the various parties are positively but moderately related. This would seem to imply that organizational interaction with the environment should be consistent, but that specific attempts to satisfy diverse groups are necessary (i.e., the Feeling function). The External Effectiveness component thus considers the relationship between the organization and its environment but not the technical or strictly informational exchange. Rather the emphasis is on the rapport or commitments that may be developed with such external clients and segments, and the extent to which the organization provides some useful and meaningful product or service—not measured simply by price and market share but by assessments of satisfaction.

MAPS may be highly instrumental in attempting to satisfy such environmental needs by including representatives of societal groups in the development of task items. This approach not only recognizes clearly various societal needs but also helps to institutionalize them within the organization design. Alternatively, MAPS can be utilized to form community groups to help environmental representatives better articulate their needs, concerns, and expectations of the organization in question. In the latter case representatives of societal groups would not only develop the task items for the MAPS questionnaire, but would also be involved in the entire design process and the resulting design.

Internal Effectiveness

The SF, or Internal Effectiveness, component contains factors relating to individual motivation. The various expectancy theories of motivation (Atkinson, 1958; Vroom, 1965) are useful in identifying some of these factors. Generally these theories hold that an individual will be motivated to the degree that he sees his efforts leading to high performance and the fulfillment of positively attractive personal goals or needs. The participatory nature of the MAPS Design Technology enables individuals to relate their personal goals to specific tasks, and thus to affect the process of task assignment by rating task items based upon ability to perform and on interest.

The impact of group processes on Internal Effectiveness is also important. Mott (1972) includes an adaptation criterion in his model of organizational effectiveness. He finds that interpersonal relations and integration are important in facilitating communication in general, and problem solving in particular. He sees these processes exemplified by the manner in which organizations anticipate problems, develop satisfactory and timely solutions, and in the promptness and prevalence of acceptance of solutions by organizational members. In other words, Internal Effectiveness is concerned with the motivation and commitment of particular organizational members to actually perform specified tasks as well as the interpersonal relationships necessary to facilitate task-related behavior.

MAPS deals with these motivational factors by clustering individuals and tasks so that most of the important interdependencies are contained within the subsystems. Therefore the potential for good interpersonal relations is increased and the need for integrative mechanisms reduced, particularly with the scientific models of MAPS that include the use of people items in the computation of people clusters: Models III through VI, as discussed in Chapter 4. The potential for good interpersonal relations may also be realized during implementation through techniques such as team building, discussed in Chapter 5.

Overall Organizational Effectiveness

The four components of effectiveness are interrelated as follows: the SF and ST components are oriented to the internal functioning of the organization, having motivated individuals perform tasks that have been efficiently designed. The NT and NF components are focused on the organization–environment interface, securing the necessary inputs for organization activity, effectively distributing the outputs, and conducting organization–environment interactions in a manner that promotes relevance, confidence, and satisfaction for affected segments of society. Together, the ST and NT components concentrate on the technical, informational, and economic aspects of organizational effectiveness (internal and external), while the SF and NF components involve the human, motivational, and qualitative aspects. This four-component conceptualization suggests that organizational effectiveness is a multiplicative function of the four components.

Organizational Effectiveness = (Internal Efficiency × External
      Efficiency × Internal Effectiveness × External Effectiveness)

The Jungian framework of organizational effectiveness does not imply that any one component is more important than another, but does suggest that the components represent distinctly different perspectives that may be in conflict. A factor in one component will affect factors in other components and trade-offs may be necessary to optimize organizational effectiveness. The relative importance of the components to an organization will differ depending upon its designs, personnel, technologies, objectives, and environment. The most obvious trade-offs exist between the efficiency and effectiveness components. Maximization of Internal Efficiency in some instances might require work flows controlled by mechanistic devices. This may negatively affect Internal Effectiveness by lowering the motivational level of organizational members. Similarly, maximization of External Efficiency through exploitation of natural resources may negatively affect External Effectiveness through increased social costs to the community. This in turn may result in reaction by the community, which will impose restrictions on Internal Efficiency.

DuBrin (1974) has presented a model of organizational climate in which he identifies several determinants of climate that may be considered as mediating variables for organizational effectiveness: economic conditions, leadership style, policy, values, organization structure, characteristics of people, nature of the business, and life stage of the organization. An examination of these variables in the Jungian framework of organizational effectiveness will emphasize the interrelated nature of the four organizational effectiveness components and provide insight for establishing evaluation criteria.

If we examine the relative economic condition of the organization on some scale of profitability, one effect will become evident in the Internal Efficiency component. Policies, particularly budgets, will tend to vary from "loose" to "tight" depending upon the relative profitability of the organization. This in turn will affect the behavior of organizational members, perhaps in terms of their approach to risk. Thus the Internal Effectiveness component may be affected by members' willingness or aversion to taking risks, and this effect may in turn be reflected in the attitudes of societal groups. These attitudes might take the form of beliefs about the relative conservativeness or innovativeness of the organization and affect the satisfaction of these groups. Consequently the External Effectiveness component may be affected. This outcome may also influence the ability of the organization to acquire resources and may therefore affect the External Efficiency component. Finally, this cycle of affects would tend to reinforce the relative economic condition of the organization.

Similarly the values held by organizational members could produce a cyclical influence on the effectiveness components. Individuals' concepts of man may be considered such a value (see Chapter 2). If the majority of individuals held similar views, for instance Theory X or Y (McGregor, 1960), this would affect the Internal Effectiveness component via leadership style. This difference in leadership style would then be reflected in the Internal Efficiency component by policies that would tend to be more restrictive or permissive. Policy type may in turn affect the External Efficiency component by the manner in which the organization acquires resources. Restrictive policies would tend to produce static acquisitions of resources, while permissive policies would tend to produce flexible acquisition procedures. This in turn may affect the External Effectiveness component by creating stable or adaptive relations with societal groups. To the degree that societal satisfaction is affected, the cycle may tend to reinforce the original value structure.

Another way of illustrating the interrelationships among the four components is by noting that if any component of effectiveness is extremely low (e.g., zero), then overall effectiveness is also low (e.g., zero), regardless of the state of the other three components (i.e., anything multiplied by zero is zero). For example, an organization may concentrate on optimizing work flows, arrangements of machinery, and specific procedures for handling materials (Internal Efficiency), but may have completely ignored the matter of motivating employees to actually perform tasks, to work the machines efficiently, and to adhere or be committed to the stated procedures (Internal Effectiveness). Totally ignoring this Internal Effectiveness component even if the Internal Efficiency component is highly attained, will render overall effectiveness low or zero, especially if there is a strike and no employee works at all! This also applies even if the external sources of effectiveness are well managed (e.g., relations with other organizations and community demand for the organization's product).

The same holds true for deficiencies in the other components. For example, work flows may be designed in an efficient manner (Internal Efficiency) and members may be motivated to perform specific tasks (Internal Effectiveness), but the organization cannot obtain the materials from suppliers to produce the firm's products (External Efficiency), or the product may simply not be wanted by consumers (External Effectiveness). In the latter case internal aspects of effectiveness are fine, but external aspects have not been anticipated or managed well. In contrast, the organization may be very effective in securing raw materials and engaging in good relations with clients and consumers (external components) but because of deficiencies in internal functioning, the product or service may be provided at a cost too high for the organization to survive.

The Impact of Interventions
on Organizational Effectiveness

A MAPS intervention will typically impact on organizational design, including job design and work flows (Internal Efficiency), and on individual commitment and group cohesiveness (Internal Effectiveness). It may also impact External Efficiency and External Effectiveness through PROBLEM-SOLVING and STRATEGIC PLANNING DESIGNS, as discussed in Chapter 4. It would be helpful, however, to be able to indicate more clearly the impact of interventions on organizational effectiveness. While the exact specification of variables will depend upon the organization in question and the MAPS implementation strategy, certain variable types can be anticipated. These types will vary from "hard" economic measures in the efficiency components to "soft" sociopsychological measures in the effectiveness components. Figure 6.3 suggests some generally applicable measures that may by used to assess performance in each of the four components.

A particular organization would naturally have to weigh the relative importance of variables within a component as well as the relative importance of components to overall effectiveness, not only in planning interventions but in evaluating the subsequent impact of these interventions. For example, an organization existing in a dynamic environment would probably emphasize the external components of effectiveness since these critically determine the adaptability of the organization to its environment, which is perhaps the prime issue for such an organization, all else being equal. Interventions are more likely to be planned that are expected to enhance the organization's adaptiveness. Where the organization's environment is fairly stable, the internal functioning will probably be the prime issue for overall effectiveness (all else being equal) and interventions will likely be planned accordingly. To evaluate the impact of these interventions, however, the organization must choose variables that can be measured easily in its own case, and must select evaluation methodologies congruent with such specific variables when the relative importance of effectiveness components and basic variable types are ascertained.

FIGURE 6.3   Measures of Organizational Effectiveness

```
                                    T
           INTERNAL                 ↑              EXTERNAL

           Units produced per man-hour        Cost of capital
           Rate of return on invested capital Market share
    EFFICIENCY
           Cost of goods sold                 Cost of raw materials
           Scrap material per unit            Labor cost
           Sales per salesman                 Product price leadership
           Sales per advertising dollar       New product development
           Inventory cost                     New market development


    S  ←─────────────────────────────┼─────────────────────────────→ N


           Employee turnover                  Community satisfaction
                                                  with organization
           Absenteeism
    EFFECTIVENESS                             Satisfaction of supplier
           Number of grievances                  with organization
           Employee attitudes                 Consumer satisfaction
           Organizational climate             Ability to identify problems
           Employee commitment                   or opportunities
           Interpersonal relationships        Social responsibility
                                              The quality of life
                                    ↓         Environmental impact
                                    F
```

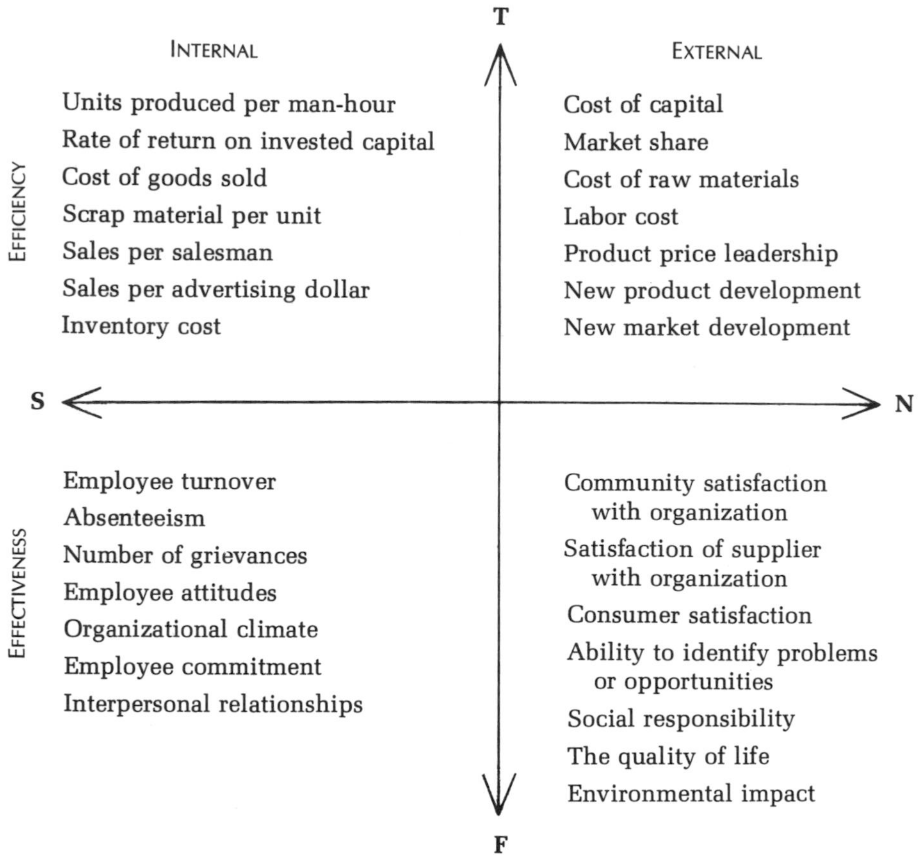

TOWARD A SYSTEMATIC METHODOLOGY

It is necessary now to consider a specific methodology to operationalize the foregoing discussion on the evaluation process and the concepts of organizational effectiveness. A judicial process may be outlined by which organizational members (including others affected by the intervention and the evaluation of the intervention) can participate systematically in conceptualizing the various aspects of effectiveness most central to their organization, in choosing evaluation methodologies to measure these components of effectiveness, and in actually evaluating the impact of an intervention designed to enhance overall organizational effectiveness. An explicit objective of this judicial process is to minimize the Type III error, that is, the probability of solving the wrong problem when one should have solved the right one (Mitroff and Kilmann, 1975b), by (a) conceptualizing the evaluation problem via different personality types and representatives for different recipient groups; (b) debating the advantages and disadvantages of the various conceptual models of, and evaluation methodologies for, the evaluation problem; and (c) deriving a synthesis that capitalizes on the strengths and weaknesses of each alternative position at each stage of the evaluation problem.

A Judicial Process for Evaluation

In the first step of this approach relevant individuals, such as organizational member representatives, the change agent, the evaluator, and societal segment representatives are requested, prior to the intervention, to develop scenarios of the organization's development up to some specified time in the future. They are to develop a different scenario for each relevant set of environmental and organizational situations. In other words, they are asked to describe how they think the organization will change, without any intervention with regard to its effectiveness. They are further requested to make such a description under various circumstances that have a reasonable likelihood of occurring. The circumstances may include variations in general economic conditions, technological change, alteration of product mix, change in consumer preferences, and so forth.

The second step requires the individuals to form Jungian groups (i.e., an ST, NT, SF, and NF group) either by their assessed Jungian psychological type (Myers and Briggs, 1962) or by a content analysis of their scenarios, to parallel the Jungian components of effectiveness. The individuals are then asked to develop a group scenario for each relevant circumstance by combining or integrating their individual scenarios. Typically this results in four very different perspectives, in which the differences may be more extreme than the initial individual perspectives (Kilmann, 1974b). Thus the ST group tends to emphasize and develop strong arguments for the Internal Efficiency component, the NT group argues for the External Efficiency component, the SF group supports the Internal Effectiveness component, and the NF group emphasizes the External Effectiveness component (Kilmann and Mitroff, 1977). The specified variables in Figure 6.3 can serve as a guide to this stage of the process.

The correlation between Jungian group and its endorsement of the corresponding effectiveness component may be only moderate, however, with additional personality or situational factors overriding the Jungian dispositions. For instance, individuals may differ in their awareness of environmental influences as well as in the way they deal with such influences (Abert and Kamrass, 1974). Actual environmental characteristics may differ between organizations as well as among differentiated segments of the same organization (Lawrence and Lorsch, 1967a). In terms of the latter it is interesting to note that individuals tend to endorse external component criteria and variables more heavily when they perceive the environment to be dynamic than when they view it as stable. While these additional factors often partially override the Jungian personality influence, they do not detract from the dialectical nature of the scenarios. Instead, these factors help to put the Jungian types into a perspective consistent with the particular organization while preserving the Jungian spokesman who best understands his own type of scenario, and consequently can generally best argue for it.

The third step examines explicitly the four differentiated group products and attempts to integrate them in some new form or synthesis. The process involves having two or more individuals from each of the four Jungian groups meet as an integrated group. This group is then asked to discuss its different scenarios, assumptions, and values. Thus a lively debate is fostered in which the different perspectives are exaggerated, challenged, examined, denied, projected, and so on. During this debate, each individual is encouraged as much as possible to critically question and confront the strengths and weaknesses of his perspective. Once each individual in the integrated group has achieved this objective, the process moves toward the synthesis stage. The atmosphere changes, and each member of the group attempts to provide integrative solutions, capitalizing on the strengths of each position while hopefully minimizing or subduing the weaknesses. Finally, this group proposes an integrated scenario for each relevant circumstance that satisfactorily confronts the issues developed by the different perspectives. The scenario that most closely approximates the actual series of circumstances in which the organization finds itself during the intervention becomes a conceptual yardstick for the remaining stages of the evaluation process shown in Figure 6.1.

This approach has certain advantages over the development of a normative model based on theory alone. The approach does not require activities that would adversely affect the intervention, since it occurs before implementation begins. The process of comparison between variables described in the scenario and those occurring during and after intervention, require no more disruptive measurement than other techniques. The resulting "yardstick" includes circumstances and perspectives particular to the organization that may be difficult to interpret from a purely theoretical standpoint. The scenario approach may actually improve the intervention by helping to identify organizational problems initially that might otherwise not be discovered until a later stage. Finally, it should be emphasized again that the judicial process may be instituted at any time throughout the intervention and evaluation process to adapt to unintended consequences, unforeseen developments, and as a general participative process for making important decisions on complex problems. This enables the process to be adaptive and proactive and not merely reactive, as are most evaluation and decision approaches.

EVALUATION AS A CONTINUOUS PROCESS

While certain quasi-experimental designs are appropriate for assessing the overall impact on organizational effectiveness, they do not generally provide a mechanism for periodic feedback of process changes. Such feedback is not only necessary for the change agent to assess the progress of the intervention but is also desirable for the organizational member to assess his own progress in adapting to the structural change. For example, Mann's (1957) approach to feedback through a concept of organizational "families" seems especially appropriate to a MAPS intervention. The initial families would consist of preintervention organizational groups to facilitate climate building prior to the boundary decision and to generate task items during the input phase. MAPS design families would be formed during the collateral phasing period to foster team building. The families would receive and evaluate feedback data in a task-oriented atmosphere to assess their capabilities. They would in turn serve as sources of data for the evaluation process as well as internally to the new organization design. Since the "families" concept provides that certain individuals will be members of more than one family, "linking" individuals will be used to assess the need for integrating mechanisms in the new design (Likert, 1961). Thus, process evaluation can occur throughout the intervention while periodically assessing organizational effectiveness.

The major objective of evaluating organizational change programs is to determine their impact on organizational effectiveness. We have provided a framework for such an evaluation and suggested methodologies to measure change. It is also important to evaluate the change technology itself. This is important not only from an academic research perspective but from an operating management perspective as well. Such evaluation can improve the technology and also provide a direction for future organizational change.

For example, the MAPS Design Technology provides clear points for self-evaluation by following a series of phases separated by explicit decisions. The first decision concerns organizational climate and is made jointly by the change agent and the organization. Implicit in this decision is an evaluation of the climate to determine whether meaningful data can be generated to facilitate structural change. Where organizational climate is low but commitment to change is high, process changes are initiated to improve climate. Explicit evaluation must be simultaneously initiated to assess changes in organizational climate.

The second decision concerns boundaries for structural change. As discussed in Chapter 3, this decision is critical to meaningful change. Evaluation of this decision must be made during and after the implementation phase. Specifically, interdependencies must be assessed to assure that most are contained within or occur at the established boundaries. The interdependencies should be identified from temporal as well as spatial dimensions. Much of this evaluation can be accomplished through the feedback process described above.

The third decision involves a choice of a scientific model of MAPS. Through evaluation of the contingency variables (particularly the environment, the individuals, and the types of technologies), a decision to approach change through one of the six MAPS models is made. Even though a thorough method of explicating and evaluating this decision has been formulated (Kilmann and Mitroff, 1975), a post-decision evaluation should be made. Evaluation during and after the implementation should utilize variables used in the decision to assess the appropriateness of the chosen model in fostering organizational effectiveness.

The fourth decision concerns a choice among alternative designs generated from the chosen model. Again, a thorough method of explication and evaluation has been formulated (Kilmann and Mitroff, 1975), but a post-decision evaluation should be made. Evaluation of this decision would concentrate on the implementation phase and assess the degree of resource and task alteration necessary to make the design viable. As discussed previously, some shifting of resources or tasks should be expected but by comparing alternative MAPS designs with the actual design, an assessment of the design decision can be made explicit.

A fifth set of decisions involves a choice of implementation strategies to accomplish the transition from preintervention to postintervention design. This phase actually may involve a series of decisions regarding appropriate approaches to process change, and each decision relies heavily on feedback from evaluation. As mentioned previously, such feedback is necessary to the change agent as well as to the organizational member. Since continuous feedback is required, special care must be taken to choose measurements that are not disruptive to the process of change itself.

Upon "completed" implementation, an assessment of organizational effectiveness can be made. As discussed previously, this is the ultimate test of a successful intervention. It is not, however, the final stage of evaluation, which should be a continuous process. As indicated with the Diamond Model applied to evaluation (Figure 6.1), inquiry (evaluation) is a never-ending process of discovery. The final feedback of information concerning organizational effectiveness should serve to identify new problem areas and opportunities for future organizational change. Thus the MAPS Design Technology then serves a final purpose: it provides a direction for organizational development and a tool to assess the need for change.

As a continuing focus on social systems design and organizational development, therefore, it is important that the design process does not stop simply because a "purposeful" design has been implemented (see Chapter 2). Aside from the many unforeseen obstacles that may be encountered during the implementation and OD programs, the new design like the old one can become outdated with changes in the social system's task environment or significant changes in members' skills and interaction desires. Consequently, the social system could well institute a periodic review of its design to keep the theory and practice of social systems designing as a recurring management process. Certainly the development of purposeful subsystems necessitates a continuing process of design assessment, design creation, design implementation, design re-assessment, and so forth.

One approach to evaluation of the MAPS design would involve periodic use of the MAPS Design Technology to retest the functionality of the design; perhaps every six months to a year, the social system's design could be reassessed via MAPS. In most cases this would not entail the use of each step of the technology. At a minimum, the same initial MAPS questionnaire could be readministered to the same bounded social system and the resulting MAPS Design Matrices (see Figure 4.8 in Chapter 4) could be compared with those of the original or preceding analyses. However, if new members have entered the social system and others have left, the people items on the MAPS questionnaire will have to be altered. With this membership change, interrelationships of task items and endorsement of task items may also change because the new members may have different task interests and /or abilities. In addition, a changed membership would also respond differently to the people items. Thus, if different members responded to the MAPS questionnaire over time, the MAPS Design Matrices could certainly be different between questionnaire administrations.

During a period of time the nature of the task environment facing the social system may also have changed, and even the objectives of the system may have shifted in response to these changes. This would suggest that the task items on the MAPS questionnaire would need to be updated, and the procedures outlined in Step 5 of the technology (see Chapter 4) could be instituted to redesign the task portion of the questionnaire. When the membership responds to this new MAPS questionnaire and when the MAPS Design Matrices are formed, there would undoubtedly be some differences between the current design of the social system and the latest MAPS design. If significant differences appear, Step 8 of the technology could be applied (i.e., the judicial process) to carefully consider the differences and whether or not some further design changes should be recommended and implemented (see Chapter 5). Furthermore, because of such environmental changes, it is also possible that the design boundaries should be altered for additional MAPS assessments, which requires members from external subsystems and /or external environmental segments to be included in designing and responding to the MAPS questionnaire. The latter case would involve Step 2 of the MAPS Design Technology to determine the most efficient and feasible decomposition of the design problem (see Chapter 3). This step would then be followed by the other steps of the technology. In any event, if the social system is facing a dynamic, complex, and changing environment and if the membership changes frequently, design changes may be required often to best adapt and manage these changes.

It should be emphasized that considerable research is needed to understand more fully the impact of a design on subsystem and total system effectiveness. Such an understanding would greatly aid the process of selecting, implementing, and evaluating a new design. It is expected that several related research studies applying MAPS to change social systems design will certainly help to explore this area further, as is discussed in Chapter 8 on current applications of MAPS.

CONCLUSIONS

Again it is worthwhile to suggest why so few organizational change programs have included a systematic and comprehensive evaluation component. Perhaps measuring and evaluating something as complex as organizational and social system change is so ambiguous and ill-defined that both change agents and academic researchers have tended to avoid the problem. However, the organizations who have decided to engage in such change programs (particularly organization design changes) are less likely to be satisfied with the avoidance of the evaluation issue, especially with the tightening and scarcity of resources. Therefore we anticipate that the development and use of evaluation processes will be demanded increasingly by organizational clients.

Furthermore, just because the evaluation of interventions is so complex and ill-defined does not obviate the development of evaluation methodologies and processes that rely on qualitative as well as quantitative assessments. The particular framework of organizational effectiveness presented in this chapter, including the judicial process of involving organizational members (as well as others) in the evaluation process, highlights the possibility of developing approaches that are appropriate to complex and ill-defined problems. Although such approaches as the judicial process will never be completely quantitative and objective, they do provide a means of addressing the problem. Once we realize that complex problems will always contain subjective and qualitative aspects and that these can be assessed (Kilmann and Mitroff, 1976), the social sciences will no longer have to avoid subjective processes or, implicitly at least, stay away from complex problems such as evaluating organizational change.

The MAPS Design Technology attempts to confront the evaluation problem directly by including the foregoing evaluation process as a formal step of the technology. The primary purpose of this chapter, however, was to raise the issue of evaluation (and, implicitly, all other aspects of the technology) beyond the fairly well-defined boundaries of MAPS. The issues of evaluation, implementation, entry, diagnosis, and so forth, are all germane to any attempt at planned social change for any technology, method, or procedure that proposes to confront complex social change problems with social science knowledge. Consequently, as stated at the outset of this book, the discussions and material contained in these chapters are as much for the social sciences in general as they are for the specific MAPS Design Technology.

PART III
APPLICATIONS, ETHICS, AND THE FUTURE

Chapter 7
Designing Problem-Solving Systems

In collaboration with Kirk P. Kelly, Marjorie A. Lyles, and John C. Ryan

Part II of this book (Chapters 3, 4, 5, and 6) presented the basic steps, components, and processes involved in the MAPS Design Technology. Part I discussed the theoretical and empirical foundations of MAPS as derived from the field of organization design, including the value premises of purposeful systems and structural interventions. The purpose now is to consider MAPS as a whole system and to suggest how it is fundamentally rooted in general systems theory and the philosophy of science, how it has been applied in a variety of organizational settings, and how it should be applied to create organizational and societal change (as based on our value positions).

Specifically, Part III of this book presents in Chapter 7 the systems /philosophical aspects of the whole MAPS Design Technology as well as its application for system-wide problem-solving objectives. Following this discussion, Chapter 8 presents a summary of the several applications of MAPS that are either completed or still in progress. These case summaries are systematically related to the previous discussions in this book by plotting the cases onto the figures that defined and portrayed various aspects and alternative applications of MAPS (e.g., the Diamond Model of problem solving, the six scientific models of MAPS, etc.). Chapter 9 concludes Part III and this book by considering not only the ethics and validity of MAPS but its future. The latter is approached by a societal simulation which illustrates the very basic and pervasive forces in our society that tend to resist the types of changes confronted by the MAPS Design Technology.

In the present chapter, however, we are mainly concerned that contemporary organizations are facing increasingly dynamic and changing environments which pose more complex and ill-defined problems than organizations have previously had to confront. These problems include the following issues: Which new international markets to explore? Which new technologies should and can be developed? Should organizational goals be altered? How should employees be effectively motivated? What social responsibility policies should the organization formulate and implement? But these problems involve the entire organization, not just one or two departments or divisions, and can never be completely resolved since they are always present. Thus these problems must be managed continually. Furthermore, the information needed to analyze them is not generally available, nor will the information ever be complete because the nature of the problem keeps changing. Actually one might argue that the basic problem is defining what the problem is, and then one can begin seeking information, analyzing the problem, and deriving and implementing strategies to manage it (Kilmann and Mitroff, 1977).

Organizations, however, are designed primarily to perform day-to-day activities and to efficiently produce well-defined products and services, not to solve complex and changing problems. Clearly, organizations are designed into operational subunits (e.g., production, marketing, finance, etc.) to pursue well-defined goals and tasks. But how can the organization engage in effective problem solving if it is primarily designed for daily concerns and if complex problems simply do not fit well into the design categories or boxes on the organization's chart? What is needed is a comprehensive approach to organizational problem solving, one that involves the entire organization or those directly affected by complex problems, and specifically designs for problem solving by mobilizing resources (i.e., people, goals, tasks, information, etc.) in a manner that does not confine the organization to handling problems within the given day-to-day OPERATIONAL DESIGN.

This comprehensive approach to problem solving also requires that the MAPS Design Technology that is proposed to design an effective problem-solving system must itself be founded on a broad philosophical and systems base. Otherwise it is quite likely that the MAPS consultant and the client system will commit a Type III error (i.e., they will have solved the wrong problem, or may even have solved the wrong problem incorrectly, simply, or narrowly). Therefore we must be assured that the technology itself meets the criteria it applies to actual social systems. Stated differently, is the MAPS Design Technology itself a total problem-solving system as well as a total information-inquiring system?

After we have considered this latter question we will explore in detail how various PROBLEM-SOLVING and STRATEGIC PLANNING DESIGNS can be created with MAPS. Although the derivation and nature of these designs was discussed in Chapter 4, because organizations will need to devote more resources and energies to problem solving and strategic activities (due to increasingly dynamic and turbulent environments), special attention is devoted to how to design these activities effectively. Included are illustrations of specific PROBLEM-SOLVING and STRATEGIC PLANNING DESIGNS that can be created by applying the MAPS Design Technology.

MAPS AS A TOTAL PROBLEM-SOLVING SYSTEM

In their paper, "Operations Research from the Viewpoint of General Systems Theory," Sagasti and Mitroff argue that both our knowledge and the application of operations research techniques (OR) have been suboptimized because the OR process itself has not been subjected to a systems approach (Sagasti and Mitroff, 1973).

General systems theory (GST) provides a framework for studying the OR process so that our understanding and effective use of management technologies may increase. GST approaches the study of phenomena from a "holistic" point of view. That is, this approach suggests a number of properties of social phenomena exist that cannot be described meaningfully in terms of the elements of any conceptual framework (or system) alone. Thus the approach taken here is to consider techniques (frameworks, etc.) such as operations research or the MAPS Design Technology as systems with several component subsystems, and to investigate not only the separate elements or subsystems but the relationships among them. These subsystems are conceptual in nature and correspond to the various phases of the OR process in general and to the defined steps of the MAPS Design Technology in particular. Also, because these techniques (frameworks, etc.) are being viewed as systems, these subsystems exist only by virtue of their relation to one another; they have little meaning, if any, when looked at strictly by themselves.

The Diamond Model of Problem Solving

The Diamond Model of problem solving has been referred to many times in earlier chapters to discuss distinct subsystems of the MAPS Design Technology (e.g., conceptual frameworks, scientific models, implementation, and evaluation) (Sagasti and Mitroff, 1973). In this section we will take a more holistic, systems approach. We will examine both the Diamond Model and MAPS as complete systems and will then argue that the MAPS Design Technology has an extremely broad foundation. The interdisciplinary approach of the MAPS Design Technology has previously been explained in some detail. However, for the purposes of this discussion it is useful to reiterate that MAPS utilizes sophisticated computer-assisted logic to develop solutions for a problem developed from a systems viewpoint. In this context, MAPS can be viewed as similar to an OR technique. But MAPS is more than a typical OR type problem solver. It includes as part of the process all those elements that are typically missing from OR techniques (Mitroff and Sagasti, 1973). Thus it is reasonable that we examine MAPS in the context of the Diamond Model of problem solving so that this contention may be substantiated.

Figure 7.1 depicts the Diamond Model of problem solving (see Figures 1, 4.2, and 6.1). We will discuss MAPS here not simply as a theoretical construct, but as a methodology being applied in a client organization. The social researcher or analyst now becomes the MAPS consultant or the MAPS consulting team. Reality becomes a real organization of real people in the real world with all the attendant "problems." This client system then becomes for us our reality. The political, economic, legal, and social constraints of the environment impact the organization and the problem definition process. The subsystem called reality thus consists of all the aspects of the real world that relate to the particular situation. Reality provides all data and initial inputs for the analyst and constitutes the starting point for the process. Initially there may be no more than a "felt" problem. Perhaps this feeling is vague in that an executive just feels that his organization could be doing things better, with no specific things in mind. The conceptual model of that situation is relevant only if the

FIGURE 7.1 MAPS as a Problem-Solving System (This model was developed by Sagasti and Mitroff, 1973)

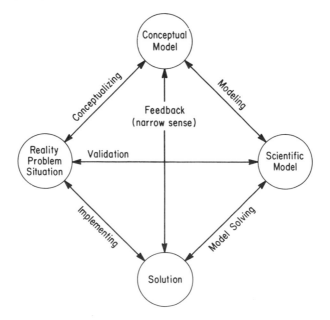

problem is seen as one of organization design. The conceptual model is identified with the design variables and the issues discussed in Chapters 1, 2, and 3. The scientific model(s) are the six models of MAPS presented in Chapter 4. The solution is the MAPS output generated by the MAPS Computer Program. Implementing the solution and evaluating whether the problem that was initially defined has been resolved (or managed) and whether new problems have emerged constitutes the fourth process of the Diamond Model (Chapters 5 and 6). Feedback is seen as a linkage between the several MAPS solutions and the originally defined design problem (conceptual model). Another relationship is the validation link between the scientific models and the client organization (the initial problem). In this context validation means the degree of correspondence between the model and the reality it purports to represent.

Reality and Problem Definition

We now consider each stage of the problem-solving process in more detail. Specifically, the concept of reality itself contains value judgments; that is, reality does not exist apart from the observer, who is himself a part of that reality. Kenneth Boulding makes the point that there are no such things as facts. He maintains that only messages exist which are filtered through a changeable value system (Boulding, 1956). The problem solver as a person is therefore a crucial determinant in this process. The analyst approaches reality with his own ideas, anticipations, values, and biases. These may be considered his knowledge, experience, or background. The interaction of the "totality of the analyst" with the "total reality" results in a specific problem perception.

That different analysts could conceive different problems for any given situation stands almost as a self-evident truth. That truth, however, has more than one dimension. Not only does the background of the analyst come into play; his personality in the Jungian sense and his epistemological preference are also involved (Mitroff, 1974). These latter aspects can have a major impact on the problem-solving process. This becomes increasingly important as one acknowledges the recent trend, particularly in the social sciences, to recognize that a primary determinant of a "solution" is how the problem has been represented or formulated initially. It is tempting to state that the most important problem is precisely the issue of how to represent problems. While we are often concerned about rejecting a null hypothesis that is true (a Type I error) or not rejecting a null hypothesis that is false (a Type II error), we often overlook the possibility of a Type III error, solving the wrong problem. This is a much more severe error because its effects are often very difficult to detect. In the social sciences the causes of a phenomenon or of a behavior are so complex that errors of the third kind are a constant threat. Frequently organizational problems will have several causal dimensions (or alternative problem definitions). Too often an "expert" will be called in to solve a problem with his particular perspective, ignoring other plausible perspectives and approaches.

The aspects of causality must be examined explicitly to accurately define the "problem reality." Only with a correct assessment and statement of the problem can we expect to produce a viable solution. For example, a common technique used in writing case studies is to present sufficient facts for several interpretations of the problem. Are the faulty products the result of machinery problems, or of poor materials, or of sloppy or angry workers? Suppose one builds a conceptual model that categorizes the problem as behavioral. A scientific model is formed which indicates that the dissatisfaction of the workers is causing them to turn out sloppy work. As an answer to the problem, steps are taken to resolve some of the issues that are causing the dissatisfaction. This then would be an example of a successful problem-solving exercise. But would it? Suppose that the issue were really a materials problem. The workers may have had some irritating issues resolved, but the products would still be faulty. This illustrates how great an impact the initial problem definition has on the subsequent problem-solving processes.

Forming a Conceptual Model

For MAPS the conceptualization process is the organizational diagnosis phase. This is a mutual learning process involving the consultants and their clients. The first phase involves the consultants teaching the top management group about some of the organization design concepts and sharing with them the values imbued in the MAPS process. A second phase reverses this order; that is, the management group teaches the consultants about their organization and, hopefully, their values. Once this normative consensus has been established, the combined groups (management and the consultants) may be able to diagnose accurately the problems in the organization. This must be an interactive process, where those whose expertise is inside the system labor equally with those whose expertise lies in the application of social science technologies. The conceptualization process allows the analyst to translate or filter the mass of inputs into a manageable number of concepts, which become the conceptual model.

Developing the Scientific Model

The relationship between the conceptual model and the scientific model is established via the modeling activity. At this point the scientific method plays its most important role: the analyst identifies the controllable and uncontrollable variables and defines them in operational terms. Where the conceptual model describes what kind of problem is being approached and what factors should be considered, the scientific model states in which ways these factors are related. In essence, concepts in the conceptual model become variables to be assessed in the scientific model. The scientific model that is developed should be capable of generating one or more solutions to the defined problem. A primary consideration in formulating a scientific model is that it can be used for testing various hypotheses and tentative solutions. The solving process that will be applied depends upon the scientific and conceptual models (and the latter, as discussed earlier, depend upon the initial definition of the problem).

Solving the Scientific Model

The model-solving process in the MAPS context is the MAPS "core," the data-gathering and computer-processing steps. (In most OR techniques these are the only steps.) Note that there will be different kinds of task items developed, depending upon the scientific model of MAPS that is utilized, and thus different kinds of data will be collected. Various computational routines will be used within the computer program. Initially it may not be apparent that the responses to the MAPS questionnaire are really a representation of an organization. But what is contained in the questionnaire responses? The organization members determined the tasks required to achieve their various goals and then they chose the items they would prefer to work on and the people with whom they would prefer to work on those tasks. Thus the data represents the collective valid information and free choices of the organization in a form capable of being "solved." The validity of this information is determined by the extent to which it replicates the reality of the situation. (See Chapters 3 and 4 for the conditions and processes that facilitate the development of valid responses to the MAPS questionnaire.) The input is then processed by the MAPS Computer Program to solve the model. The solution of the model is the output from the program showing several alternative designs for the organization.

Implementing the Solution

The selection of one of several possible designs is the first step in the implementation process. The effect of the implementation is the creation of a new reality. However, this new reality might also include the effects of changes in other "realities" internal or external to the boundaries of the MAPS analysis. This is the ultimate test of the problem definition and conceptualization efforts. The evaluation of the implemented design must determine if the design "fits" the current reality. If not, there is another problem to be solved. Is the mismatch due to changes in the external environment or to errors/omissions in definition and conceptualization? The evaluation process is needed on a regular basis, for even if the design fits today's environment it may not be in tune with tomorrow's. If the difference between today's situation and tomorrow's is great enough, there may be reason to repeat the entire MAPS process; on the other hand, perhaps only selected steps might be warranted, as discussed in Chapter 6. This is of course a highly situational, dependent judgment.

The conclusion to be drawn from this exposition is that the MAPS Design Technology is more complete than other OR techniques. MAPS is a total problem-solving system. An integral part of the technology is the process of minimizing the Type III error, as well as steps to ensure that Type I and Type II errors are also minimized. The diagnosis and design boundary steps confront the former issue; the core steps (i.e., input, analysis, and output) and the design decision process address the latter two. Thus MAPS is distinct from most OR techniques since it integrates qualitative subsystems with the typical quantitative subsystems, and is therefore referred to as a technology (a total system) rather than merely a technique (see Figure 4.1 in Chapter 4).

MAPS AS A TOTAL INFORMATION-INQUIRING SYSTEM

Having discussed the MAPS Design Technology from a systems point of view, it may be helpful to describe further what we mean when we speak of a system. It was stated that general systems theory (GST) approaches the study of phenomena from a holistic point of view. That is, GST suggests that there exist a number of properties of techniques (technologies) that cannot be described meaningfully in terms of their separate elements. This suggests that to fully understand and appreciate MAPS it must be studied in relation to interdependencies among its own subsystems and with other systems (i.e., other techniques, technologies, and philosophies). It should now be apparent that *just as the design of social systems entails the specification of subsystems and their interrelationships to understand the behavior of the total social system, the technology that is applied to assess or design such a social system is itself viewed as a system containing interacting subsystems. In other words, the technology is as much subject to systems analysis as the actual social system: both the technology and the phenomena are analyzed by the same systems approach.* We now need to consider the makeup of MAPS vis à vis information and inquiring systems concepts by which the design of social systems are also approached by general systems theory.

Information and Organizations

Katz and Kahn (1966: 223) refer to the nature of subsystems interdependency as follows:

> When one walks from a factory to the adjoining head house or office the contrast is conspicuous. One goes from noise to quiet.... One goes in short from a sector of the organization in which energic exchange is primary and information exchange secondary, to a sector where the priorities are reversed. The closer one gets to the organizational center of control and decision making, the more pronounced is the emphasis on information exchange.

Buckley (1956) expands this concept of energy versus information as the binding forces of subsystems and shows that in a continuum or hierarchy of systems there exists a point he refers to as "organized complexity," which describes our socio-cultural system. By applying Buckley's concept to organizations within our society, "organized simplicity" (a point in the hierarchy that depends on energy as the binding force maintaining the subsystems) may be seen as analogous to the lower levels in the organization, where automation is prevalent. Here both Buckley and Katz and Kahn refer to the energy exchange as the nature of the interrelationship. As we move into supervisory and management levels, we approach "organized complexity", and the subsystems become increasingly dependent on information exchange until at some point information is the only linkage of the subsystems. It follows from this that when we concern ourselves with the design of organizations (particularly the design of complex organizations), we become concerned with designing an information system.

Mason and Mitroff (1973) have identified the key variables of an information system as follows:

> An information system consists of at least one PERSON of a certain PSYCHOLOGICAL TYPE who faces a PROBLEM within some ORGANIZATIONAL CONTEXT for which he needs EVIDENCE to arrive at a SOLUTION (to select some course of action) and that the evidence is made available to him through some MODE OF PRESENTATION.

Defining a problem as a discrepancy between what is (i.e., reality) and what could or should be (i.e., values, goals, objectives) and then qualifying this via the concept of an organizational context is necessary in understanding a total information system. At the same time we must realize that an organization faces a tremendous variety of problems that vary considerably in degree of complexity. A framework identifying the differing complexities is that used by decision theorists, in which they refer to a problem as structured or unstructured (Mitroff and Sagasti, 1973). Briefly, a structured problem is one which can be well defined in the sense that the key variables, such as the various states of nature, possible actions, possible outcomes, and utility of outcomes, are known. The structured problem is then further refined by subdividing it into three categories as follows (Raiffa, 1968):

1. Decisions under certainty, where the variables are known, and the relation between the action and the outcomes is deterministic.
2. Decisions under risk, where the variables are known, and the relation between the outcome and the action are known probabilities.
3. Decisions under uncertainty, where the variables are known but the probabilities for determining the outcome of an action are either unknown or cannot be determined with any degree of certainty.

The unstructured, or wicked, problem is one which cannot be clearly defined. That is, one or more of the variables discussed is either unknown or cannot be determined with any degree of confidence. So decision making must deal with problems that run the gamut from simple to complex and beyond that to the ambiguous.

Imposing the concept of the "hierarchy of system" on organizational problems, the operational day-to-day problems are viewed as oriented more toward the structured, inflexible, mechanically linked systems with few degrees of freedom. Here we are generally concerned with completion of tasks, and efficiency is the key concern (Internal Efficiency, as discussed in Chapter 6). Emerging problems, that is, the discrepancy between what is and what should be, are normally clearly defined where the action–outcome relationship is either deterministic or of a known probability, thus decision making under certainty or risk.

As we progress up the hierarchy of the organization, the next level is concerned with ascertaining that the operational subsystem is functioning for the benefit of the overall system. Here we are concerned with the short-range planning (i.e., budgets, scheduling, etc.) and the control of the OPERATIONAL DESIGN. Inputs from the larger system (i.e., the executive and external environment) are conceptualized and then integrated by the internal environment. At this point information becomes the prime linkage, as energy transfer is generated in the operational area by the information from this intermediate subsystem. At this level the degrees of freedom are increased exponentially in comparison to the operational level. The problems will be of the structured variety, but tend increasingly toward those under conditions of uncertainty. There will also be issues of the unstructured variety.

At the highest organizational level all dependence on the energy transfer is eclipsed to maintain the system. We are solely interested in information. Here, the degrees of freedom continue to increase exponentially, offering an abundance of options for alternative behavior. The problems, or discrepancies between what is and what should or could be, are increasingly difficult to define; problems in which all the possible "states of nature" are not known (indeed, cannot be known) and a single 'best' answer does not exist. At this organizational level the "error of the third kind" is most salient. Also, the information required to define problems is always incomplete.

For the most part information systems are designed around the operational level, where the problems are clearly defined or structured. The paucity of research at the strategic level leads to the ironic conclusion that where information is most important to the existence and survival of an organization it is least available or sought after. Furthermore, what has been described as the imposition of the hierarchy of systems on organizational problems is also analogous to Anthony's (1965) three major problem categories of strategic planning, management control and operational control, where:

1. Strategic planning is the process of deciding on objectives of the organization, on changes in these objectives, on the resources used to attain these objectives, on the policies used to attain these objectives, and on the policies that are to govern the acquisition, use, and disposition of these resources.
2. Management control is the process by which managers assure that resources are obtained and used effectively and efficiently in the accomplishment of the organization's objectives.
3. Operational control is the process of assuring that specific tasks are carried out efficiently and effectively.

Imposing the decision typology on Anthony's problem categories yields Figure 7.2. The X's indicate where the majority of decisions fall for the designated problem area and are not intended to mean that operational or managerial decisions are not occasionally of the unstructured type. Clearly the "process of assuring that specific tasks are carried out efficiently and effectively," the description of operational control, includes some aspects of performance evaluation. To the extent that we do not know all the possible behavioral effects of a particular performance evaluation on an individual, we may view this decision as unstructured.

Clearly there is a distinction in the types of information needed for the different decision situations. The main difference is probably in the degree of interaction with the external environment as we progress from operational to strategic control. With the increased need of external information comes a decrease in the degree of certainty, since so many options or alternatives exist from which to choose. Accepting Boulding's premise that "reality does not exist apart from

FIGURE 7.2 Problem Type and Decision Structure

| | PROBLEM TYPE | | |
DECISION STRUCTURE	Strategic	Management	Operational
Structured under certainty			×
Structured under risk		×	
Structured under uncertainty		×	
Unstructured	×		

the observer, who is himself a part of that reality" (Boulding, 1956) it is clear that recognition of a problem in a given situation depends on the individual observer. Inherent in this process are the impact of the individual's psychological type and the inquiry system used in gathering or producing information about the problem.

Information and Individuals

The Jungian typology utilized throughout this book (see Chapters 1, 2, 4, and 6, and Figure 1.3) is also useful in highlighting some key distinctions, particularly among the different ways that individuals acquire and act upon information. The four personality types are as follows (Jung, 1923; Kilmann and Mitroff, 1977):

1. The Intuition-Thinking (NT) type person is one who observes and inputs data from a holistic or system type of framework. He sees things perhaps not as they are but as they can be: as possibilities. His output or evaluation of these possibilities is judged in accordance with some formal rules, and he tends to be impersonal in his judgment. That is, the possibilities he sees are either truly or not truly possible. There is a tendency to model or formalize his output.

2. The Intuition-Feeling (NF) type will observe input data the same way as the NT, but the information will be judged in a personal or value-laden manner, such as good or bad, pleasant or unpleasant. This personality does not follow formal rules of logic and, as a result, may be more exploratory and considerably more qualitative.

3. The Sensation-Thinking (ST) type is one who sees information as concrete facts. He will then turn the specific facts into a formal solution according to some well-defined set of rules. He is desirous of working on specific, clear problems and will probably be characterized by a low tolerance for ambiguity.

4. The Sensation-Feeling (SF) type also prefers to observe concrete facts apart from their totality, but is less formal in his evaluation of the data. He does not apply the facts to a formal solution or model, but utilizes instead a subjective, value-laden assessment.

The need for all four personality types within an organization should be apparent. Organizations have definite needs for both the intuitive and sensation modes of perceiving reality, if only because one can provide a different perspective for defining problems than the other. An organization so bound to the "facts" of a sensation type would soon be lost in the day-to-day operations, coupled with a total lack of creative planning. The opposite extreme of this would be all intuitive individuals with no attention to the detail necessary for effective control of the operational aspects of the organization. Such an organization would eventually go bankrupt amid all the glorious plans of the future. Similarly, a strictly thinking type of organization would probably represent a military authoritarian regime, running the risk of severe labor unrest. At the other extreme, the feeling organization would be the happiest group of people on welfare. However, it is essential to view these personality functions as four factors that combine to make up the various information needs and problem perspectives of an organization. While each personality may show a tendency or preference for one model against the other, the other should not be totally excluded.

Information and Inquiring Systems

That a problem is viewed differently by each observer is a function of the individual background, psychological type (as discussed above), and the inquiring system used to generate the information. This latter function refers to how the information was gathered or produced in formulating the problem, that is, the different epistemological approaches used by the observer or researcher. This point is well developed by Churchman (1971) in his book *The Design of Inquiring Systems*. According to Mitroff and Sagasti (1973: 701):

> To represent (conceptualize or model) a problem is to conduct an inquiry into its nature—to conduct an inquiry into a problem is to gather (or produce) some information on it. In this sense information is not different from inquiry (or epistemology) because what we know (i.e., information) is not independent of how we have obtained that knowledge, i.e., the particular inquiry system we have adopted.

Mitroff describes five "archetypal" philosophically based information systems as follows:

1. The Leibnitzian Inquiring System is characteristic of a formal symbolic, mathematical system. It starts from a set of elementary, primitive, analytic truths, and from these are built a network of ever-expanding and increasingly more general formal

propositional truths. It is earmarked by consistency, completeness and comprehensiveness. The Leibnitzian Inquiring System is most useful on clear, well-defined, structured problems, and would most likely be the preference of an ST personality.

2. The Lockean Inquiring System is one which is consensual in nature being initiated from a general premise or truth which has wide consensual agreement. From this base, data is collected and modeled in accordance with the consensual agreement of the problem. Accounting is a characteristic example of this type of system of inquiry, being based on a simple generally accepted principle and depicting a problem through the collection of empirical evidence. The Lockean Inquiring System is most useful for well-structured problems and would be found most useful or preferable to an ST or SF type personality.

3. The Kantian Inquiring System is characterized by a complementary multimodel approach. This system presupposes at least two alternate scientific theories for which it then builds empirical "fact nets" to show several different views of a problem. That model which best fits the empirical data to the theoretical model is the best model or representation of the problem. This inquiring system seems best suited for mildly unstructured problems, and may be the preference of an NT or NF type personality.

4. The Hegelian Inquiring System is characterized by a conflictual multimodel approach. Starting from at least two strongly contrary models, a debate is developed (arguments and counterarguments) to expose the underlying assumptions of both models, and one or the other (or a third "creative synthesis") of the first two models will be chosen as representative of the problem. This system seems best suited for the ill-structured problem and will also probably be preferred by the NT or NF personality.

5. The Singerian-Churchmanian Inquiring System is extremely difficult to describe in a limited space, and for this reason the reader is referred to Churchman's (1971) book for an in-depth discussion. This inquiring system is based on the Hegelian inquirer in that it is dialectic, but its emphasis lies in the belief that no one inquiring system is the correct or "best" approach to any problem. By using only one system we necessarily constrain our inquiry. Fundamental to the Singerian-Churchmanian system is the use of all known inquiring systems, recognizing that each approaches the same problem differently, and that each is intended for a different type of problem (i.e., well-structured versus ill-defined). The Singerian-Churchmanian Inquiring

System is thus a metasystem—a systems view of inquiring systems including application of the ethics of each and all inquirers.

MAPS and the Inquiring Systems

Since the MAPS Design Technology is meant to be applicable to a wide range of design problems across a wide variety of organizational and social settings, it is important that MAPS is not simply based on one philosophical inquiring system (or the wrong inquiring system). Rather, it is virtually essential that a technology such as MAPS be designed by incorporating various aspects of all the inquiring systems to minimize the possibility of solving the wrong problem (Type III error) the wrong way, or of simply viewing the world or creating the world to reflect only one or a few philosophical perspectives. Let us briefly suggest how the steps in MAPS reflect these basic philosophical notions, as summarized in Table 7.1.

The Leibnitzian Inquiring System (IS) is contained in MAPS via the eloquent mathematical model inherent in the multivariate procedures in the MAPS analysis (e.g., complex factor analysis, operations research assignment algorithms, etc.). If MAPS were purely Leibnitzian, however, the design process would merely be a mathematical simulation of task and people combinations with little reliance on any input data. The designer(s) (e.g., representatives from the social system and a team of MAPS consultants) would have to run the design simulation and infer how the results of the simulation relate to the specific, real world case of concern. Thus real data would not be readily integrated into the model.

The Lockean IS is illustrated via the actual collection of data from responses to the MAPS questionnaire, which serves as a major input to the MAPS analysis. However, without the MAPS Computer Program, designers would be lost in trying to infer from MAPS questionnaire responses what an effective organization design would be. They would perhaps develop some model from the data, but the model would not approach the sophistication represented in the elaborate statistical procedures of MAPS.

The Kantian IS is incorporated via the six explicit models of MAPS from which the designer(s) must choose. Each scientific model of MAPS portrays a different type of input data, different multivariate analyses, and different outputs of organization designs. Each model thus represents a different view of the design problem and different proposed solutions. This gives the designer(s) a basis for explicitly comparing and contrasting different world views, and consequently a

Table 7.1   The Philosophical Inquiring Systems Underlying The MAPS Design Technology

INQUIRING SYSTEM	STEPS OF MAPS	RATIONALE
1. Lockean (S)[a]	1, 2, 5, 6	MAPS Questionnaire (development of task items); Responses to the MAPS questionnaire as key input to design analyses
2. Leibnitzian (T)	7	Multivariate Analysis; Logic underlying the MAPS Computer Program
3. Kantian (NT)	3, 4	Six models of MAPS to choose from providing alternative views of the design problem
4. Hegelian–Dialectic (NT–NF)	8	Procedure utilized to select a particular model and design of MAPS enabling a well-informed choice and/or an informed synthesis
5. Singerian—Churchmanian (ST,NT,SF,NF)	9–12 (including previous steps)	Incorporates aspects of all four inquiring systems and explicitly considers ethical issues in further developing and using the technology

[a] The Jungian counterparts of the inquiring systems.

better basis for understanding the underlying objectives, assumptions, and values of each model. If the MAPS process only presented one model, the social systems designers could only consider MAPS versus no MAPS, which would not help them examine the many subtle aspects of the technology.

The dialectical, or Hegelian, IS is utilized at several steps in the MAPS Design Technology, but the most important use is when the designers consider the several models of MAPS available and have to decide which model would best manage the organization or design problem. Here a dialectical debate can be generated that actively encourages a management team (or representatives throughout the organization) to examine critically the values, assumptions, and positions implicit in each model and to move toward some design choice or synthesis. Without this active debate, designers might choose a particular model of MAPS based on a superficial understanding of the various models and their different implications for the organization.

The Singerian-Churchmanian IS seeks to include all four preceding inquiring systems in a holistic approach to inquiry. The MAPS Design Technology, because of its explicit inclusion of these different philosophical systems, approaches what is intended by the Singerian-Churchmanian system. What is also required or emphasized by this holistic approach, however, is that the developer and users of MAPS remain reflective about the technology, in particular, the ethics of its further development and use. The last chapter in this book, Chapter 9, will consider in detail the ethics of the MAPS Design Technology, for such a discussion deserves special attention.

DIFFERENT PROBLEM-SOLVING
AND INFORMATION-INQUIRING SYSTEMS

As has been discussed previously, most organizations have one formal design generally represented by the organization chart, and this design is for performing day-to-day activities and efficiently producing well-defined products and services, not for solving complex and changing problems. Thus far this chapter has argued that problem-solving, information, and inquiring systems are the important linkages and processes which bind the organizational subsystems together, especially at the higher levels, where complexity is greatest. General systems theory (GST) emphasizes the importance of these informational and problem-solving linkages, Jungian psychology suggests which types of individuals are most comfortable with various information systems, and the philosophy of science concept of inquiring systems articulates the different kinds of information systems that are applied to various kinds of problems (well-defined and ill-defined).

It is our contention that an organization, or any social system, must explicitly design some problem-solving or strategic planning system if it is to function effectively (particularly if it is to achieve External Efficiency and External Effectiveness, as discussed in Chapter 6). Using the Diamond Model of problem solving, we suggested that the MAPS Design Technology is a total system of problem solving, that is, the twelve steps of MAPS encompass all the states and processes indicated on the Diamond Model (see Chapter 4, and particularly Figure 4.2). Furthermore, the five inquiring systems (Leibnitzian, Lockean, Kantian, Hegelian, and Singerian-Churchmanian) are all incorporated in the MAPS Design Technology, and therefore MAPS is not confined to one type of information system or one mode of inquiry. Rather, since MAPS is based on such quantitative and qualitative components (i.e., ST, NT, SF, and NF components), the technology itself is congruent with the diversity and complexity of the social systems which it seeks to design (or redesign). Consequently we now propose how MAPS may be applied to create particular problem-solving and information systems, being reasonably confident that MAPS has a broad philosophical foundation and can therefore explicitly manage the Type III error.

Chapter 4 presented the scientific models of MAPS and proposed three models as appropriate for designing problem-solving and information systems: the PROBLEM-SOLVING DESIGN (Model II), the STRATEGIC PLANNING DESIGN (Model VI), and the INTEGRATED PROBLEM-SOLVING–STRATEGIC PLANNING DESIGN (Model IV). These models vary according to the input data utilized to form people clusters (task items, people items, or both, respectively) and whether task clusters are not shown to the designers, or if task clusters are shown but the items composing the clusters are problem or strategic items (versus operational task items). Chapter 4 briefly discussed the distinguishing characteristics of these three models of problem-solving systems and gave some indication of instances in which each might be applied. It was suggested, however, that organizations would generally not have as many as four distinct designs (except for special circumstances when the organization's environment is extremely complex and dynamic), but would instead have two designs: the INTEGRATED OPERATIONAL–INFORMAL DESIGN and the INTEGRATED PROBLEM-SOLVING–STRATEGIC PLANNING DESIGN. These two designs could manage in a synthesized manner all four components of organizational effectiveness (Chapter 6) while keeping the costs of designing and maintaining a number of designs from becoming too high. Consequently the remainder of this chapter will concentrate on the INTEGRATED PROBLEM-SOLVING–STRATEGIC PLANNING DESIGN (Model IV) for designing different problem-solving and information systems for the organization or social system. For convenience, we will refer to Model IV (and Models II and VI) as simply PROBLEM-SOLVING DESIGNS or problem-solving systems, and in each instance we will not distinguish problem-solving from information systems since the two are so interrelated.

Alternative Choices for the Designers

Even with a focus on the integrated model, however, there are a number of alternatives open to the designer. In particular, several questions arise that pertain to the design of a problem-solving system: (1) who will be involved, (2) for how long, and (3) will the individuals be working in the design part-time or full-time? The first question is usually handled by having representatives selected or elected (or volunteer) from each of the OPERATIONAL DESIGN categories in the organization (e.g. marketing, finance, production, etc.), based on some assessment of the individual's motivation and expertise to perform various problem-solving activities. The organization can also hire individuals from the outside to engage in problem-solving functions, who would then be involved in the MAPS design process.

The second and third questions noted above provide some interesting alternatives to the designers of the problem-solving system, and the decisions on these two questions may actually help decide the first question of who will be involved. Figure 7.3 shows a matrix of four alternative PROBLEM-SOLVING DESIGNS that can be created with the MAPS Design Technology by varying two dimensions.

The first choice for the designers is whether the PROBLEM-SOLVING DESIGN is to be permanent or temporary. The permanent design means that the subunits created by MAPS remain intact over time, while the temporary design implies that the subunits only exist

FIGURE 7.3   Problem-Solving Systems

Continuity of Design

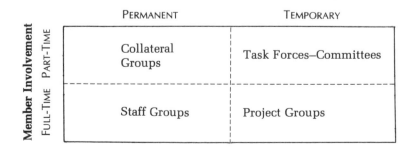

	PERMANENT	TEMPORARY
PART-TIME	Collateral Groups	Task Forces–Committees
FULL-TIME	Staff Groups	Project Groups

Member Involvement

as long as a particular problem (or a specified set of problems) is being handled. With the temporary design, when the problem is resolved or viewed as managed, the subunits disband.

The second choice for the designers is whether the members are participating in the PROBLEM-SOLVING DESIGN on a full-time or part-time basis. If full-time, the members are working exclusively on problem solving and do not have any explicit involvement in the OPERATIONAL DESIGN of the organization. If part-time, the members spend not only several hours per week in the PROBLEM-SOLVING DESIGN but also have formal roles and responsibilities in the organization's OPERATIONAL DESIGN.

The two choices above (two dimensions) result in four possible alternatives for problem-solving systems. Specifically, the temporary–part-time design is referred to as task forces or committees. In this design, members who maintain involvement in the OPERATIONAL DESIGN spend several hours per week (or per month, etc.) working on a specified set of problems. Once these problems are solved or managed, the task force is disbanded and the members again spend all of their time in the OPERATIONAL DESIGN. The temporary–full-time design is known as project teams. Here the members devote their entire time in the organization to a set of problems, and do not return to their operational positions until the problems are resolved or managed. The permanent–part-time design is called collateral groups (Zand, 1974). In this case the members are continually involved in two designs, the OPERATIONAL DESIGN and the PROBLEM-SOLVING DESIGN. The members divide their time between the two designs but the collateral groups are not disbanded as problems are solved. Instead, they begin searching for new problems to define and confront within the collateral groups. Finally the permanent–full-time design is termed staff groups. This design is not disbanded as problems are solved, but contains members that have no explicit involvement in the OPERATIONAL DESIGN. These members devote all their time to the staff groups on a continuing basis.

It should be emphasized that these four PROBLEM-SOLVING DESIGNS are pure types and that a variety of hybrid forms could also be considered. For example, it may be worthwhile to have rotating group memberships in the permanent designs so that more people in the organization will become familiar and appreciate the problem-solving process. Such rotating involvements are similar to the objectives of job rotations within OPERATIONAL DESIGNS. Another possibility is for the temporary designs not to disband totally but to begin defining new problem areas and then designing new "temporary" designs to confront these new problems. There would then be a sequencing of temporary designs that would approach the intention of the permanent ones. The part-time, full-time distinction could also be combined by having members work in either mode depending on the extent to which problems need attention—there can be lulls or crises in problem solving just as for operational activity.

Characteristics of the Four Designs

In considering the four pure PROBLEM-SOLVING DESIGNS, each has different advantages and disadvantages for the organization; therefore the decision of which one to institute requires a careful examination of the specific environment facing the organization and the types of conflicts that may arise because of different designs. For example, an organization facing a dynamic and changing environment will probably need a permanent design rather than a temporary one because problems emerge frequently in such an environment and it would be too costly to create a new temporary design for each new problem that is generated. On the other hand, an organization facing a fairly stable environment might not be able to justify supporting a permanent problem-solving system since such a design would be underutilized. Fewer problems tend to emerge in a stable–static organizational environment.

The part-time, full-time dimension affects the types of interdesign conflicts that are created and the kinds of implementation problems likely to be encountered. The designers need to assess the relative trade-offs among these issues in choosing one of the PROBLEM-SOLVING DESIGNS. For example, the advantage of the full-time designs is that the members are not generally biased by vested interests; that is, they do not have an interest in how a particular problem is solved since they are not members of the OPERATIONAL DESIGN. However, a full-time setting makes it difficult to implement solutions since the problem solvers must rely on others to understand and accept their recommendations. Actually the full-time problem solvers may have difficulty even in obtaining the necessary information and feeling for the problem since they may be removed from the day-to-day source of the problem. The classical case of this type of conflict is the staff-line conflict (Dalton, 1959). A part-time design, on the other hand, has members in both operational and problem-solving activities, which enhances the likelihood that solutions will be implemented and that the information needed to solve the problem in the first place is available. Basically the part-time designs have the members working on the problems they have actually been experiencing in the OPERATIONAL DESIGN. But this tends to foster vested interests—members may have a definite stake in the outcome or proposed solution of the problem, or they may be "too close" to the problem to suggest creative, alternative solutions.

Consequently, if the designers feel that members can be objective and that their support is crucial in implementing solutions, a part-time design should be chosen. However, if vested interests are strong (because of the types of problems expected) and if members in the OPERATIONAL DESIGN are willing to foster and support the problem solvers' efforts, one of the full-time designs may be instituted. Once the part-time, full-time distinction is chosen, the designer may select either the temporary or permanent design mode (or some combination) depending on the assessment of the organization's environment—how frequently complex problems are likely to emerge, and the corresponding need for an ongoing PROBLEM-SOLVING DESIGN. As a result of a dialectical debate of these design issues (Chapter 5), some synthesis or hybrid form may be derived, as was suggested earlier.

Once a particular PROBLEM-SOLVING DESIGN is chosen (i.e., one of the four alternative problem-solving systems shown in Figure 7.3), the MAPS Design Technology may be applied to actually create the chosen design. Then the members develop the task items for the MAPS questionnaire and proceed through the succeeding steps of the technology (see Chapters 3, 4, 5, and 6).

It should be emphasized, however, that to be effective all of the systems require a climate of trust and openness within the organization so that ideas and feelings may be shared (Argyris, 1962). The information needed for problem solving must be forthcoming, and considerations of effective group decision making must be taken into account. These problem-solving systems cannot be tied to the authority, reward, and power structures of the OPERATIONAL DESIGN, and the evaluation process must be adequately modified for tasks that do not have a defined output. It is extremely difficult to evaluate individuals on the number of new ideas that they have per month or the number of solutions the problem-solving system suggests. Since MAPS is more than a mathematical analysis, however, and since it includes climate building, an educational process, and the development of trust, many of these problems can be overcome, particularly at the diagnostic and implementation stages of the technology.

EXAMPLES OF DESIGNING PROBLEM-SOLVING
AND INFORMATION-INQUIRING SYSTEMS WITH MAPS

Now that the philosophical and theoretical frameworks for designing problem-solving systems have been discussed, it seems appropriate that some examples be given for designing the problem-solving systems with the MAPS Design Technology. The following will illustrate how MAPS can be used to design a committee system, a strategic planning system, and a nonsubstantive problem-solving system. These systems can be represented within the NT-NF quadrant in the Jungian model, since they attempt to define and manage ill-defined problems and would fit Model IV with the inclusion of task items (problem and strategic items) and people items (the INTEGRATED PROBLEM-SOLVING–STRATEGIC PLANNING DESIGN).

Committee Systems

Many organizations rely on a system of committees as a vehicle for participative decision making and idea generation. Without the proper climate and acceptance by top management, the committee system can be merely a figurehead hiding the fact that decisions are made entirely by top management. Usually it is automatically assumed by everyone serving on the committee that decisions will be democratically derived within the committee and proposals will then be made to a more powerful decision group. Nevertheless many organizations within our culture rely heavily on a system of committees for whatever reason. The United States Senate, most academic departments, and professional organizations are examples. MAPS can be used by these organizations to identify the committees (tasks) on which able people are interested in working and to identify the people who are motivated to work together.

As an example, a committee structure for university departments will be discussed. The committees are ongoing and membership generally rotates. Some objectives for designing the task items would be the following:

1. Establishing policies and admission standards for the doctoral program.
2. Establishing policies and admission standards for the masters program.
3. Recommending modifications in courses currently being offered.

4. Identifying new courses.
5. Exploring possibilities for research opportunities.
6. Establishing recommendations for long-term planning.
7. Recruiting new faculty.
8. Reviewing undergraduate program.
9. Continuing education programs.

These objectives or major categories of activities would then be used as the basis for the development of the task items for the MAPS questionnaire. The faculty would respond to those task items and to the people items. The result would be groupings based on the interests and abilities of the faculty and with whom each was interested in working. The results might not correspond to the committees that originally existed, and new committees with new thrusts might be identified. By utilizing MAPS to construct these committees, the results would be more efficient since the redundancies across committees would be eliminated. People would be more highly motivated because they would be involved in areas of their own choosing. In most cases the committee system would fit into the temporary–part-time classification, although some committee systems are permanent–part-time and have rotating memberships.

Strategic Planning Systems

Many organizations have begun to develop subunits for long-range planning, but few have approached it from a total systems view in which many members would participate directly in the long-range planning process. Traditionally it has been left almost entirely as the task of those at the very top of the corporate hierarchy, with the planning staff serving only in an operational role (Thompson, 1967). Perhaps what is needed to foster commitment is a more participative planning process involving members of the OPERATIONAL DESIGN within a problem-solving system for long-range planning.

Strategic decisions have not been easily managed by OPERATIONAL DESIGNS. The short-range tasks and decisions become more important than the handling of strategic problems that are ill-defined, long-range and ongoing. An appropriate design and people who are committed to this type of problem are necessary. The strategic planning process must involve a monitoring of the environment to predict such things as economic trends, international developments, consumer tastes, and government spending. This would involve the utilization of all the inquiring systems and the skills necessary for each type of activity. The planning process must provide a holistic view of the organization and its relationship to the environment; therefore divergent interests and skills must be represented so that a synthesized total view may be formulated.

However, because of the nature of the problem, even when this environmental information is gathered and combined with the internal data about the organization, there will be no clear path for the organization to pursue. From the same data base it will be possible to support several alternative solutions. The individuals involved in the planning process will be bringing to it their own perceptions and basic assumptions. People representing the different Jungian personality types will have different world views and will reach different conclusions about solutions from the same data (Kilmann and Mitroff, 1977). The planning process must include a design that will allow the exposure of these underlying assumptions in a constructive manner. Thus since both the collection of data and the strategic decision-making process itself cannot be routinized, but are dynamic and undefined, an organic-adaptive design would seem appropriate. Cleland and King have suggested that a matrix design be used for strategic planning (Cleland and King, 1974). Another suggestion might be a dual design: one for operational activities and one for strategic planning. In any case the design must allow for the exposure of underlying views and the development of relevant planning objectives by a dialectic debate (Mason 1969).

Through the use of the MAPS Design Technology, the necessary task interdependencies and people relationships for strategic planning can be formulated. Since the individuals will have participated in the process and in the definitions of the tasks, there will be more of a sense of commitment and acceptance by the task and people clusters. Those individuals most able and interested in monitoring government activities will probably be involved in the cluster with that as a major thrust. There will be a climate that will allow for individuality and risk taking because the people have chosen each other and acknowledge each individual's expertise to work on the tasks endorsed. Through MAPS, then, a process of design can be accomplished that will foster open channels of communication and permit creative ideas. The strategic planning process needs this kind of design if the organization is going to manage itself effectively in a changing environment in the long run.

It is possible to speculate that some of the tasks on the MAPS questionnaire might include the following:

1. Assessing the values of the organization.
2. Establishing corporate goals and objectives.
3. Providing special studies for management.
4. Assessing the competitive environment.
5. Assessing organization and community relationships.
6. Assessing government trends.
7. Assessing international trends.
8. Forecasting and mathematical modeling.
9. Formulating action plans.
10. Deciding which plans to pursue.
11. Integrating long-range plans into short-range plans.
12. Providing feedback on plans.

Thus it may be seen from these task items that the strategic planning process must search for new market opportunities, assess a dynamic environment, and deal with multiple conflicting objectives. Kilmann and Ghymn state: "In essence, most of the environmental variables that were mentioned are subjective, ill-defined, and highly qualitative, i.e., they are heavily future-oriented and are therefore based on peoples' perceptions, intuitions, feelings, values and expectations" (Kilmann and Ghymn, in press). By using MAPS to design the strategic planning system, a systems approach to the problem can be taken and a design appropriate for considering the qualitative as well as the quantitative aspects of the problem will be developed. A strategic planning system might fit several of the design characteristics shown in Figure 7.3. In most cases, however, the system would be either permanent–full-time or permanent–part-time unless the system has a specific planning horizon to consider and is then disbanded upon completion of its mission (e.g., developing a five-year plan).

Nonsubstantive Problem-Solving Systems

Zand, in his article on collateral organizations (1974), discusses the need for a design to manage ill-structured problems. He describes this design as being capable of identifying a problem, of having little formal structure, of being highly interactive with the OPERATIONAL DESIGN, of being highly creative, and as being capable of solving the problem. There will not be any conventional means of measuring the productivity of this design since it cannot be measured in the number of solutions it manufactures per week, and the results of its decisions will not be apparent until long after the decision has been made.

While this type of design may at first seem similar to the strategic planning systems just described, it is in fact much broader. Not only is the nonsubstantive design not rooted toward any type of problem (i.e., not just strategic users), but the design is meant to address the complete problem-solving process (i.e., not merely to recommend strategic plans). The collateral design is meant to address all types of problems and to include the implementation of recommended solutions as well as the initial problem formulation.

MAPS can be used to design the nonsubstantive PROBLEM-SOLVING DESIGN that Zand described. It would be a design that was not created to solve an existing problem but to identify and implement solutions to any problem that it recognizes. MAPS can bring together people from a variety of backgrounds and places within the OPERATIONAL DESIGN of the organization, permitting the development of an interdisciplinary and multiperspective approach, by forming a design based on the activities necessary to identify and solve a problem. As a framework for this discussion and for the various activities involved, we will use the Diamond Model of problem solving shown earlier in this chapter, in which the processes were identified as problem recognition and conceptualization, scientific modeling, model solving, and implementation.

Regarding a design for problem solving, the problem recognition phase offers a tremendous challenge. The process of perception is so individualized that two people may not agree on the reality of the situation and thus may not agree when, or if, a problem exists. The people assigned to the task of problem definition should choose each other with certain factors in mind. They must be aware, prior to answering the MAPS questionnaire, of the fact that individual perceptions of the problem are based on various factors which include personality, needs, values, and cultural biases. An ST will not perceive the problem in the same way that an NF would. It may be necessary to have a heterogeneous group so that problem definition can consider different perceptions of the problem. A dialectic process might be encouraged as a means of identifying the underlying assumptions and of reaching agreement.

Another means of problem recognition and identification is to reevaluate the organization's goals and criteria. It may be that what the organization proposes as ideal long-term goals may differ from what it is actually working toward. Problems may be defined by the disparity between the real and the ideal, and the organization may wish to redefine its goals and ideals.

The development of the conceptual model involves identifying the variables or issues. This is attempting to control and to predict the environment as much as possible by managing uncertainties. The variables identified and in fact the whole conceptual model will depend on the perception of the problem definition as influenced by the individual's personality and world view. Inherent in this process is a definition of the nature of the problem and identification of the interrelationships and information that must be gathered. The intuitive personality type would be best suited for this kind of activity because people of this type can best appreciate undefined situations and view them holistically. Conceptualization also involves the utilization of the Kantian and Hegelian IS in the formulation of the problem.

The next process involves the choice or development of the scientific or formal model. Since the scientific model will be the basis for a solution, it is necessary that the scientific model include the information needed to reach a solution. This process and the model-solving process will identify the variables within the conceptual model that lend themselves to data collection. The purpose of the scientific model is to clearly define the assumptions made in the conceptual model. It is an analytical process and is best performed by the thinking types utilizing the Lockean and Leibnitzian IS.

The solution process will involve solving the scientific model and might also involve running a computer program that processes all the data via mathematical equations. For more complex problems it may involve the qualitative weighing of several parameters and issues, implying a particular solution. This model-solving process may involve a unanimous decision or a dialectical confrontation. Usually, however, it will be performed best by the thinking, analytical personality types, and therefore the Lockean or Leibnitzian Inquiring Systems are highly satisfactory for this process.

The implementation process involves the intervention into reality (e.g., the organization) to bring about change. It is action-oriented and involves overt behavioral steps. It also involves the decision of how to put the solution into action. Inherent in this is the decision of whether to implement the solution in the form that was suggested or to tailor the solution by making modifications. The individuals best suited for the implementation process are those of the SF-NF type. Feeling is utilized, since this step involves the development of behaviorial action plans, the generation of commitment, and overseeing that the change process is not too rapid or too much of a shock to the organization. The individuals involved in this process must be able to relate to the members in the OPERATIONAL DESIGN. Those involved in the

PROBLEM-SOLVING DESIGN must interface between the two designs so that successful negotiation of the solution and implementation can occur. In attempting to implement the solution a new problem may be identified, and the process of problem solving then becomes cyclical and adaptive.

With the explanation of the processes now completed, the following will serve as examples of tasks that might appear on the MAPS questionnaire for the development of a nonsubstantive problem-solving system:

1. Seeking others' views of what problems exist.
2. Searching for better ways of performing a task.
3. Identifying variables related to the problem.
4. Identifying interrelationships of variables.
5. Evaluating organizational goals versus reality.
6. Asking the "right" questions.
7. Building models or strategies for outcomes.
8. Collecting data.
9. Solving the scientific model.
10. Engaging in a process to decide on a solution.
11. Evaluating the solution in terms of reality.
12. Developing a plan for implementation.

After the individuals have responded to the MAPS questionnaire, the MAPS Computer Program is run, and the design solution is implemented, an ongoing problem-solving system would be formed to identify, define, and confront different kinds of problems. In most cases, as has been suggested, the nonsubstantive problem-solving system would fit the permanent–part-time category, as shown in Figure 7.3.

CONCLUSIONS

The foregoing has presented the philosophical and systems perspectives for designing problem-solving systems and has identified the various needs for problem solving within an organization or social system. Since MAPS is a broadly based technology rooted in the various inquiring systems and including all the steps in the Diamond Model of problem solving, using MAPS to design the various problem-solving systems is likely to minimize the Type III error (i.e., the probability that MAPS solved the wrong problem, designed the wrong problem-solving system, or utilized only a single and inappropriate inquiring system to actually design a problem-solving system).

An important theme in this chapter, however, is that one formalized OPERATIONAL DESIGN may be greatly restrictive for contemporary organizations because this one design cannot hope to mobilize all the potential resources of the organization: the varied motivations, skills, perspectives, and problem-solving abilities of the members. Even if an INFORMAL DESIGN should emerge to satisfy the various needs and functions not confronted by the formal OPERATIONAL DESIGN, this informal organization would probably be designed in an implicit, evolutionary manner without the benefit of rigorous testing and debate.

Thus we propose that organization designers consider the possibility of implementing several simultaneous designs to extract and activate the potential resources in the organization. This may require that the organization develop two different types of designs, an OPERATIONAL and a PROBLEM-SOLVING DESIGN (or the integrated models). An explicit attempt at these designs may highlight and draw attention to resources the organization was not even aware of, namely, information, decision-making, and problem-solving skills of its members, who are constrained by the requirements of the single OPERATIONAL DESIGN not to solve or participate in such problem-solving activities. In other words, just as human relations consultants and organizational development specialists have attempted to mobilize resources within a given organization design, we advocate that designers begin at the more basic level, the very structure of the organization, to consider in which ways and by which different designs the potential resources can be clustered and mobilized before they are developed. Such a philosophy and practice would create resources as much as simply identifying those apparently available.

Basically we propose that the MAPS Design Technology has the capability of creating such different organization designs and mobilizing the resources necessary to confront complex problems. Currently we know of no other systematic methodology that even purports to do this. Organization design is a very complex decision and process in its own right, and certainly a technology such as MAPS is required to approach these complex design issues in a manner that derives from the substantive, methodological, and philosophical contributions of the social sciences. Consequently the MAPS Design Technology, with continuing research and examination, can become an important approach to designing effective problem-solving systems.

Chapter 8

Current Applications and Research with MAPS

In collaboration with Joseph Seltzer

The previous chapters in this book have discussed the MAPS Design Technology mainly from a normative point of view. While this innovation in the field of organization design is quite recent, a number of organizations have already participated in a MAPS analysis for a wide variety of purposes. In fact, most of the conceptual models and discussions of the technology in prior chapters have developed directly from the experience of applying MAPS in a number of settings, some of which were established partially for empirical research, while others were initiated primarily to bring about changes in existing organizations. However, it should be stated that it is only to achieve a certain logical sequence in presenting the material in this book, i.e., a reconstructed logic vs. a logic in use (Kaplan, 1964) that the applications and research of the MAPS Design Technology were not examined earlier. Basically it was felt that the reader could better understand and appreciate the nature of the several applications after the underlying theory and steps of the technology were presented.

This chapter will first provide a brief background of the organizations involved in MAPS applications that includes the design boundaries, the characteristics of the MAPS questionnaires, and the relative time in the steps of the technology for each application. Next, we will attempt to show the relationship between several conceptual models presented in earlier chapters as they pertain to the various MAPS applications. These models include the four Jungian organization designs (Chapter 1), the six scientific models of MAPS (Chapter 4), the four components of organizational effectiveness (Chapter 6), and the different problem-solving systems that can be designed with MAPS (Chapter 7). In essence, relating MAPS applications to these conceptual models provides a summary of some of the material discussed in prior chapters. The focus will then shift to the applications of MAPS as instances of research studies, and we will summarize the variety of research methodologies utilized to address the problem of internal and external validity of research results (Campbell and Stanley, 1963). This chapter thus considers the dual and interrelated objectives of illustrating how MAPS can be applied to redesign social systems while simultaneously (with particular research assessments) subjecting these applications to scientific investigation. The latter objective not only fosters the development of substantive knowledge in organization and social systems design, but also helps to further the development of the MAPS Design Technology.

CURRENT APPLICATIONS OF MAPS

There are a number of organizations in which the MAPS Design Technology has been or is currently being applied. Each case will be briefly described in terms of the nature of the organization, the design objectives for which MAPS was considered, the types of participants, and the process of the application. The applications of the MAPS Design Technology are summarized in Table 8.1 and briefly described below. Cases 1–9 represent organizational applications, and cases 10–13 are examples of some special classroom utilizations although these were explicitly applied to generate some "real" organizational activity.

Table 8.1   Applications of MAPS: Types of Organizations and Design Objectives

CASE NUMBER	ORGANIZATION	DESIGN OBJECTIVES
1	Educational (A)	Develop study centers
2	Educational (B)	Curriculum redesign
3	Community Service	Create an organization structure
4	Industrial (A)	Reduce interface conflict
5	Industrial (B)	Task design for MBO
6	Financial	Structural diagnosis
7	Retail	Form teams and goals for OD
8	Public Agency	Strategic planning
9	Scholarly Journal	Effectiveness and structure of editorial board
10	Eighth Grade Class	Team formation and research
11	Executive Class (A)	Problem-solving system
12	Executive Class (B)	Management education in year 2000
13	Doctoral Seminar	Experience MAPS, write this book

Cases

1. A school of business in a large university (A) used MAPS as an aid in the development of "study centers" (i.e., faculty interest groups) for faculty members. The output from the MAPS

analysis was presented to the faculty (only two of the possible solutions) with a memo from the dean suggesting at least one meeting of the MAPS groups. Study centers could be proposed to the dean. After 20 months, seven such study centers had been established (McKelvey and Kilmann, 1973).

2. A school of business in a large university (B) used MAPS as part of a task force on curriculum redesign. An analysis was conducted using 71 learning modules, 20 criteria for evaluation of curricula, and the 36 faculty members who responded to the MAPS questionnaire. The learning modules were clustered into 15 groups corresponding to 15 individual courses, and a grouping of curriculum criteria factors and several clusters of faculty were also presented. The MAPS analysis was used as input for the report the task force was developing (Kilmann, 1974c).

3. A community service organization associated with a business school decided to use MAPS to create an organizational structure. This organization was primarily voluntary and utilized the services of MBA students to aid small businesses. Almost the entire organization changed membership from year to year although its goals had some stability through a board of governors. This organization used the MAPS Design Technology in an initial attempt to develop a structure, and task items were generated with regard to 10 general goals at a two-day workshop. The output was presented to the organization, modified slightly, and then adopted. Organizational development activities were conducted for several months to help in the establishment of the structure (Kilmann, 1975a).

4. A division of a large industrial firm (A) applied MAPS to help reduce interface conflicts between sales, marketing, and engineering functions. The vice-president and department heads developed five general goals and in a meeting presented these to all managers in the division, which employed a total of over 2,000 persons. Each manager was asked to develop specific task items, and a total of about 1,200 items were generated. A representative group of managers and members of the industrial relations staff met to edit the items and developed a list of 64 task items. All managers responded and the results were fed back to the organization. Discussions of implementation are in progress (Keim and Kilmann, 1975).

5. A department in a large industrial firm (B) considered MAPS to aid in the development of new task objectives in connection with a concurrent MBO implementation. The department manager distributed a list of department objectives (previously de-

veloped), and individual managers (two levels below the department manager) developed a large number of task items. The department manager edited these into a list of 93 rather detailed tasks. Both the department manager and his subordinates were unwilling to be involved in the MAPS analysis and, further, disapproved of the use of the people items. Thus only the managers (two levels down) responded to the questionnaire which consisted of strictly task items. The results were returned to the organization through the department manager and, to date, he has not distributed them to his subordinates or to the people who responded to the questionnaire.

6. A service division in a large financial institution utilized MAPS primarily as a diagnostic tool. The assistant vice-president developed 35 task items from the job descriptions in the division. Then all the people in the division responded to the MAPS questionnaire. The results were fed back to the participants. After a period of time changes in personnel and the division's scope within the organization (not attributable to the MAPS Design Technology) necessitated a second analysis, with the result again used for diagnostic purposes.

7. The president of a retail business became interested in MAPS to help identify appropriate groups and goals for an organization development effort. Initially he identified four work groups and held meetings to introduce MAPS and to develop task items in line with a listing of general organization goals that he prepared. All persons in the organization were involved and a total of 20 meetings were held. A number of task items were generated by the four groups, and a coordinating group of six people was elected to edit the questionnaire. All persons in the organization were expected to respond to the questionnaire, but internal organizational problems halted the process. For research purposes only, the president responded to all questionnaires as he felt the employees would. This organization may possibly continue to apply the MAPS Design Technology.

8. MAPS was utilized in a large public agency to form temporary teams to develop a strategic plan for the year 2000. Several workshops were held to introduce MAPS and to generate 18 rather general task items about the future concerns and problems of this agency. All persons in the workshop responded to the MAPS questionnaire (the director of the agency, his staff, and representatives throughout the organization). The results were returned to the organization and a solution for five groups

was adopted. These groups met periodically for about ten months, using the task clusters from the MAPS analysis as the basis for long-range planning reports. These reports were presented to the governing board of the agency.

9. The editor-in-chief of a scholarly journal wanted to investigate the impact of the journal on the field and on its readership. A diagnosis suggested that MAPS might be utilized to develop internal and external effectiveness clusters (see Chapter 6). The existing structure included 16 departmental editors and about 40 associate editors. It was suggested that a new structure of editors might be more responsive to the authors and readers of the journal and better able to anticipate future developments in the field. A meeting was conducted for the 16 departmental editors, and they were asked to indicate specific areas of future development and importance in the field, to identify a number of "futurists" who could add to this list, and finally to define the current departmental responsibilities. Each of the "futurists" was then asked to generate a list of specific topics that would grow in importance. In all, over 500 items were developed and a panel of "experts" from a management school was convened that edited these into 87 task items (in this case people items were not deemed relevant). Three groups were asked to respond to the MAPS questionnaire: the editors and associate editors (respondents = 50), a sample of authors who have published in the journal (respondents = 80), and a sample of the readers of the journal (respondents = 550). Three separate analyses were presented to the editorial board suggesting an organization design for authors, readers, and editors, and a synthesis will be developed and proposed (Kilmann and King, 1975).

10. For research purposes, two eighth grade classes in school were given a MAPS questionnaire consisting of people items and task items relating to a number of science projects. The students responded and the MAPS analysis was used to form student groups to work on the projects. Several hypotheses concerning group composition were also tested.

11. Executives from a number of firms in a graduate level course in management (A) used MAPS to create a nonsubstantive problem-solving system as described in Chapter 7. Task items were developed to fit each part of the Diamond Model of problem solving.

12. Executives in another graduate level course (B) used MAPS to form teams to explore "the needs of management education in

the year 2000." From a total of 30 task items, task clusters were used to develop reports recommending what the graduate school of business should be doing differently in the year 2000.

13. Students from several disciplines and interest areas taking a doctoral seminar used MAPS to create a learning organization (see Introduction and Overview). The goals of the organization were to provide the students with an opportunity to experience the MAPS Design Technology and to write this book.

Design Boundaries of the MAPS Applications

The applications can be classified in terms of design boundaries of a MAPS analysis (Chapter 3), which relates to such questions as: Is MAPS applied to all persons in an organization or to some subunit or division of the total organization? Is MAPS used to provide a structure for a new or an already existing organization? Figure 8.1 represents each case in terms of these questions. For cases 4, 5, 6, and 8, it has been indicated that not all persons in the organization participated. In case 5 only one level of managers were involved in the MAPS analysis. In case 8 a task force of interested persons from the agency participated. All persons within an organization subunit participated in cases 4, 6, and 8.

In Figure 8.1 we note that only in cases 3, 11, 12, and 13 were applications used in developing new organizations. All of these cases were in educational settings, yet an untapped potential of MAPS may be the creation of new organizations in other settings as well. The full technology requires that a new organization first define its overall goals and, from that, its operational and strategic tasks. Since MAPS

FIGURE 8.1 Applications of MAPS: Inclusion of Organization Members (Design Boundaries)

	NEW ORGANIZATION	EXISTING ORGANIZATION
All Persons in the Organization Included	Cases 3,11–13	Cases 1,2,7,9,10
Not All Persons in the Organization Included		Cases 4–6,8

is a participatory process, all organization members will be aware of, and begin to develop commitment to, the tasks that the organization must perform. As clusters of tasks are provided by the MAPS Design Technology, members will be able to develop clearer goals and job definitions and thus reduce any felt ambiguity. New tasks, which would not otherwise have been identified, may become evident from the interrelationships within the task clusters. Since MAPS is an educational process, the organization will become more aware of the importance of design on the workings of the organization and better able to provide for flexibility in future redesigns as they become necessary. Finally the qualitative aspects of the MAPS Design Technology, which are related to OD methods (organizational development), should help develop a climate in the organization that fosters individual satisfaction and performance.

A special issue arises concerning the design boundaries of the MAPS applications. At present there is a limitation on the MAPS Computer Program (maximum of 100 task items, 100 people items, 100 respondents) that prevents a large organization from being involved as a single MAPS analysis. One can argue, however, that even if any number of task items, people items, and respondents could be included in one MAPS analysis, this would probably not be desirable. For large organizations considering a change in their OPERATIONAL DESIGN, top management (or even middle and lower management) would not relate at all to the types of specific tasks that first-line supervisors or "production" workers would endorse, and vice versa. Thus the distribution of responses to many task items on the MAPS questionnaire would be skewed to the "not at all" point on the seven-point Likert scale, which violates the statistical assumption of "normality," even with the standardization procedures in the MAPS Computer Program (see Chapter 4).

More appropriately, in a conceptual vein, the entire organization could be decomposed into certain hierarchical sections (natural "breaks" in the substantive nature of the tasks), and these sections would then be subject to a sequential set of MAPS analyses. For example, the total management group would respond to a separate MAPS questionnaire, then a "second order" MAPS analysis would be performed for those members who are in the province of the newly formed MAPS design, and so on, to specify a further "breakdown" of the design into finer categories. This is the decomposition problem discussed in Chapter 3 under design boundaries. This problem will be given some qualifications in Chapter 9. Specifically for ethical and value criteria, it will be argued that the design problem should not be decomposed for the reason of automatically maintaining the status quo of power distribution—that top management will always remain on top and that workers will always be on the bottom line. Finally, it should also be stated that this decomposition problem (and scope limitations of the MAPS Computer Program) is more pertinent to an OPERATIONAL DESIGN (which is more likely to have many members and a formalized power distribution) than to a PROBLEM-SOLVING DESIGN (which generally involves representation throughout the organization in one design analysis and has fewer persons than the OPERATIONAL DESIGN).

Characteristics of the MAPS Questionnaire

The reader is referred to Appendix B for a sample of the task items from the MAPS questionnaires (see Chapter 4) used in the MAPS applications. Some of the items on these questionnaires have been modified slightly so that the organization in question cannot be identified. Because of the variety of design boundaries, design objectives, and organizational settings represented in the cases, the task items as a whole are quite varied.

For each of the cases, the number of respondents to the MAPS questionnaire and the number of task and people items in the initial MAPS anlysis have been summarized in Table 8.2. Several aspects of this table should be noted. The first is that the MAPS computer analysis only includes those persons who responded to the questionnaire. Thus the relationship between the number of respondents and the number of people items should be considered. The latter includes all those individuals defined within the boundaries of the MAPS analysis, while the former are these individuals less those who did not respond to the MAPS questionnaire. If the number of respondents is far less than the number of people items, many persons in the organization will be excluded from the MAPS output. This implies that the new structure will be neither entirely relevant nor easily implemented in the organization. However, it can be anticipated that if the MAPS process is performed appropriately in the early stages of the technology, then sufficient commitment among the people in the organization will ensure a high response rate. It should be noted that this was the case in most of the industrial applications. Cases 5 and 9 are especially noteworthy because no people items were included in the analysis. In case 5 the goal was to develop a "task" design similar to an OPERATIONAL DESIGN and thus only task items were considered in the MAPS analysis. Since people who used the scholarly

Table 8.2   Applications of MAPS: Respondents and Structure
of MAPS Questionnaires

CASE NUMBER	NUMBER OF RESPONDENTS	NUMBER OF TASK ITEMS	NUMBER OF PEOPLE ITEMS
1	74	31	99
2	36	39	59
3	40	45	41
4	51	64	57
5	14	93	0
6	29, 21 [a]	35, 31 [a]	29, 21 [a]
7	1	35	30
8	40	18	59
9	50, 700 [b]	87	0
10	31, 31 [a]	16	31, 31 [a]
11	24	60	25
12	22	30	22
13	25	60	25

[a] Number of respondents, people and task items in second MAPS analysis.
[b] Number of respondents from the organization's environment (i.e., authors and readers of the journal).

journal were included in case 9 (those in the environment of the organization, as readers and authors), only task items relating to current and future research topics were used.

A second aspect of Table 8.2 is the relative number of task and people items for each case. If the number of items is approximately equal, then both task and people items have the same importance in determining the formation of people clusters (e.g., cases 3 and 4). If the number of items is not equal an imbalance occurs, with either the people items (cases 1, 8, 10) or the task items (cases 2, 5, 11) having more importance in people cluster composition. Therefore, in developing task items, consistency must be maintained between the relative numbers of task and people items and their importance to the goals for which the MAPS Design Technology was applied (i.e., a decision should be made regarding the relative extent of integration of task and people items in determining people clusters for the integrated designs discussed in Chapter 4).

If the design objective is to develop a new organizational structure in which the individuals can work well together productively and interpersonally (as in cases 1, 3, 8), there should be a greater number of people items. If task performance is to be emphasized (as in cases 2, 5, 11), then more task items should appear. The number of task items might also reflect the specificity with which they were developed. There were 93 specific task items in case 5, while case 8 had only 18 general tasks. Thus the relative number of task and people items may be varied in terms of the specificity of the task items. Consistency with design objectives should be maintained in making the decision of numbers of task versus people items on the MAPS questionnaire.

RELATIVE TIME IN THE STEPS OF THE TECHNOLOGY

Just as several chapters have used the Diamond Model of problem solving (Sagasti and Mitroff, 1973) to discuss the construction and processes of the MAPS Design Technology, we may consider each application of MAPS in terms of the problem-solving processes that occurred. Using the headings from Part II of this book, Figure 8.2 represents the length of time spent in each portion of the MAPS Design Technology classified as follows: Slight (no time or almost instantaneous), Short (days or weeks), Long (months), or occasionally, Not Yet Completed (if the application has not yet been reached or if only a portion is completed).

Figure 8.3 indicates the relationship between the phases of the MAPS Design Technology and the Diamond Model. The entry and diagnosis phase involves the initial contact with the organization, the educational process that allows the organization to develop its own diagnosis and, finally, a decision by the organization and the consul-

FIGURE 8.2 Applications of MAPS: Relative Time in Steps of Technology

Time Spent in Phase	Entry and Diagnosis Steps 1 through 4	Input, Analysis, and Output Steps 5 through 7	Implementation and Evaluation Steps 8 through 12
Slight	Cases 1, 2, 10 −13	Cases 1, 2, 10	Cases 2, 6
Short	Cases 3–7	Cases 3, 11–13	Cases 3, 10 −13
Long	Cases 8, 9	Cases 4–6, 8, 9	Cases 1, 8
Not yet completed		Case 7	Cases 4, 5, 7, 9

Note. See Figs. 1, 4.2, 7.1 and Table 7.1.

FIGURE 8.3 The Diamond Model of Problem Solving Applied to MAPS as Discussed in Chapter 3 (Entry and Diagnosis), Chapter 4 (Input, Analysis, Output), Chapter 5 (Implementation), and Chapter 6 (Evaluation)

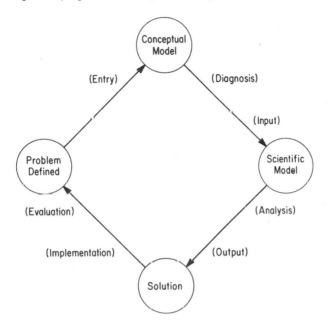

tant to proceed with the MAPS Design Technology. The input, analysis, and output phase (the core of the technology) includes the development of the task items and the final MAPS questionnaire, the response by organizational members, analysis by the MAPS Computer Program, and the output showing a number of alternative designs. The implementation and evaluation phase consists of the choice by the organization of a design, the enactment of procedures to implement the chosen design and, finally, an evaluation of the implemented design.

The diagnosis phase was reasonably short in many of the educational applications because of the research nature of the study. Many of the noneducational applications had shorter diagnosis phases because of the initial commitment of a key person in the organization to the MAPS Design Technology. The MAPS consultants were approached by the key person at a time when the individual, rather than the MAPS consultant, had already determined that MAPS would assist in solving a particular organizational problem (cases 3, 4, and 5) or in providing impetus to a program of organization change (cases 6 and 7). In case 8 MAPS consultants were asked to study the question of evaluating the impact of the journal. Initial diagnosis and discussion suggested that design was an important issue. This decision was made by both the organization and the MAPS consultant. Similarly, in case 8, the initial purpose was to aid the agency in planning for the year 2000. Along with a variety of other educational processes, the MAPS Design Technology was suggested as a method for establishing task force groups and topics for strategic planning.

The length of the input, analysis, and output phase was largely determined by the time required to develop the MAPS questionnaire. In the educational applications, special workshops of one or two days' duration were held to develop the task items. In cases 1 and 2 existing concepts (study centers, curriculum criteria, and learning modules) were used for the questionnaire. The research design in case 10 required that the task items be developed by persons other than the participants. In the noneducational applications considerable time was spent developing task items and then editing them into a questionnaire. In cases 4, 5, and 8 an extraordinary number of task items were developed (as many as 1,200), and required the formation of a special committee to remove the redundancies and state the task items in a manner that could be understood by all persons in the organization.

The implementation and evaluation phase has not yet been reached in many of the noneducational applications. In some of these a decision may be made to implement a new organization design. In cases 2 and 6 the output was used by the organization (for a task force report and for diagnosis, respectively), but not to provide a new design. The educational applications had short implementations because of the research and learning nature of the experience. However, in cases 3 and 13, the MAPS output was modified somewhat in developing the organization design.

In case 1, study centers, as suggested by the MAPS analysis, were adopted by the organization over a period of 20 months (McKelvey and Kilmann, 1975). In case 8 task force teams created by the MAPS Design Technology met for ten months to develop strategic planning reports. It can be seen that in industrial and public applications the decision to implement a new design is neither taken lightly nor made rapidly. Further, since MAPS is a participative process, the organization will spend additional time in making the decision and building commitment among its members.

Conceptual Models and Applications of MAPS

In previous chapters of this book various conceptual models were presented to show the facets and nuances of the MAPS Design Technology. In this section we will present several of these models and show how the applications may be classified in each. Frequently, one or more cells of a model will not have current applications and will suggest areas for future research.

The Four Jungian Designs

The Jungian dimensions of Sensation-Intuition and Thinking-Feeling were first introduced in Chapter 1 and have been used extensively in constructing various conceptual models of organization design. Figure 8.4 represents the various applications in terms of the four Jungian designs. As originally conceived, the MAPS Design Technology was for the OPERATIONAL DESIGN of an organization, and a number of applications are of this type. In case 3, for example, general statements of goals were translated into 45 organizational tasks. The output was considered by the organization and, after modification, adopted as the organization design. During the year-long life of this particular student group, the design was used for the

FIGURE 8.4   Applications of MAPS: Types of Designs (See Fig. 4.10)

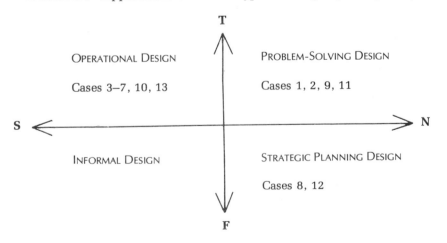

T

OPERATIONAL DESIGN

Cases 3–7, 10, 13

PROBLEM-SOLVING DESIGN

Cases 1, 2, 9, 11

S

N

INFORMAL DESIGN

STRATEGIC PLANNING DESIGN

Cases 8, 12

F

day-to-day activities of the organization. To provide leadership, one member from each of the task groups was elected to a steering committee.

As the MAPS Design Technology developed, applications other than those for OPERATIONAL DESIGN were begun. An example of a PROBLEM-SOLVING DESIGN is case 9, where MAPS was used in an attempt to translate the future into the present so that the organization's design would be more responsive to current and newly developing areas of scholarly research. This was accomplished by having the task items generated not only by the journal editors but also by a number of "futurists," and by having the editors, a sampling of authors, and a reader sample respond to the MAPS questionnaire. Several designs will be presented to the organization for a decision on implementation. To further differentiate OPERATIONAL and PROBLEM-SOLVING designs, consider the task items in case 1. If an OPERATIONAL DESIGN were required, a number of task items relating to teaching duties would have been included. However, the concept of study centers was to foster research, and thus only strategic items relating to intended research topics were considered.

In the strategic planning applications, differences were noticeable in the emergent designs and the task items. Operational tasks require specific and day-to-day definitions as task items (ST). To be concerned about the year 2000 (as in cases 8 and 12), task items must be general and based on personal and subjective feelings (NF) since no more specific information or perspectives are available. Thus, for case 8, a few general items were generated (see Appendix B) and the task clusters were used as the basis for extensive strategic planning. The issues raised would be of concern to the agency over the next 25 years rather than the next several months. Similarly, in case 2, the information was for future changes in the curriculum.

Finally, we should look to the SF cell of the model and the possibility of forming an INFORMAL DESIGN. Some research is planned to examine this cell, but it raises a myriad of questions. For example, can the MAPS Design Technology be modified to suggest friendship patterns within the organization? Secondly, if one conceives of the INFORMAL DESIGN as providing necessary information flows, can MAPS develop better channels of information by combining formal and informal paths? MAPS does provide a technology for assessing and comparing the formal and informal designs. We are not aware of previous attempts to specifically create an INFORMAL DESIGN in an organization.

The Scientific Models of MAPS

Chapter 4 provided an extended discussion on the six scientific models of MAPS as derived from different combinations of inputs, analyses, and outputs from the core of the technology. While most applications of MAPS have collected responses to both task and people items (except cases 5 and 9), the ouput could reflect people clusters based on only people items, only task items, or both. The task clusters would always be formed only from the task items. Most applications of MAPS have given task clusters, people clusters, and their assignment (except, cases 5 and 9) to the organization.

Chapter 4 also presented a variant of the six models of MAPS. Rather than distinguishing whether task clusters and their assignments to people clusters (Models I, II, V) or only people clusters (Models II, IV, VI) would be shown, the latter could be approached by developing problem or strategic task items, while the former would specify operational task items. Operational task items would thus be specific, day-to-day, tasks (ST and SF), while problem-solving tasks would be future-oriented, general, and intuitive-type tasks (NT and NF). The applications in terms of the types of task items used in the questionnaire are summarized in Figure 8.5, which shows that the

FIGURE 8.5   Applications of MAPS: Scientific Models of MAPS
(See Figs. 4.11 and 4.12)

INPUT DATA UTILIZED TO DETERMINE PEOPLE CLUSTERS	NATURE OF TASK ITEMS	
	Task items specify operational activities	Task items specify problems and strategic issues
Responses to Task Items	Case 5	Case 9
Responses to Task Items and People Items	Cases 3, 4, 6, 7, 10, 13	Cases 1, 2, 8, 11, 12
Responses to People Items		

T

F

S ⟵————————⟶ N

integrated designs have been utilized most. Only cases 5 and 9 have been based on responses to task items only, the former for operational purposes and the latter for strategic purposes. Figure 8.5 also highlights the models of MAPS that have not been applied and therefore need to be researched in the future.

Organizational Effectiveness

The Model of organizational effectiveness presented in Chapter 6 provides a framework for consideration of the areas in which the MAPS Design Technology can enhance the functioning of the organization. The economic attributes of Internal Efficiency may be affected by the new OPERATIONAL DESIGN. Internal Effectiveness will improve as organization members are given a greater chance to participate in the design of their organization by being involved in the MAPS process. External Efficiency can be seen in terms of increased ability to deal with external factors, and to plan, so as to predict future environmental problems and opportunities. Finally, External Effectiveness will improve if the client is involved in the development and response to the MAPS questionnaire (as in case 9). These four types of effectiveness and efficiency combine to determine overall organizational effectiveness. Figure 8.6 shows the approach taken in each application to improve organizational effectiveness. For example, MAPS was applied in case 5 to get a better understanding of the interrelationships of the tasks, and case 6 used MAPS as a diagnosis of the interrelationships of the people and the tasks they perform to address Internal Efficiency.

Several of the applications, however, address more than one type of organizational effectiveness. In case 1, for example, the new study centers were intended to improve the ability of faculty members to work jointly on research and also their motivation to do so. In case 8, the strategic planning was to better anticipate problems that would occur in the future (NT) and to consider societal needs and areas of potential conflict with these needs (NF). Thus an important feature of the MAPS Design Technology is that it can have an impact on several aspects of organization effectiveness (see Chapter 6). By using the Jungian model (see Figure 8.4) and the model of organization effectiveness (see Figure 8.6), we can see that different design objectives lead to different designs (via the scientific models of MAPS; Figure 8.5) to have the greatest impact on the different components of organizational effectiveness.

FIGURE 8.6   Applications of MAPS: Components
of Organizational Effectiveness (See Fig. 6.2)

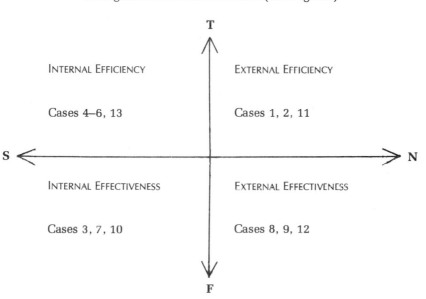

INTERNAL EFFICIENCY

Cases 4–6, 13

EXTERNAL EFFICIENCY

Cases 1, 2, 11

INTERNAL EFFECTIVENESS

Cases 3, 7, 10

EXTERNAL EFFECTIVENESS

Cases 8, 9, 12

Problem-Solving Systems

The applications on the right side of Figures 8.4, 8.5, and 8.6 (cases 1, 2, 8, 9, 11, and 12) can be classified in terms of the problem-solving systems first shown in Figure 7.3, and discussed in Chapter 7, and now illustrated in Figure 8.7. The use of the MAPS Design Technology to form task forces that are both temporary and part-time can be seen in case 8, where 40 members from all levels and sections of the public agency met to develop plans for the year 2000. These persons still retained their roles in the OPERATIONAL DESIGN, although time was released to work on the strategic issues. Both examples of project groups (cases 11 and 12) need further explanation. Since both these cases were in educational settings, and the class was only part-time for its members, it should be stated that for a temporary period of time (several class sessions) all effort was devoted to the task force objective (developing a problem-solving system and planning for management education in the year 2000, respectively). Future applications in this cell might include the assignment of personnel to project teams from a pool of available organization members, the

FIGURE 8.7   Applications of MAPS: Problem-Solving Systems
(See Fig. 7.3)

Continuity of Design

		PERMANENT	TEMPORARY
Member Involvement	PART-TIME	Collateral Groups	Task Forces–Committees Cases 2, 8
	FULL-TIME	Staff Groups Cases 1, 9	Project Groups Cases 11, 12

creation of teams that would travel from location to location in a large organization, or the movement of personnel through a number of temporary assignments in a multinational corporation.

The creation of an organization design for research planning is seen to some extent in cases 1 and 9 in the development of staff groups that are more responsive to the future as well as in the current demands of the internal and external environment of the organization. The development of collateral groups for problem solving and /or strategic planning suggests strong possibilities for future applications (Zand, 1974). Some organizations may be unwilling to undergo a complete organization redesign (OPERATIONAL DESIGN), but may be willing to develop a collateral PROBLEM-SOLVING DESIGN.

RESEARCH STUDIES WITH MAPS

The introduction to this chapter indicated that the various applications of the MAPS Design Technology have had a major impact on developing the many conceptual models of MAPS and organization design presented throughout this book. While the present chapter has provided a summary of the thirteen applications as they pertain to these conceptual models, it seems appropriate to consider the important, interdependent relationship of research and applications regarding the MAPS Design Technology. In particular, it seems important to address the need for a variety of research studies to further test and develop the technology.

In Chapter 2 we stated that our ethics and values regarding social systems change take priority to the findings of research studies since the latter are largely rooted in the past. Available research knowledge will be utilized so that the MAPS Design Technology and its interventions will be more effective in bringing about our terminal values: to design effective and purposeful social systems. This does not mean, however, that a proactive stance cannot be taken toward research studies. That is, specific research studies involving the MAPS Design Technology can be undertaken to test its specific effects and to derive implications for revising the technology so that it is more effective for a variety of design objectives in different organizational settings. In other words, we do not have to rely solely on the research studies of others; we can conduct such studies ourselves.

A study by Kilmann and Seltzer (1975) is an example of such research but was not included as an application of MAPS because it used the technology only for research purposes. That is, there was no intention in this study of using MAPS to design actual organizational activity. Instead, the research study sought to test several hypotheses experimentally on homogeneous versus heterogeneous composition of subsystems designed by MAPS (see Chapter 4). The thirteen applications reported in this chapter, however, were not merely for the purpose of applying MAPS to foster design changes. Several involved specific research assessments to ascertain the process of the design change, the extent of the design change and, in some cases, the effectiveness of the resulting design. Actually some of these assessments were part of the evaluation component of MAPS (step 11, as discussed in Chapter 6), which was as much for the benefit of the organization as for the benefit of the MAPS consultants and researchers. Furthermore, even those applications that did not entail formal research assessments may be viewed as case studies—an intensive qualitative examination of the MAPS design process for the organization, accomplished mainly by observations, interviews, and anecdotal information. But before we suggest how the various applications of MAPS are also instances of research investigations, it is necessary first to consider the variety of different approaches to research (i.e., research methodologies) and how each deals with different aspects of the accumulation of valid social science knowledge.

Research Methodologies

For the purposes of this discussion, we wish to separate research methodologies into the following five categories: controlled laboratory experiments, laboratory simulations, comparative field studies, longitudinal field studies, and case studies. Although there are other taxonomies for classifying research approaches, these five represent methodologies that are frequently used to study organizational phenomena and are well documented (Campbell and Stanley, 1963). The essential issue for each type of research methodology is to what extent it contains the potential for high internal and external validity, assuming that the particular methodology is applied as intended. Internal validity concerns whether the results of the study can be confidently interpreted according to the variables, concepts, and theories purported to explain the results (e.g., that MAPS was responsible for the organization becoming more effective). External validity concerns whether the results from the given study are actually generalizable to other research and organizational settings (e.g., will the effects that MAPS produced in one particular organization also take place in another organization?) (Campbell and Stanley, 1963). Briefly, we can define each research approach as follows.

Controlled laboratory experiments generally involve an experimental "group," which receives some treatment and is then compared to an equivalent control group. Each of these has randomly assigned individuals, and the experimenter attempts to control all variables except the experimental treatment. The results of the experiment can therefore be more confidently explained by the treatment and not by other variables or alternative explanations. Although such laboratory experiments have a potential for high internal validity, their external validity is questionable since the laboratory setting is highly contrived and often quite different from real life settings (e.g., where all other variables are not controlled and the results of the activity are real). Thus it is not always clear how generalizable the findings are from laboratory to other settings even if the internal validity is high (Campbell and Stanley, 1963).

Laboratory simulations are also contrived by the experimenter but they tend to be closer to real life settings. For example, there is often greater ego involvement on the part of the individuals, and they have more discretion about their behavior during the simulation. Internal validity is lower, however, than controlled laboratory experiments since there are more alternative explanations. On the other hand, external validity is higher since the behavior of the individuals in the simulation is not as controlled and artificial. The major advantage of the simulation is that the researcher can create the conditions and behavior he wishes to examine, and therefore he does not have to wait around for some organization to participate in a design process, nor does he have to convince the organization to go through a design change. Instead, the simulation can compact real life processes in a setting that can be easily observed in a short period of time. Doubtless this is not as genuine as a real setting, where time and people move at their own pace via their own objectives.

Comparative field studies involve real organizations engaging in real design processes. Assuming that a researcher can obtain access to such organizations and can monitor the dynamics of the design process, external validity will be moderately high. However, since the research cannot control the many variables operating along with the design variables, there always are a number of alternative explanations of what occurred and why, which limits the internal validity of the study. This may be compensated somewhat by the use of control groups (e.g., other departments or organizations) similar to the organizational units undergoing design changes, but these control groups do not undergo the changes, perhaps leading to the "Hawthorne Effect" (Roethlisberger and Dickson, 1938). Generally, however, there is not a random selection of departments and organizations that are placed in the experimental or control group category, and the two groups are also usually different in a number of other variables. Furthermore, comparative field studies examine characteristics or outcomes of organizational behavior (or work group behavior, etc.) at one point in time by the use of descriptive statistics (e.g., means, correlations, analysis of variances). Without taking into account the dimension of time, it is difficult to discern cause-and-effect relationships, and hence, what really did determine the effectiveness or ineffectiveness of the design or the design change. Thus comparative field studies can suggest characteristics, outcomes, states, and so on, which are associated with each other, but cannot provide strong evidence of what caused what to occur. Consequently, external validity is only moderate while internal validity is low.

Longitudinal field studies circumvent some of the shortcomings of comparative studies. For example, assessments are made over a period of time (e.g., one month, six months, one year, several years) to isolate the factors that actually caused the dynamics in the design process or the outcomes of the resulting design. Thus external validity is high while internal validity is still questionable, since the researcher cannot control all other variables nor can he randomly place organizational units in various environmental settings (i.e., organizations come with their environments), nor can he randomly select which units are to go through the design process. The latter is usually determined by top management and the MAPS consultants, with a view toward design change and not merely design research. Furthermore, as with comparative field studies, the researcher may have to wait around for the opportunity to apply the MAPS Design Technology, and it may be quite difficult to obtain a large enough sample size to calculate various statistics. In other words, it is quite difficult to find fifteen real life organizations that wish to participate in equivalent design changes (assuming that the organizations are similar enough to warrant summarized statistical calculations).

The fifth research approach we have identified is the case study. This is an intensive, clinical assessment of one organization, work group or team, and so forth. The study is usually longitudinal and often includes assessments on a number of variables, both behavioral and traditional accounting data. Generally, however, the case study emphasizes such nonquantitative assessments as interviews, anecdotal information (e.g., organizational stories [Mitroff and Kilmann, 1975b]), critical incidents, and clinical observations. Since the sample size is $N = 1$, much reliance must be placed on the observational skills and insights of the researcher(s), and consequently it is difficult to assess both internal and external validity—statistical calculations are not possible and there are no other organizations or units to which to compare the given study. The advantage of the case study, however, is that quantitative measures do not always capture well the dynamics of a design change since aspects of organization designing do not lend themselves to valid, quantitative assessment. Insights from intense observation of a design process can often lead to a better understanding of what occurred than some elaborate statistical calculation on less meaningful variables. For example, the actual reasons why a top manager felt the need for a design change can sometimes be better expressed and captured in an intensive interview than as a single number on a seven-point Likert scale.

Sequential Utilization of Research Methodologies

The important consideration in these different research approaches is to realize that each has its advantages and disadvantages in regard to the ease of obtaining research samples, as well as constraints on internal and external validity. Thus to further develop the field of social systems design and the MAPS Design Technology, it is necessary to apply a variety of research approaches to combine the advantages and minimize the disadvantages of each.

For example, the case study approach is usually most helpful for investigating complex phenomena that have not been well understood and articulated previously. As a result of the case study (or studies), specific hypotheses may be formulated and tested in a controlled laboratory setting. When some confidence has been developed in regard to useful explanation of the phenomenon (in the controlled laboratory setting), a laboratory simulation can then be set up to see if the same explanation, prediction, or control of behavior will also occur in a less constrained setting. If the various laboratory findings and explanations are still plausible (although these will undoubtedly have been modified during the course of previous studies), and thus support some internal validity, the organizational design phenomenon may then be investigated in a comparative field setting to test for the external validity of the laboratory findings. Various cycles of such different research approaches would continue to further both the internal and external validity of the emerging theory or technology to explain, predict, control, or bring about the phenomenon of interest, where refinement and modifications can occur at each stage. An intensive case study might then help to document whether the anticipated organizational behaviors have actually changed during subsequent design processes, which would imply that the developed theory has been put to practical use through the design technology. The latter is presumably the goal of social science knowledge. What is most important, however, is not the particular sequence of research studies (i.e., first a case study, then laboratory studies, then field studies, then further case studies, etc.), but that some sequence does take place. Both internal and external validity cannot be assessed in one research study or by one research methodology alone.

Research Methodologies Utilized in MAPS Applications

Figure 8.8 summarizes the key distinctions discussed thus far in this section via a matrix that shows the five research approaches. (See Kilmann, Pondy, and Slevin [1976] for a more elaborate discussion of this matrix as applied to a collection of research studies on organization design.) In each cell of the matrix the relative internal and external validity of each research methodology are suggested. It should be emphasized that the relative validities in each cell are simply qualitatively and subjectively assessed, but do follow from the preceding discussion on research approaches to studying organization design. In making the qualitative expectations on internal and

FIGURE 8.8   Research with MAPS: Methodologies and Validity

RESEARCH	LABORATORY EXPERIMENTS	LABORATORY SIMULATIONS	COMPARATIVE FIELD STUDIES	LONGITUDINAL FIELD STUDIES	CASE STUDIES
Internal validity	High	Medium	Low	Low	Medium
External validity	Low	Medium	Medium	High	Low
Studies	Kilmann and Seltzer, 1975	Cases 10–12	Case 3	Cases 1,4,6,8	Case 2, 5,7,9, 13

NOTE. See the summarization of these cases at the beginning of this chapter for the references to these studies.

external validity, it is also assumed that each research methodology is applied appropriately to maximize its potential advantages and to minimize its disadvantages (e.g., utilization of reliable and valid measures, randomization where possible, etc.).

Also shown in Figure 8.8 are the thirteen applications of MAPS sorted into the five cells according to the research methodology that was utilized. The Kilmann and Seltzer (1975) study, which was not an organizational application of MAPS, is also included. As can be seen, each research methodology has been used in applications and research studies with MAPS.

The Kilmann and Seltzer study was a controlled laboratory experiment. Cases 10, 11, and 12 are instances of laboratory simulations of the MAPS design process. Case 3 is an example of a comparative field study; that is, certain outcomes of the organization designed via MAPS were compared with other organizational units not utilizing any design technology. Cases 1, 4, 6, and 8 were longitudinal field studies since assessments were made over time about the effects of the MAPS design process. Finally, cases 2, 5, 7, 9, and 13 are classified as case studies because they did not entail quantitative research assessments. Instead the results of the five cases stem from observation, interviews, and anecdotal information informally collected (and experienced) while MAPS consultants and researchers were interacting with each organization.

Furthermore, a particular sequence of research methodologies was utilized in the MAPS applications to determine both internal and external validity. The first application was a longitudinal study in an educational system over a 20-month period, where the predictive validity of the MAPS Design Technology was tested (Case 1 [McKelvey and Kilmann, 1975]). The study found that the best design solution suggested by MAPS (via the coefficient of purposefulness, as discussed in Chapter 4) predicted not only the right substantive theme, which was derived by the subsystems, but also predicted with 82 percent accuracy which members would actually select themselves for the evolved subsystems. The external validity of this study was suggested, since the members never saw the best MAPS-designed solution of subsystems and the MAPS consultants (researchers) did not involve themselves in any stage of the implementation. Basically the organizational members were given considerable freedom by the top administrator in choosing which subsystem they wanted to be identified with, and the members could switch in and out of subsystems while making their "final" choices over the 20-month period. The only information the members had before they began making subsystem choices were two very different MAPS designs (i.e., a five-cluster solution and an eleven-cluster solution), both of which varied considerably from the eight-cluster solution that had the highest coefficient of purposefulness.

The second application (case 2 [Kilmann, 1974c]) involved a case study to replicate and examine more thoroughly the effects of MAPS in a similar organizational setting. The third application (case 3 [Kilmann, 1975a]) was a comparative field study, again in the same organizational setting (an educational system), to more quantitatively assess the effects on an organization using MAPS as compared to control groups not using MAPS.

The next applications utilized MAPS in different types of social systems. Cases 4 and 5 took place in industrial settings; the former was a longitudinal study (Keim and Kilmann, 1975), the latter a case study. Case 6 entailed a financial organization case study. Case 8 was a longitudinal study that involved a large federal government agency, and case 9 utilized MAPS in a scientific organization via a longitudinal study (Kilmann and King, 1975).

Cases 10, 11, and 12 focused on special purpose design objectives in more controlled settings (i.e., laboratory simulations). The thirteenth study concerned the very specialized application of writing this book. Finally, the study by Kilmann and Seltzer (1975) was the first pure research study that did not involve any real organization in any sense of the term, and it was also the first controlled laboratory experiment using the MAPS Design Technology that concentrated on internal validity.

A number of the applications cited above (particularly the longitudinal studies) are still in progress, and other studies are constantly being initiated, as indicated in several chapters in this book. What is most important, however, is that these and other research studies are conducted to develop an accumulated base of knowledge of social systems design and the MAPS Design Technology, and to continually modify the technology as based on these studies so that it is constantly being refined, improved, and expanded. Thus MAPS applications and MAPS research studies not only test the current state of the technology but also serve to provide ways of enhancing its practical usefulness in designing effective social systems in the future.

CONCLUSIONS

In this chapter we have shown the applications of the MAPS Design Technology in a variety of settings, and have indicated how some of the conceptual models relate to these applications. Implicit in these models are a number of potential applications, only some of which are currently being explored. In addition, the applications provide a number of findings of particular interest and importance. Looking back to Table 8.1, we note that the settings where the MAPS Design Technology has been applied include educational, business, and public organizations. Other opportunities in the health professions and religious communities, as well as additional applications in various business and public sector organizations, will lead to expanded learning about the technology.

We can also observe in Table 8.1 the variety of design objectives for which MAPS has been considered. These could be classified in terms of operational activities, strategic planning, organizational diagnosis, organizational development, and organizational problem solving. The MAPS Design Technology is well suited for the creation of new organizations but, as can be seen in Figure 8.1, there have been few implementations in this area and additional experience is needed. Similarly, as noted in Figures 8.4, 8.5, and 8.7, the applications of the MAPS Design Technology for strategic planning and problem solving have a high potential, although some areas, such as the development of collateral designs, will need to be explored further.

An important point is that MAPS can have impact on several areas of organizational effectiveness (Figure 8.6), and through modification of the type of design (Figure 8.4) and the number and content of the task items (Table 8.2), identified aspects of effectiveness can be enhanced. This linkage provides the crucial step in the development of a systemic approach to social systems design. The MAPS Design Technology, which is based on many conceptual models and social science frameworks, can be used in a variety of settings, to meet a variety of goals, through a variety of methods to augment all facets of organizational effectiveness. The applications to date have begun to show these multiple uses, and therefore the MAPS Design Technology is developing into a broad, interdisciplinary approach for designing effective social systems.

The last section of this chapter presented the applications of MAPS as instances of research studies. That is, while the primary purpose of an application was to bring about some design change or to design some organizational activity, various research assessments were made to ascertain the process and outcome of the design intervention. It was noted that the applications could be classified by one of five major research methodologies: laboratory experiments, laboratory (organizational) simulations, comparative field studies, longitudinal field studies, and case studies. A combination and sequencing of these methodologies over a long period of time are necessary to test and obtain internal and external validity for the MAPS Design Technology (as well as for any other theory or technology).

Even if such a comprehensive set and sequencing of research studies were conducted, however, the validity of MAPS would still not be conclusive, nor can the validity of any theory or technology ever be conclusive. Not only do the complexities and dynamics of social systems behavior preclude unequivocal explanations of that behavior, but the design of research studies and especially the interpretation of research results are very much affected by the values of the researcher (as discussed in Chapter 2). Therefore some criteria must be applied in decisions to utilize the technology both before and after extensive research studies are conducted. These dilemmas are examined explicitly in the next chapter of this book, where ethical and value positions will be presented, which serve as criteria for utilizing the MAPS Design Technology: before extensive research studies are completed and to override the results of research based upon other ethical and value positions.

Chapter 9

The Ethics, Validity, and Future of MAPS

We believe that any individual who has significant personal and /or positional influence over another ought to explicate his or her ethical stance toward that person or situation. By "ethical" is meant how one ought to behave toward others, what standards and guidelines one ought to live by, and what ends or objectives one ought to pursue. Thus our first ethical position is to be explicit concerning these matters and not to simply assume that everyone has the same ethics or that such a discussion is not relevant to social change. Ethics, to us, is the sine qua non of planned social change, for our ethical positions greatly determine what we see as important and appropriate (as well as possible) and consequently determine what we attempt to do.

The MAPS Design Technology brings to the forefront the ethics of social change and social intervention as we have not often seen before. It is one thing to talk about organization design in some descriptive or theoretical manner, or to discuss the general steps involved in a five-year organizational development program. It is quite another to suggest that as a result of questionnaire data (i.e., the MAPS questionnaire) people will be sorted by some elaborate computer program into a new organization design, and that the output of MAPS is so specific as to indicate which group of people (by name) is to work on which cluster of tasks. It seems then that a computer program that processes "hard," objective data, as is the case with management information systems or operations research algorithms, is experienced quite differently from a computer program that utilizes subjective, personal data for management decision making. Perhaps individuals question subjective data more than objective data because the latter seems more valid. This, of course, overlooks the possibility that the wrong objective data was collected or that the analyst may be solving the wrong problem (Mitroff and Featheringham, 1974).

The remainder of this chapter will explore the ethics underlying the MAPS Design Technology, first by stating as explicitly as is now possible the objectives we have in mind in applying MAPS; second, by considering how these ethics affect our decision to apply MAPS in different situations; and third, by discussing how MAPS ought to be developed further in the future. While we do not have the answers to all the ethical questions raised by MAPS, nor perhaps may we ever have, the best we can do is discuss these issues and be conscious of the various ethical dilemmas as MAPS is being applied and as decisions are being made. The following discussion therefore builds upon many of the value and research issues raised earlier in this book, particularly those in Chapters 1, 2, and 3, and suggests the need for a continuous dialogue and debate of these fundamental social science issues.

AN ETHICAL STANCE TOWARD MAPS

The MAPS Design Technology was developed to further the following ethical and value position: allowing individuals greater choice and control over their behavior as it affects their involvement and meaningfulness in personal and organizational life, to the extent that such choices are based on valid information and are consciously desired by the individuals; and that these choices are to be integrated with organizational and societal goals. This perspective is similar to Argyris' concept of valid information, free choice, and commitment (Argyris, 1970a). It is also similar to the values and ethical positions taken by others involved in organization development programs (Bennis, et al., 1969; Margulies and Raia, 1972). The difference, however, is that the stated values are meant to be operationalized by member influence and control over the design of the social system (i.e., the objectives and tasks to be pursued as well as the assignment of people to tasks), and not just control and influence within a given design and structure. Thus, if the design of the social system is a major determinant of the behavior that occurs, then giving members an opportunity to affect the design of their system by having them provide information and choices concerning the design can foster their meaningfulness and involvement in the organization.

A major assumption of this value position is that giving individuals greater control over the design of their social system will not only benefit the individuals but also the organization and even society itself. But there may necessarily be trade-offs between the individual and the organization. Research on participative management, for example, has suggested that the organization does not always benefit from allowing individuals greater freedom and influence (Leavitt, 1975; Vroom, 1965). Also, some findings on organization design research suggests that for stable environments the organization designed in a bureaucratic manner (i.e., having greater control over members' behavior) is a more effective one (Lawrence and Lorsch, 1967a). Although such research results are certainly not conclusive, they do raise the issue of who will benefit from application of the MAPS Design Technology.

Ethical Violations of MAPS

The foregoing poses a particular dilemma: should change agents of organization design (or any other framework) be guided by the results of scientific research or by their values and ethics? Although research may suggest that the organization will benefit most if certain decisions are made by top management, if these decisions are expected to diminish the amount of valid information and choices of participants in the organization the change agent may decide not to help top management formulate and implement such decisions. Or, should the change agent put his values aside and help top management implement a plan that would make the organization more profitable, if only in the short run?

Our ethical stance regarding the application of the MAPS Design Technology is as follows: we will be guided primarily by our ethics and will not implement MAPS in a social system if we anticipate that it is being done to further control participants and to manipulate their behavior in the organization. It should be stated that this ethical position and, particularly, choosing ethics over research results, derives from the kind of world we wish to see and live in. On the one hand, research findings stem from the way things have been conceptualized and the way things are, while on the other, ethics stipulate how we want things to be. The latter acknowledges the possibility and the motivation to actually alter the way things are, and consequently the use of a technology and other social interventions are then applied to bring about our terminal values (Rokeach, 1969). Therefore a major reason for us to apply the MAPS Design Technology is to help develop those conditions in organizations and society that operationalize our values. Available research results on organization design, organization theory, and so on, are relied upon to develop the technology so it may have the intended effects.

The Possibilities of Ethical Violations

Even though the stages of the MAPS Design Technology are meant to be conducted in a manner consistent with the underlying values and ethics of MAPS, this does not have to be the case. Figure 9.1 shows the Input-Response Matrix for the MAPS questionnaire. The "Y" shows for which process MAPS was primarily intended; that is, where members and /or clients develop the task items of the questionnaire and where all members respond to the questionnaire. The "X"

shows where the technology could be used most to manipulate organizational members: where top management assumes it is in the
best position to determine task items, and where top management
(either one individual or a group) endorses the questionnaire for each
member of the organization (because top management again feels it is
in the best position to judge members' expertise and interests).

In the "X" case, top management could, in a very short time,
develop the MAPS questionnaire, respond to it, and then unilaterally
implement a design change following the MAPS analysis and output.
This could be done before the members of the organization could even
understand, appreciate, or truly accept the design change. It should
be noted that this is the way that performance evaluation is often
conducted (i.e., management determines the criteria and then uses a
rating scale to evaluate each individual). The difference is only that
top management's similar use of the MAPS questionnaire can be
processed to suggest alternative organization designs via the MAPS
Computer Program. In fact, top management could look at all the
alternative designs of each scientific model of MAPS (Chapter 4) and
then choose the one design that comes closest to what it wants to see
rather than what might be best for the entire organization (via the
participative process of MAPS involving organization members).
From our ethical standpoint (although not from a research point of
view) this would represent a misuse of the technology.

Furthermore, in applying MAPS, some managers have asked if they
could use the technology to eliminate unnecessary or undesirable
organizational members. It has been proposed, for example, that the
factor loadings of members on the people clusters be made known to
top management so that they could determine a cutoff point for each
people cluster and then eliminate 10 percent, 20 percent, and so on, of
the members. To us, this would also represent a misuse of the technology from an ethical standpoint, but not from a research or even
from an organizational viewpoint (i.e., the organization might be
more effective if it eliminated certain people and reduced costs, etc.).

In both of the above cases, however, we have not permitted the use
of MAPS as a top management tool for its own design needs and
objectives and, with regard to the second case, we do not provide the
organization with such individual information (i.e., factor loadings
on the people clusters) even though the information is available. Our
basic ethical stance is that MAPS is not to be applied other than to
mobilize available resources as optimally as possible and to make use
of all the resources in a manner that furthers valid information,
individuals' choices, and greater control over their own behavior. If

FIGURE 9.1 The Input-Response Matrix for the MAPS Questionnaire (X indicates the possibility of using MAPS to further control and manipulate organizational members; Y indicates the greatest likelihood of using MAPS as was intended via ethical considerations)

Those Developing the Task Items	Those Responding: Top Management	Those Responding: All Members
Top Management	X	
All Members		Y
Clients and All Members		Y

management wants to make certain decisions about individual members (hiring or firing), management will have to use some other method or technology. At the very least, the validity of employment decisions is based on much more and different information from that contained in the MAPS questionnaire and processed by the MAPS Computer Program.

The Consequences of Ethical Violations

Consider what could happen if MAPS were in fact used in the above cases. Future users of MAPS would probably not trust the technology since it had been used against them. Responses to the questionnaire would perhaps be sabotaged so the technology could not be applied, or individuals might refuse to fill out the forms. A primary condition for obtaining valid information and choice on the MAPS questionnaire (or any other questionnaire) is that people trust the process and take the time to give accurate information. Violating this trust would limit the validity of the data. Such a development might not be too different from the cases of psychological experiments in which the subject has been deceived to create some experimental condition. The same subjects (as well as future subjects who may learn of this deception) easily become uncooperative or even deceiving subjects for future experiments. To use MAPS in a deceptive or manipulative manner may not only limit its application to other client systems, but may also limit the use of other technologies in the future because of the mistrust that will become associated with such technologies. What will it take, for example, to reverse the negative reaction that college sophomores have when they must participate in psychological experiments? The same rationale applies in convincing organizational members that they should respond honestly and accurately to a questionnaire when they have been deceived in the past. Consequently, misusing the MAPS Design Technology may have a significant effect on the climate of the organization in addition to many unintended consequences.

Validating the Use of MAPS

All along we have been assuming that the MAPS Design Technology is valid, that it does what it purports to do. While some validity has been established in the early studies (see Chapter 8), MAPS is proposed as a broad, interdisciplinary technology having many potential sources of application (e.g., mobilizing resources for social and organizational problem solving) and research is needed to test its applicability in different settings, under different conditions, and for different design objectives.

As we have stated, research is not the final criterion in applying MAPS, just as the fact that the atomic bomb works (i.e., is valid) is not the sole criterion of whether it should be used. An ethical stance may often override research results. Even then, however, what would it take to demonstrate that MAPS is valid, whether or not it is to be used in certain situations?

Issues in Validating a Technology for Social Change

There seem to be some qualitative differences between validating a theory and a technology. The former may be accomplished, at times by not making a major intervention and change in some social system, but can be approached by laboratory experimentation and field observation. One can argue, however, that even a laboratory experiment constitutes some social intervention and social change. Perhaps we need to consider more the ethics of conducting research on theory, as highlighted by the Milgram experiments (1965). Nevertheless, validating a technology explicitly requires the use of that technology, a definite social intervention. In this case scientists or the public may insist that the technology should not be applied even for purposes of testing, for the very act of testing may violate social norms and values.

Placing ethics aside for the moment, to validate a technology such as MAPS is certainly a major undertaking, as was discussed in the previous chapter. Research would have to demonstrate continually that MAPS does in fact generate more valid information for the social system and gives members greater choice and control, and simultaneously that MAPS does enhance a social system's effectiveness by a design that better integrates individual and organizational objectives, skills, processes, information needs, and so on. To demonstrate this, however, requires longitudinal assessments with many organizations. Some organizations would go through design changes with MAPS, others would go through other changes, and still others would undergo no change. These organizations would then have to be followed up with various measurements to ascertain changes in certain outcome variables. This may take as long as several years or a decade. (See Bowers, 1973, for this type of rare longitudinal study with many organizations.)

Even if one could obtain such samples, the researcher cannot control all variables and all contingencies or even measure all these parameters over such a period of time. The environments of organizations change, membership changes, culture changes, and it becomes more and more difficult over time to identify confidently the cause of certain outcomes, only one of which is the treatment condition (i.e., the MAPS design change). Actually, the various statistical and research methods that were developed via agricultural applications (where the setting remains very constant and stable) may not be appropriate for research investigations of phenomena seen in a dynamic, complex, and changing environment, even if samples are available.

This state of affairs further confounds the dilemma presented earlier, that is, the ethics of using a technology before it is fully developed, and yet our research methods cannot even substantiate such developments in a convincing manner. And even if controlled experiments were applied via simulations of design changes, there is still the issue of how generalizable the results are to large-scale organizations, where other variables are not controlled and where the results for the members are real. Consequently, although Chapter 8 considered the variety of research methodologies that may be applied to the study of organization design and the MAPS Design Technology (i.e., controlled laboratory experiments, organizational simulations, comparative field studies, longitudinal field studies, and case studies), we must realize that not only are such a use and sequencing of research approaches a long-term endeavor, but even the results of many studies are never unequivocal. In addition, the results are still subject to differing interpretations, as influenced by the values and ethics of the researcher (as discussed in Chapter 2).

Managing the Validity Dilemma

Our way of managing this dilemma relies on the content or face validity of MAPS rather than on external validity (Loevinger, 1967). We believe MAPS does permit more generating and processing of valid information if the MAPS Design Technology is applied as intended. Also, from the applications we have been involved with thus far (see Chapter 8), our qualitative, intuitive experience suggests that MAPS does foster greater member choices and member control of their own behavior if MAPS is applied as intended. Finally, again from our experience, MAPS does enhance the effectiveness of a social system by mobilizing the commitment and resources of participants (e.g., by containing the important interdependencies within the task clusters, and by bringing those people together in people clusters who can work well with one another in the tasks) as long as MAPS is applied as intended. While we make every effort to collect research data to address issues of external validity, we are at least for the time being (until various longitudinal studies are 'complete'), relying most heavily on our qualitative, subjective assessments of the validity of MAPS and on the face validity of the technology. Chapter 6 describes a methodology for evaluating the impact of interventions (i.e, the judicial process). This methodology could also be applied to the more general problem of evaluating longitudinal research rather than relying on traditional experimental research designs.

It can also be argued that MAPS works in spite of itself. That is, regardless of the validity of the MAPS design (the formation and assignment of people clusters to task clusters), a major aspect of MAPS is the process that is set in motion. MAPS is fundamentally an educational process, which is expected to occur before organizational members develop the MAPS questionnaire, endorse it, and adopt one of the MAPS designs. The expectation of using MAPS appears to develop a need in the social system for knowledge about organization design, organization development, leadership styles, power distribution, and so forth. It seems that the core of the technology and its concreteness (input, analysis, output) raises issues about managerial and organizational behavior that generally do not arise as readily or as strongly when other change programs are being considered. Sorting people via a computer program apparently makes people ask more questions. Consequently, one aspect of the validity of MAPS is the educational process that is not only recommended as a formal part of the MAPS Design Technology, but is generally demanded by the social system when it decides to use MAPS.

Furthermore, regardless of the validity of the MAPS design, the technology sets up a process of information gathering, influence, participation, choice, and so on. In other words, a behavioral change is seen that is consistent with the values and ethical positions underlying MAPS—to give people greater choice and influence over their behavior in the organization. In fact, a major intervention for a social system may be simply to go through the process of MAPS, whether or not a MAPS design is selected or implemented. MAPS contains a step-by-step procedure to enhance conscious choice and valid information in the social system, and therefore validity is suggested since the process of MAPS is consistent with its objectives, i.e., structural validity (Loevinger, 1967).

TOWARD A FORMAL CODE OF ETHICS

The foregoing discussion on the ethics and validity of the MAPS Design Technology can be summarized according to a set of guidelines. It is expected that further experience with the technology, along with intensive reflection concerning the ethical implications of the many decisions involved in applying MAPS, will enable the development of a formal code of ethics. The guidelines are as follows:

1. The process of applying MAPS must be consistent with the values of valid information, free choice, and members' control over their own behavior.
2. The diagnostic phase of MAPS will include an explicit assessment (though a subjective one) of the Type III errors of defining

the organization's problem as one of organization design as opposed to some other framework.

3. Before the core of MAPS is applied (i.e., input, analysis, output), considerable effort will be made to educate the client system as to the process, values, and expected outcomes of MAPS. While this does not necessitate that the client has an understanding of multivariate analysis, the client should know enough about MAPS and organization design to meaningfully develop and respond to the MAPS questionnaire and to choose among alternative organization designs.

4. Individual choices concerning which group to be assigned to via a MAPS design will not be succombed to statistical analysis. Individuals will be permitted to choose a group different from the one they were assigned by MAPS (an individual may be statistically assigned to one group over another because of a very small numerical difference). Previous experience with MAPS, however, has found that less than 5 percent of individuals actually wish to change their assignments.

5. Information concerning individual responses to the MAPS questionnaire, or statistics indicating an individual's centrality on a people cluster, will not be given to a client system and will be used only for research purposes in a confidential manner.

To assure that the above ethical guidelines will not be violated, we have made every effort to control the use of MAPS. Although this control includes being very selective about MAPS applications, perhaps even more important is the fact that we have not distributed (nor will we) the MAPS Computer Program, which is the core of the technology. Thus any application of MAPS must be processed through our organization (Organizational Design Consultants, Inc.). While others may independently develop a computer program to design organizations that is significantly different from MAPS, this might result in a superficial approach to clustering tasks, people, or some other set of variables. The intricacies of the MAPS Computer Program in taking into account response biases, data skews, reassignments of tasks and people to more purposeful clusters, and alternative scientific models of analysis, is deemed necessary for so important and critical a process as social systems design.

As others develop design technologies, we hope that they will also be explicit concerning the ethics of their technology and that their ethics will be similar to ours. We will be among the first to criticize severely the use of a technology that can bring significant and major change to social systems if the processes and /or results of the technology violate the ethical positions outlined here regardless of the "validity" of the technology.

MAPS AND POWER EQUALIZATION

Applying MAPS to its potential uses will seriously confront some of society's most established norms and practices. For one thing, MAPS represents power equalization on a large scale (Leavitt, 1965). The technology does not take into account members' present status, authority or power position, or members' salary and seniority. Instead MAPS utilizes equally all members' perceptions as to task abilities, interests, and interpersonal compatibilities. Thus some organizations have been extremely fearful of using the technology because it threatens the very basis of top management being on top. In fact, it can be argued that top management often spends large sums of money on management workshops, management education, and various organization development programs (e.g., job enlargement, team building, leadership training, etc.) because subconsciously perhaps they know that these activities will not cause significant changes—these programs will not alter the power structure of the organization. Stated differently, how can a small change in some microvariable such as job design have a major impact on such macrooutcomes as overall organizational effectiveness? MAPS does, however, confront management's most prized possessions (at a macrolevel), and consequently the technology challenges management's and society's sincerity and commitment to real social change.

To illustrate the forces in society that resist application of the MAPS Design Technology, a behavioral simulation of institutional power is described below. It will be suggested that these various forces will have to be examined and altered if social scientists ever expect to significantly enhance the effectiveness of our organizations and the quality of life for organizational participants. The issues that will be considered in the behavioral simulation will have to be managed in the future of MAPS.

A Simulation of Society: "Star Power"

The simulation is generally referred to as "Star Power," and is often utilized with a population of 30 to 50 participants (managers). The total time for the simulation is usually two to three hours and it is administered by one or more trained staff members.

The population of participants is first divided into three groups: the Circles, the Squares, and the Triangles. Individuals are given name tags with the appropriate symbol of their group to identify them. Each person is given an envelope containing a number of chips of different colors. The staff members provide a chart indicating the worth of each chip (in points) as well as the types of color combinations that result in additional points. The objective of the simulation (game) is for each individual to maximize his point total by engaging in favorable bargains with other individuals (either in his own group or in the other groups). Bargaining tends to increase the points received from particular combinations of colored chips.

A bargaining round lasts for 10 minutes, and participants are given certain rules on how to approach one another, how to engage in a "trade," and how to end the negotiation. At the end of each round, the point totals for each individual and group are tabulated and displayed so that the relative standings are known to all. Although the staff members indicate that individual scores count in announcing the winners, the totals are shown to illustrate the ranking of each group as a whole. Once the totals are shown, the staff members have each group exchange one member: the lowest scoring member in the best group is transferred to the next highest group, the best member in the worst group gets "promoted" to the next highest group, and so on.

The essence of this simulation is that the game, just as real life, is predetermined mainly by inequalities among the three groups. Initially the Squares are given a significant advantage, since their chips have higher point totals and their color combinations are more valued than the individuals in the other groups. There is also some initial difference between the Circles and the Triangles in the value of chips that they receive. (The ethics of deceiving the participants in this simulation should perhaps be questioned, as was discussed earlier!).

After several rounds it becomes quite clear that not only do the Squares have the highest point totals by far (presumably because of their better bargaining skills), but as the rounds continue the Squares get "richer" while the Circles and Triangles get "poorer." It is interesting to observe how the Squares stay relatively involved in the game while the others become disenchanted.

When it becomes apparent that the Circles and Triangles will never catch up to the Squares, the staff members intervene with the following instructions: "Since the Squares have done so well in their bargaining, they will be in charge of the rules of the game from now on, and they may make whatever changes they like." The authoritative stance of the staff generally makes this and other instructions acceptable to the participants (Milgram, 1965).

At this point the Squares usually form a physically closed circle of members as they enthusiastically plan the fate of the other two groups. Often the first rule that the Squares announce is that the Squares will always be in control of the game, or they proclaim themselves the winners and terminate the game. Sometimes they decide to change the value of the colored chips so that they have even higher point totals than the other two groups. When a member of the Squares suggests that perhaps they should change the rules so that the other groups may have an equal chance of winning the game, the outspoken individual is called a communist by the other Squares. Often a Square will make a comment such as, "I have never been able to make the rules before, and I am not going to give it up now!"

The game generally ends shortly after the Squares take over the rules. At this point the staff members attempt to suggest what occurred during the simulation and to draw analogies to real life situations. Frequently, however, the game ends with the participants wondering what the purpose of the game was and how it is at all relevant to their roles as managers. Then the staff asks such questions as, "How is the game similar to the distribution of wealth and power in society, and how do the various subgroups in society (i.e., upper class, middle class, lower class) respond to this distribution?" Also, "How did the participants feel when they were forced to move to a lower level group at the end of a round?" Or, "How did the participants feel toward their former group after they were permitted to move to a higher level group?"

Given these types of questions, participants will soon realize that in a short period they have recreated the attitudes, prejudices, and behaviors of those at various power and wealth stratas of society. And although these same educated managers advocate equality and express displeasure about the state of society, it is easy for them to forget or ignore these value statements and lose themselves in the competitive power dynamics of the simple game. If such behavior can be simulated with colored chips and staff instructions in so short a time, one must seriously consider the impact of forces and the inertia in real society where there is real money, real power, and a continuous stream of enforcements for the status quo. If participants can manifest their socialized behavior in a game setting so easily, what does it take to change these internalized (and partially unconscious) behaviors in actual society?

"Star Power" and MAPS

The "Star Power" simulation is extremely relevant to the issues of applying MAPS in our organized society. Consider two applications: (1) mobilizing the resources of the Circles and the Triangles to counteract the inefficiencies and motivational problems created by the Squares' control of money and power, and (2) mobilizing the total population of Squares, Circles, and Triangles into a more effective society.

Power Equalization at the Microlevel

Regarding the first application of MAPS mentioned above, in the simulation it is rare for the Circles and Triangles to unite and decide to combine their resources to overcome the Squares. It seems that the designation of groups (as Circles and Triangles) tends to keep them apart and dispersed. One application of MAPS would be for the Squares to indicate that they will remain the Squares and in control of the game, but that they do wish to create a more effective system by better mobilizing the resources of the Circles and the Triangles, by redesigning them into more cohesive and productive groups. In some ways this strategy is analogous to top management's use of job enrichment and morale building for those below them in the hierarchy.

Various experiences with MAPS, however, raise some doubts as to the likelihood of the Squares actually using MAPS for this purpose. There was an actual case in which the corporate offices of a large organization contained approximately 300 women who were dissatisfied with their impact and role in the organization (i.e., possibilities for promotion, influence on corporate decisions). Top management had engaged several behavioral scientists to counsel the women and to process their views. However, the women were dispersed throughout the corporate offices and could not often agree among themselves about what the key issues were and how they could best approach the issues with top management.

At this stage, MAPS was proposed to organize the women into viable action groups, since the women in each group could agree on the issues to be pursued and could work with one another on these issues. The task items would contain the issues that the women felt were important to them, and the MAPS analysis would cluster these issues into common themes so that the clusters could be independently pursued. The resulting action groups could then prepare effective recommendations to top management concerning the enhancement of women's roles and influence in the organization. When this approach was actually presented to top management, however, they responded by stating: "But what will happen when we start turning down the action recommendations of all the groups?"

It was not surprising that top management decided not to use MAPS but continued with counseling and process sessions for the women. Apparently top management did not want to utilize a technology that would mobilize the power and resources of the women and then have the women's groups confront them with their articulated and supported concerns. In this case, the Squares wanted to keep the Circles and the Triangles immobilized, yet attempted to pacify the needs of the lower level members with superficial activities.

Power Equalization at the Macrolevel

The second application of MAPS to consider involves the redesign of the total system. What would it take for the Squares to decide to include themselves in some grand MAPS analysis and make their influence in the final design no more or less than that of the other groups (i.e., the Circles and the Triangles). Such an application would be the ultimate in power equalization.

Thus far, no MAPS analysis has included the top decision makers in the design boundaries. In the largest application of MAPS to a division of 2,000 individuals (case 4 in Chapter 8), the first stage of MAPS involved the five levels of managers totaling 50 persons but did not include the vice-president and general manager of the division at the latter's own request. Thus the desire to stay on top seems to dominate the willingness to examine how a new design might redistribute resources more effectively. This was further shown in the Star Power simulation when individuals could advance from a lower group to the highest group after each round depending on their performance. In subsequent rounds, however, these individuals totally divorced themselves from their earlier memberships and did all they could to maintain themselves in their new, higher status group.

Perhaps the most fundamental test of top management's commitment to apply the MAPS Design Technology and to institute major change in the organization, is for top management to include themselves in the MAPS analysis. It might even be argued that the ethical stance discussed earlier in this chapter should require everyone within a division or department to be involved in the design assessment, including the top decision maker, otherwise the MAPS Design Technology should not be applied. In another actual case, the top manager decided to use MAPS for his division but would not include himself (case 5 in Chapter 8). When the issue of using MAPS was presented to the several department heads, they too decided that it would be more appropriate for their subordinates to be involved and not themselves. As it turned out, the subordinates did want to participate in MAPS but without the inclusion and full support of the top manager and the department heads, MAPS could do no more than work-group redesign and could not truly be a case of organization design. While the MAPS Design Technology was applied in this limited manner for research purposes, if such a situation occurred again, MAPS would probably not be utilized.

Ethics and Power Equalization

It may be too restrictive to indicate that everyone within some organizational boundary (i.e., a division) must be included if MAPS is to be applied since few organizations may meet this level of commitment. Therefore MAPS would not be applied where it still could foster the values it was intended to foster. On the other hand, it seems clear that if MAPS is downgraded in the hierarchy until only lower levels of the organization are willing (or required) to participate in the design process, then the objectives of MAPS will probably not be realized. An awareness of this power and status phenomenon could aid in explicitly confronting the Squares (i.e., top management) as to the reasons for their noninvolvement, and thus lead to the adoption of a definite stand when MAPS consultants feel that too many of the Squares are uninvolved. The latter situation seriously limits the potential usefulness of MAPS and most clearly violates its ethical guidelines.

It should be emphasized that with the two examples of MAPS applied to the simulation game (mobilizing the Circles and Triangles, and redesigning the total system) it was not intended to suggest that the objective of MAPS is power equalization per se. Power structures will always be a part of our institutions and organization designs. The issue is, however, power based on what and controlled by whom? We would argue (and some management literature supports this) that contemporary power structures are not based as much on competence, expertise, and valid information as they could be, and the structures themselves seem to be controlled more by those at the top of the hierarchy. MAPS is intended to reexamine the functionality of a given power structure (as well as of the information and decision-making structures) and to create new designs that more effectively distribute not only expertise (i.e., horizontal design categories) but also the control of individual and organizational behavior (i.e., vertical design categories). Thus the future of MAPS critically depends on whether organizations and society itself will be able to confront both substantive and ethical issues and be willing to implement new social systems designs. To facilitate such confrontation and experimentation is currently as much a part of the MAPS Design Technology as are the formal steps of the technology for actually creating and implementing new designs.

While Star Power highlights the issues involved in changing an organization's OPERATIONAL DESIGN, these same issues are slightly mitigated when MAPS is applied to create a PROBLEM-SOLVING or STRATEGIC PLANNING DESIGN. The latter two designs, as discussed in Chapters 4 and 7, are created to coexist with the organization's OPERATIONAL DESIGN. Thus the collateral design permits members to retain their power, status, and security positions in the formal day-to-day design (Zand, 1974). Increasingly, applications of MAPS (see Chapter 9) are using the collateral approach for the reasons suggested in the Star Power simulation: organizations are obviously more comfortable keeping their OPERATIONAL DESIGN intact and adding on a second design. This does not, however, eliminate all the problems inherent in the OPERATIONAL DESIGN, even though the PROBLEM-SOLVING DESIGN may help solve or manage some of these problems. At some point the members of the organization, while partaking in their PROBLEM-SOLVING DESIGN, might very well suggest the need to question and change the OPERATIONAL DESIGN. Perhaps this is more feasible than first approaching the redesign of the operational system because the members will have had some experience with the MAPS Design Technology (when they designed and implemented their PROBLEM-SOLVING DESIGN) that might make them more confident and willing to examine the functionality of the OPERATIONAL DESIGN and even attempt to change it!

THE FUTURE OF MAPS

At the outset it was stated that MAPS is intended to be a broad-based, interdisciplinary technology. Currently MAPS includes computer science, techniques of organization development work (e.g., diagnosis, management by objectives, team building, interteam building), inquiring systems from the philosophy of science, and elements of management information systems. As MAPS is applied to different social systems in different settings for different design objectives, the need to consider more formally and explicitly how MAPS must be linked with other social science ideas, concepts, and technologies will be further demonstrated.

A systems approach to organization and societal change thus requires the integration of concepts, methods, and technologies that address the many facets of social systems design. Each conceptual framework and technology will generally be limited in its impact if other technologies that address other variables are ignored or pursued independently. The classical method is for an organization to hire an organization development specialist, a personnel selection consultant, a specialist in pay and reward systems, a staff to conduct management education, an organization designer, and so on, and expect each to pursue his own specialty in working with the organization. The interdependencies among these approaches almost guarantee the failure of each program in meeting even its own objectives. Consequently, what is needed is a combined and integrated approach to assessing and then altering the many types of organizational parameters that influence organizational effectiveness (as discussed in Chapter 6).

It is expected that the MAPS Design Technology can serve as the foundation for such an integrated set of concepts and technologies. MAPS has shown the ability to highlight the need for integrating organizational practices as well as explicitly raising the issues concerning the ethics of social change. Also, MAPS seems to motivate organizational members to learn more about management and organizational knowledge, and to inquire how other technologies can be integrated with MAPS.

The future of the MAPS Design Technology can be represented schematically as several philosophical and substantive options (or possibilities) for MAPS researchers. The distinction between the quantitative (ST) versus the qualitative (NT, SF, NF) aspects of social science (Kilmann and Mitroff, 1976) and how these aspects may be further integrated with MAPS are illustrated in Figure 9.2. The overall design of MAPS as presented in this book is shown as Case A, which was first discussed in Chapter 4 and schematically shown in Figure 4.1. Case A reveals that the quantitative portions of MAPS, while central to the technology, is in a broader sense not as important as the

FIGURE 9.2   The Future of the MAPS Design Technology: Quantitative versus Qualitative Portions

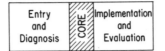

Case A.   Same as Figure 4.1 (The Present MAPS)

Case B.   Expanding the Core of MAPS

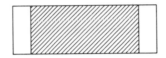

Case C.   An Extensive Core of MAPS

Case D.   Expanding All Portions for the Future of MAPS

qualitative aspects. Entry and diagnosis determine the validity of the data utilized for the MAPS Computer Program, while implementation and evaluation determine whether the potential of the MAPS design output will actually be manifested.

Case B portrays a possible future for MAPS that places a heavier emphasis on the quantitative aspects of the technology. Some of the MAPS methods that are currently qualitative and clinical can perhaps be incorporated in the core of MAPS (input, analysis, output) or even in the MAPS Computer Program.

For example, while the current MAPS analysis can suggest which groups of people should work on which cluster of tasks, the assignment must often be modified to consider resource capabilities (i.e., are five people really necessary to successfully address a particular task cluster?). As was discussed in Chapter 5, reassignments are often made during the implementation process as resource requirements and expectations are qualitatively considered in the negotiation steps. However, it is quite conceivable that resource issues can be formally incorporated into the core of MAPS. An additional section of the MAPS questionnaire might ask organizational members to indicate how much effort, time, or importance is attached to each task item, and then the resulting task and people clusters could be quantitatively adjusted (weighted) by such resource expectations and people and tasks could be reassigned to foster a better match-up of resources and needs. The additional section on the MAPS questionnaire could even be expanded by weighting a person's responses to each task item (his assessment of its resource demands) according to how well the individual feels he can make such an assessment (i.e., how well he actually understands the nature of the task).

As shown in Case B, a considerable portion of the MAPS Design Technology would still be qualitative. Case C, however, illustrates a future of MAPS in which the technology has become increasingly quantitative and less reliance is placed on qualitative methods. For some social scientists (Mitroff, 1974) Case C might even represent the epitome of a technology, because less emphasis is placed on subjective and value-laden criteria. In fact many traditional operations research (OR) techniques strive for complete quantification to eliminate such "imprecise" methods, and are criticized to the extent that quantification has not been fully achieved. It is our contention, however, that Case C is not only impossible to achieve (because social phenomena by their very nature will always contain subjective elements), but would not be desirable even if it were possible (according to the values of purposeful systems and free choice discussed in Chapter 2). Time, perhaps, may eventually disprove this, but extreme quantification seems to remove the unique feeling components of man, in the Jungian sense, that we may wish to retain (Jung, 1923).

Case D, shown in Figure 9.2, represents best where we would like to see MAPS develop for the future. One objective is to expand the core of MAPS (as shown in Case B) to include those additional aspects of social systems design that can reasonably and validly be quantified. Case D, however, recognizes that some aspects (and these are significant aspects) will always be qualitative in nature and in method, yet seeks to include and integrate a broader array of social science ideas, concepts, and technologies, as discussed earlier. The incorporation of these additional components would naturally broaden MAPS abilities and applications.

For example, a key issue that generally arises in the implementation of MAPS is how pay and reward systems will be affected or altered by a new design. If individuals are relocated to different groups and are working on different tasks, perhaps they should not only receive different salaries but the type of incentive system (bonuses, promotions, etc.) may also need to be different to provide the kind of reward conducive to individual and organizational effectiveness. Thus far, applications of MAPS have not attempted to manage this issue except to provide general discussions or to assure members before MAPS is used that their salaries will not be affected. It has become apparent, however, that a pay and reward system that is not consistent with the new design can serve to limit the potential impact of a design change. Certainly, if rewards reinforce behaviors more appropriate to the old design (e.g., individual vs. team objectives), the new design may only exist in theory and not in practice.

Similarly, a question generally arises about the method of hiring new people for the new design. For example, can a method be devised to recruit personnel that is more consistent with the behavioral objectives of the MAPS Design Technology (e.g., valid information and free choice) and that would not be confined by old design categories (stereotyped specializations) but would explore expertise which could be applied appropriately in the new design categories (Torbert, 1973)? In line with this, can members' ability and expertise be better assessed and utilized in the MAPS Design Technology? Currently MAPS attempts to make the most of given resources, and seeks to attain organizational effectiveness primarily by task arrangements, maximizing motivation and commitment, and by appropriate task and people combinations (although the ST instructions to the MAPS questionnaire involve an individual's assessment of his own expertise to perform each task item, and his assessment of the expertise of others via the people items; see Figures 4.5 and 4.6). But why take resources as given? Perhaps MAPS can incorporate not only the selection of individuals to enhance overall ability levels (in line with the nature of organizational tasks) but can also incorporate the training and development of relevant skills and abilities of organizational members in a more systematic manner than that described by the implementation process in Chapter 5.

CONCLUSIONS

The foregoing discussion and illustrations of alternative futures of MAPS pose a major challenge to social scientists. It is hoped that this book has laid the foundation for a significant social science technology, one that can address the important problem of social systems design. Although MAPS is still quite new, it is hoped that the ideas and discussions throughout this book will encourage others to engage in further research to investigate and expand the quantitative and qualitative portions of MAPS, or to develop other social science technologies. One thing is quite clear, however. Such technologies are needed if social science knowledge is to yield more effective social systems and, conversely, the development of technologies is incumbent on the integration of social science knowledge.

The Implemented Organization Design for Writing the MAPS Book

CHAPTER 1: ORGANIZATION DESIGN

Rose Constantino,
Afzalur Rahim,
Jerzy Zderkowski

Historical Development of Organization Design
Purpose of Organization Design
Cross-cultural Organization Design
Process versus Structural Approaches to Organizational Change

CHAPTER 2: PURPOSEFULNESS AND STRUCTURAL INTERVENTIONS

Steven E. Bangert,
David Breyer,
Dorothy M. Hai,
Hugo M. Schmidt

Models of Man
People can Design their own Organizations
Individual versus Organizational Values
Value Assumptions of MAPS
Existing Types of Organization Structure
Frequency of Structural Interventions
Designing a Matrix Organization by MAPS
Dynamics of Structural Interventions
Different Approaches for Structural Intervention

CHAPTER 3: DESIGN BOUNDARIES

Michael A. Belch,
Donald W. Dieter,
Frederick J. Slack,
David A. Smethers,
Rajendra K. Srivastava

Definition and Types of Boundaries
External Constraints on Design Boundaries
Need for Organizational Diagnosis
Implications of Design Boundaries for MAPS Effectiveness
Developing a Taxonomy for MAPS Technology
Development of Users Manual for MAPS
Training to be a MAPS Consultant

CHAPTER 4: THE CORE OF MAPS

Samandar N. Hai,
Robert T. Keim,
Ralph H. Kilmann,
Walter P. McGhee

Describe and Defend Questionnaire and How It Was Developed
Validity and Reliability of MAPS Questionnaire
Routinizing the Questionnaire Development Package
Possibilities for Other Variables on Questionnaire
Methods of Mathematical Analysis
Alternative Analytical Techniques—MAPS Analysis
Other Design Technologies
MAPS Computer Program
Output Format (Description)
Implications of Format for Design Decisions
New Information on MAPS Output

CHAPTER 5: IMPLEMENTATION

Rajaram B. Baliga,
Shankar R. Kapanipathi,
Vadake K. Narayanan

Selection Criteria for Design Decisions
Dynamics of Decision-Making Process
Implications of Design Decision for Implementation
Change Strategies for Implementation
Barriers to Design Change
Implementation Transition Process
Monitoring the Implementation Process

CHAPTER 6: EVALUATION

Richard P. Herden,
Jerome A. Kleinman

Feedback Mechanisms for Evaluation
Criteria and Measurement Devices for Evaluation
Limitations of MAPS
Need for Evaluation of MAPS Design
Frequency of Evaluating MAPS Design

CHAPTER 7: PROBLEM SOLVING

Kirk P. Kelly,
Marjorie A. Lyles,
John C. Ryan

Conflict Management in Problem Solving
Information System as a Function of Organization Design
Designing a Decision-Making System

CHAPTER 8: APPLICATIONS

Ralph H. Kilmann,
Joseph Seltzer

Current Application of MAPS
Sufficient Conditions for Application
MAPS for New Versus On-Going Organizations
Benefits of Applying MAPS

INTRODUCTION AND CONCLUSIONS; COORDINATION AND LEADERSHIP OF ENTIRE PROJECT

Ralph H. Kilmann,
Afzalur Rahim,
Dorothy M. Hai,
David A. Smethers,
Walter P. McGhee,
Shankar R. Kapanipathi,
Richard P. Herden,
Marjorie A. Lyles

Coordination of Literature Search
Coordinating Group Products
Coordinating Objectives of Subsystems
Monitoring the Performance and Satisfaction of BA 347 Members
Assessing Resource Needs of BA 347 Subsystems
Literature Support of MAPS
Coordination of Computer Editing
Editing and Reviewing Manuscript
Monitoring Organization Effectiveness of BA 347
Providing for Group Maintenance of BA 347

Appendix B

Task Items from Selected MAPS Questionnaires*

CASE 1
(Educational)

1. Educational innovation
2. Public systems research
3. Public and private market systems
4. Information systems
5. Business forecasting
6. Social control of management
7. Human resources, manpower, and industrial relations
8. Policy and environment research
9. Measurement
10. Operations research
11. Comparative and international studies
12. Development of human systems
13. Decision processes
14. Urban systems
15. Competition and business policy
16. Human being or person oriented studies
17. Institutional–organizational change
18. Accounting
19. Behavioral science
20. Business economics
21. Business and society
22. Computing sciences and applications
23. Finance
24. Housing, real estate and urban land economics
25. Insurance
26. Management theory and policy
27. Marketing
28. Operations management
29. Personnel management and industrial relations
30. Quantitative methods
31. Socio-technical systems

CASE 3
(Community Service)

1. Determining who should participate in SCP conferences
2. Evaluation of present BA 251 and BA 252 program (behavioral science)
3. Determining common needs of minority businessmen
4. Determining relationship of SCP experiences to the entire GSB
5. Deciding on resource allocation and reward structure
6. Determining the decision making process in the SCP organization
7. What sources are available for funding SCP
8. Getting relevant information on to potential clients of SCP
9. Determining the editorial policy of the SCP newsletter
10. Determining the type and scope of research activities in SCP

*See Table 8.1 for Cases 1, 3, 4, 6, 7, 11, and 13.

11. Determining the allocation of resources and funding of the SCP newsletter
12. Design accredited undergraduate course relating to minority enterprises
13. Coordinating agenda of SCP conferences
14. Designing curriculum of courses for minority businessmen
15. Matching of SCP students to SCP clients
16. Designing a temporary structure for SCP
17. Planning for future funding of SCP
18. Compiling the mailing list to reach clients
19. Relating the SCP newsletter to public relations
20. Obtaining and allocating resources for support of research in SCP
21. Examining relationship between SCP and individual career orientations
22. Integration of specific problems of minority business into other GSB classes
23. Handling financial matters of SCP conferences
24. Planning the instruction of courses for minority businessmen: teachers and teaching methods
25. Determining the size and composition of teams that provide service to clients
26. Building a flexible SCP organization
27. Getting faculty more involved in SCP
28. Helping clients make competitive bids for contracts
29. Handling the administrative aspects of the SCP newsletter
30. Designing research activities in SCP
31. Assessing issues and problems that developed last year in SCP
32. Guiding changes and transitions in the SCP organization
33. Providing continuity of service to SCP clients
34. Evaluation of organizational structure
35. Fostering faculty and administrative support of SCP
36. Evaluating the bidding system
37. Getting input from other MBA students on curriculum changes
38. Evaluating SCP conferences
39. Evaluating the impact of courses for minority businessmen
40. Defining client-consultant role
41. Planning for a continuing organizational structure of SCP
42. Generating greater community involvement in SCP
43. Evaluating effect of client-consultant relationships

CASE 4
(Industrial)

1. Provide customer reports covering resolution of problem areas
2. Insure uniform internal job scope understanding between marketing and engineering
3. Acquaint or sell customer on proposed system capability
4. Furnish technical support in meetings with the customer

5. Prepare marketing abstract and justification for new products
6. Analyze present products for standardization opportunities
7. Analyze present system designs and application for standardization opportunities
8. Review proposal for cost reduction before giving to customer
9. Review purchase order and define areas not in agreement with proposal scope
10. Submit preliminary drawings of new applications to customer for approval
11. Prepare actual operating performance documentation
12. Establish price of proposal to customer
13. Obtain customer concurrence with detailed system description
14. Prepare selling strategy to influence customer on best / profitable approach
15. Gather information and analyze competitive products
16. Determine standard equipment
17. Establish design approach standards
18. Estimate hardware content, materials, engineering content and cost
19. Prepare detailed system description
20. Meet with customer on final job close out
21. Determine what products can be obsoleted as a result of development
22. Establish new product parameters
23. Develop selling and promotional programs for new products
24. Determine effort and resources

to be expended in developing systems proposal
25. Provide project status information to customer
26. Establish system acceptance test and get customer agreement
27. Participate in specification review with customer
28. Monitor new product development program
29. Review customer specifications and assure understanding of same
30. Evaluate alternate design approaches to new products
31. Resolve technical problems with designated customer representative
32. Develop market plans for systems for the served market
33. Negotiate with customer for money to cover scope change
34. Develop and implement close out strategy to sell customer
35. Conduct market research type activity to determine new product requirements
36. Decide that customer must pay for scope change
37. Determine system delivery date
38. Evaluate new product performance
39. Recommend design changes to simplify, reduce cost and standardize
40. Establish system design standards
41. Develop new product sales promotion and literature
42. Verify technical completion of the job in accordance with scope and specifications
43. Analyze and determine cause of an unsuccessful bid
44. Resolve technical differences in job scope with customer

45. Coordinate new assemblies to utilize standard parts
46. Estimate new product cost
47. Determine effect of scope change on project schedule and delivery
48. Meet with customer, identify and develop probable sales opportunities
49. Make presentation of proposal to customer
50. Prepare service manuals for customer
51. Determine market conditions influencing product standardization
52. Establish component and device standardization design guidelines
53. Plan customer approach, analyze competitive and commercial factors
54. Develop system concept or adapt existing concept to customer need
55. Introduce new products to the customer
56. Establish component standards
57. Assure that all cost considerations are resolved on final job close out
58. Estimate cost involved in a scope change
59. Develop selling plan for customer buying influences aimed at closing the order
60. Attempt to influence customer specifications
61. Prepare technical abstract including cost and schedules
62. Identify present product deficiencies
63. Determine if all customer obligations have been met
64. Identify new product opportunities

CASE 6
(Financial)

1. Account reconciliation
2. Audio system
3. Corporate bondholders
4. Corporate interface
5. Central information files
6. Certificates and bonds
7. Charge account checking
8. Commercial loans
9. Community office procedure manual
10. Cost and time analysis
11. Data processing standards and procedures
12. Demand deposits
13. Edutronics coordination
14. Financial control
15. Fixed assets
16. Floor plans
17. Installment loans
18. Management assistance program
19. Charge plates
20. Mortgages
21. Microfiche support
22. Payroll
23. Personal savings
24. Personnel system
25. Portfolio analysis
26. Referral system
27. Savings club
28. Shareholders
29. Software support
30. Special projects
31. Teleprocessing systems
32. Teleprocessing training
33. Test time coordination
34. Trust
35. Work order system

CASE 7
(Retail)

1. New car sales
2. Used car sales
3. Developing a customer relations and customer satisfaction program
4. Implementing a customer relations and satisfaction program
5. Mechanical repairs
6. Service selling
7. Service management
8. Developing service and parts merchandising programs
9. Body and fender repairs
10. Clerical responsibility (general office)
11. Accounting responsibility
12. Office management
13. Titling and licensing responsibility
14. Developing a daily rental program
15. Implementing a daily rental program
16. Developing a leasing program
17. Implementing a term leasing program
18. Developing a finance and insurance department
19. Implementing a finance and insurance program
20. Organizing the social aspects of the company, employee parties, etc.; recreation, etc.
21. Serving on an employee-management relations committee
22. Develop an advertising program
23. Implementing an advertising program
24. Develop new and used car merchandising program
25. Develop incentive programs
26. Parts selling
27. Parts management
28. Body and fender shop management
29. Maintenance department
30. Detail shop duties
31. Serve on a committee for future development and expansion
32. Gather information and analyze competitive products and prices
33. Develop marketing strategies and programs
34. Develop employee improvement programs—I. C. training, special courses, testbooks, etc.
35. Committee for civic activities

CASE 11
(Executives)

1. Environmental change
2. Personal anxiety
3. External imposition
4. What changed
5. Why anxiety
6. Who is involved
7. Problem specificity
8. Data assembly
9. Examining alternatives
10. Testing alternatives
11. Analyzing results
12. Selecting solutions
13. Program change
14. Establish system
15. Review progress
16. Review records for variances or abnormalities
17. Look for better ways of doing something

18. Seek other views of what problems exist
19. Analyze areas where a problem is potentially applicable
20. Determine how critical a problem is
21. Conceiving alternative approaches to a problem
22. Determine and organize available data and resources
23. Develop problem-solving strategies
24. Integrate data and strategies available
25. Data collection
26. Testing validity of data and models
27. Perform mathematical manipulations and analysis
28. Write procedures
29. Train people
30. Introduce innovative mechanisms
31. Examination of outside factors that have impact
32. Comparison of problems with others in our field
33. Setting up goals and standards
34. Determining cause-effect relationships
35. Placing problems into approach categories
36. Matching problems to corporate resources and impact
37. Locating needed expertise

38. Definition of what constitutes a solution
39. Examination of previous models
40. Documentation of time and task structure
41. Examination of resources
42. Study of model reliability
43. Matching available resources to model
44. Organization of task forces
45. Progress reporting
46. Disturbance of personal state of equilibrium
47. Objective inputs or constraints—five senses
48. Subjective recognition—intuition
49. Formation of mental images from a perceptual trigger
50. Focusing on potential problems, contingency planning
51. Find root cause of problem
52. Definition of root or source of problem
53. Define objectives, strategies and tactics
54. Developing model that is pragmatic and realistic
55. Recognition of variables
56. Reconciliation of variables
57. Resolution of variables
58. State solution precisely and concisely
59. Sell solution to gain agreement
60. Synergistic acceptance of solution and self-implementation

CASE 13
(Doctoral Seminar)

1. Historical development of organization design
2. Existing types of organization structure
3. Models of man
4. Definition and types of boundaries

5. Describe and defend questionnaire and how it was developed
6. Methods of mathematical analysis
7. Selection criteria for design decisions
8. Output format (description)

9. Change strategies for implementation
10. Feedback mechanisms for evaluation
11. Conflict management in problem solving
12. Current applications of MAPS
13. Coordination of literature search
14. Purpose of organization design
15. Frequency of structural intervention
16. People can design their own organizations
17. External constraints on design boundaries
18. Validity and reliability of MAPS questionnaire
19. Alternative analytical techniques—MAPS analysis
20. Implications of format for design decisions
21. Dynamics of decision-making process
22. Barriers to design change
23. Criteria and measurement devices for evaluation
24. Information system as a function of organization design
25. Sufficient conditions for application
26. Coordinating group products
27. Need for organizational diagnosis
28. Coordinating objectives of subsystems
29. Routinizing the questionnaire development package
30. Designing a matrix organization by MAPS
31. Other design technologies
32. Limitations of MAPS
33. Monitoring the performance and satisfaction of BA 347 members
34. Process vs. structural approaches to organization change
35. Assessing resource needs of BA 347 sub-systems

36. Literature support for MAPS
37. Dynamics of structural interventions
38. Individual vs. organizational values
39. Implications of design boundaries for MAPS effectiveness
40. Possibilities for other variables on questionnaire
41. MAPS computer program
42. New information on MAPS output
43. Implications of design decision for implementation
44. Implementation transition process
45. Need for evaluation of MAPS design
46. Designing a decision-making system
47. Developing a taxonomy for MAPS technology
48. Coordination of computer editing
49. Editing and reviewing manuscript
50. Value assumptions of MAPS
51. Monitoring the implementation process
52. Cross-cultural organization design
53. Development of users manual for MAPS
54. Different approaches for structural intervention
55. Frequency of evaluating MAPS design
56. Training to be a MAPS consultant
57. MAPS for new vs. on-going organization
58. Benefits of applying MAPS
59. Monitoring organization effectiveness of BA 347
60. Providing for group maintenance of BA 347

References

Abert, J. G., and M. Kamrass

1974 *Social Experiments and Social Program Evaluation.* Cambridge, Mass.: Ballinger Publishing Company.

Ackoff, R. L.

1967 "Management misinformation systems," *Management Science,* 14:B147–156.

1970 *A Concept of Corporate Planning.* New York: Wiley.

1971 "Towards a system of system concepts," *Management Science,* 17:661–671.

Ackoff, R. L., and E. Emery

1972 *On Purposeful Systems.* Chicago: Aldine-Atherton.

Alexander, C.

1964 *Notes on the Synthesis of Form.* Cambridge, Mass.: Harvard University Press.

Ansoff, H. I.

1965 *Corporate Strategy.* New York: McGraw-Hill.

Ansoff, H. I., and R. G. Brandenburg

1971 "A language for organization design: Part I & II," *Management Science,* 17:705–731.

Anthony, R.

1965 *Planning and Control Systems: A Framework for Analysis.* Boston: Harvard University Press.

Argyris, C.

1957 *Personality and Organization.* New York: Harper.

1962 *Interpersonal Competence and Organizational Effectiveness.* Homewood, Ill.: Richard D. Irwin.

1964 *Integrating the Individual into the Organization.* New York: Wiley.

1970a *Intervention Theory and Method.* Reading, Mass.: Addison-Wesley.

1970b "T-Groups for organizational effectiveness," in G. W. Dalton, et al. (Eds.), *Organizational Change and Development.* Homewood, Ill.: Dorsey.

Argyris, C., and D. Schon

1975 *Theory in Practice, Increasing Professional Effectiveness.* San Francisco: Jossey-Bass.

Atkinson, J. W.

1958 *Motives in Fantasy, Action, and Society.* Princeton, N.J.: Van Nostrand.

Babbage, C.

1969 "Division of labor," in J. A. Litterer (Ed.), *Organizations*, vol. I, 2nd ed. New York: Wiley.

Barnard, C. I.

1938 *The Functions of the Executive.* Cambridge, Mass.: Harvard University Press.

Bass, B. M.

1970 "When planning for others," *Journal of Applied Behavioral Science*, 6:151–171.

Beckhard, R.

1967 "The confrontation meeting," *Harvard Business Review*, 45:149 –153.

1972 "Optimizing team-building efforts," *Journal of Contemporary Business*, 1:23–32.

Bennis, W. G.

1966a *Changing Organizations.* New York: McGraw-Hill.

1966b "Theory and method in applying behavioral science to planned organizational change," in J. Lawrence (Ed.), *Operational Research and the Social Sciences.* London: Tavistock.

1969a *Organization Development: Its Nature, Origins, and Prospects.* Reading, Mass.: Addison-Wesley.

1969b "Unresolved problems facing organizational development," *The Business Quarterly*, 34:80–84.

Bennis, W. G., K. D. Benne, and R. Chin

1969 *The Planning of Change*, 2nd ed. New York: Holt, Rinehart and Winston.

Blake, R. R., and J. S. Mouton

1961 *Group Dynamics—Key to Decision Making.* Houston, Texas: Gulf.

1964 *The Managerial Grid.* Houston, Texas: Gulf.

Blake, R. R., J. S. Mouton, and R. L. Sloma

1965 "The union-management intergroup laboratory: strategy for resolving intergroup conflict," *Journal of Applied Behavioral Science*, 1:25–57.

Blau, P. M., and R. A. Schoenherr

1971 *The Structure of Organizations.* New York: Basic Books.

Bobbitt, H. R., R. H. Breinholt, R. H. Doktor, and J. P. McNaul

1974 *Organizational Behavior.* Englewood Cliffs, N.J.: Prentice-Hall.

Bouchard, T. J.

1969 "Personality, problem-solving procedure and performance in small groups," *Journal of Applied Psychology Monograph,* No. 53.

Boulding, K. E.

1956 *The Image.* Ann Arbor, Mich.: University of Michigan Press.

Bowen, D. D., and R. H. Kilmann

1975 "Developing a comparative measure of the learning climate in professional schools," *Journal of Applied Psychology,* 60:71–79.

Bowers, D. G.

1973 "OD techniques and their results in 23 organizations: The Michigan ICL Study," *Journal of Applied Behavioral Science,* 9:21–43.

Bradford, L. P., J. R. Gibb, and K. D. Benne

1964 *T-Group theory and laboratory method.* New York: Wiley.

Buckley, W.

1967 *Sociology and Modern Systems Theory.* Englewood Cliffs, N.J.: Prentice-Hall.

Bucklow, M.

1966 "A new role for the work group," *Administrative Science Quarterly,* 11:59–78.

Burns, T., and G. M. Stalker

1961 *The Management of Innovation.* London: Tavistock.
1969 "On mechanistic and organic systems," in J. A. Litterer (Ed.), *Organizations,* vol. II, 2nd ed., New York: Wiley, 345–348.

Business Week

1973 "Where being nice to workers didn't work," January 20, 99–100.

Campbell, D. T., and J. C. Stanley

1963 *Experimental and Quasi-Experimental Designs for Research.* Chicago: Rand McNally.

Campbell, J. P.

1968 "Individual versus group problem solving in an industrial sample," *Journal of Applied Psychology*, 52:205–210.

Carey, Alex

1967 "The Hawthorne studies: A radical criticism," *American Sociological Review*, 32:403–416.

Catell, R. B.

1952 *Factor Analysis: An Introduction and Manual for the Psychologist and Social Scientist.* New York: Harper.

Chandler, A. P., Jr.

1962 *Strategy and Structure.* Cambridge, Mass.: M.I.T. Press.

Churchman, C. W.

1971 *The Design of Inquiring Systems.* New York: Basic Books.

Clark, P. A.

1972a *Organizational Design.* London: Tavistock.
1972b *Action Research and Organizational Change.* London: Harper & Row.
1976 "Key problems in organizational design," in R. H. Kilmann, L. R. Pondy, and D. P. Slevin (Eds.), *The Management of Organization Design: Volume I, Strategies and Implementation.* New York: Elsevier North-Holland.

Clark, P. A., and J. R. Ford

1970 "Methodological and theoretical problems in the investigation of planned organizational change," *Sociological Review*, 18:403–416.

Cleland, D. I., and W. R. King

1974 "Organizing for long range planning," *Business Horizons*, 17:25–32.

Coch, L., and J. R. French, Jr.

1948 "Overcoming resistance to change," *Human Relations*, 1:512–532.

Collins, B. E., and H. S. Guetzkow

1964 *A Social Psychology of Group Processes for Decision Making.* New York: Wiley.

Conant, E. H., and M. D. Kilbridge

1965 "An interdisciplinary analysis of job enlargement: Technology, cost, and behavioral implications," *Industrial and Labor Relations Review*, 18.

Conference Board

1974 Planning and the Corporate Director, Report No. 627, New York: Conference Board.

Coons, W.

1967 "The dynamics of change in psychotherapy," *Canadian Psychiatric Association Journal*, 12:241.

Cowan, T. A.

1972 "Paradoxes of science administration," *Science*, 177:964–966.

Cronback, L. S.

1951 "Coefficient alpha and the internal structure of tests," *Psychometrika*, 16:297–334.

Dalton, M.

1959 *Men Who Manage*. New York: Wiley.

Davis, K.

1967 *Human Relations at Work*. New York: McGraw-Hill.

Davis, L. E.

1971 "The coming crisis of production management: Technology and organization," *International Journal of Production Research*, 9:65–82.

Davis, L. E., and R. R. Canter

1956 "Job design research," *Journal of Industrial Engineering*, 71.

Davis, L. E., and R. Werling

1960 "Job design factors," *Occupational Psychology*, 34.

Davis, S. A.

1967 "An organic problem-solving method of organizational change," *Journal of Applied Behavioral Science*, 3:3–21.

Delamter, J.

1974 "A definition of group," *Small Group Behavior*, 5:30 – 44.

Derr, C. B.

1972 "Successful entry as a key to successful organization development in big city school systems," in W. W. Burke, and H. A. Hornstein (Eds.), *The Social Technology of Organizational Development*. Fairfax, Va.: NTL Learning Resources.

Deutsch, M.

1951 "Task structure and group process," *American Psychologist*, 6:324–325.

Dickson, J. W., and D. P. Slevin

1973 "The use of semantic differential scales in studying the innovation boundary," Working Paper No. 46, Graduate School of Business, University of Pittsburgh.

Dill, W. R.

1958 "Environment as an influence on managerial autonomy," *Administrative Science Quarterly*, 2:409 – 443.

Drucker, P. F.

1954 *The Practice of Management*. New York: Harper.

DuBrin, A. J.

1974 *Fundamentals of Organizational Behavior*. New York: Pergamon.

Duncan, R. B.

1972 "The implementation of different decision making structures in adapting to environmental uncertainty: An expansion of contingency theories of management," *Academy of Management Proceedings*, 39 – 47.

Eells, R.

1972 "Multinational corporation: The intelligence function," in C. C. Brown (Ed.), *World Business: Promise and Problems*. New York: Macmillan.

Emery, P. E., and E. L. Trist

1971 "The causal texture of organization environments," in J. G. Maurer (Ed.), *Readings in Organization Theory: Open Systems Approaches*. New York: Random House.

Etzioni, A.

1964 *Modern Organizations*, Englewood Cliffs, N.J.: Prentice-Hall.
1965 "Organizational control structure," in J. March (Ed.), *Handbook of Organizations*. Chicago: Rand McNally, 650 – 677.

Evans, Martin G.

1974 "Failure in OD programs—what went wrong?," *Business Horizons*, 17:18–22.

Fayol, H.

1949 *General and Industrial Management*. Trans. by Constance Storrs, London: Pitman.

Feldman, J., and H. E. Kantor

1965 "Organizational decision-making," in J. G. March (Ed.), *Handbook of Organizations.* Chicago: Rand McNally, 614–649.

Fenno, R. F.

1964 "The House Appropriations Committee as a political system," in J. H. Leavitt and L. R. Pondy (Eds.), *Readings in Managerial Psychology.* Chicago: University of Chicago Press, 354–381.

French, W.

1972 "Organizational development: Objectives, assumptions, and strategies," *California Management Review,* 12: 37–52.

French, W., and C. H. Bell, Jr.

1973 *Organization Development: Behavioral Science Interventions for Organization Improvement.* Englewood Cliffs, N.J.: Prentice-Hall.

Friedlander F., and N. Margulies

1969 "Multiple impacts of organizational climate and individual value systems upon job satisfaction," *Personnel Psychology,* 22:171–183.

Fuick, S. L., et. al.

1971 "Organizational crisis and change," *Journal of Applied Behavioral Science,* 7.

Galbraith, J.

1970 "Environmental and technological determinants of organizational design," in J. W. Lorsch and P. R. Lawrence (Eds.), *Studies in Organization Design.* Homewood, Ill.: Dorsey-Irwin, 113–139.

1973 *Designing Complex Organizations.* Reading, Mass.: Addison-Wesley.

Gantt, Henry L.

1919 *Organizing for Work.* New York: Harcourt, Brace, Howe.

George, C. S., Jr.

1968 *The History of Management Thought.* Englewood Cliffs, N.J.: Prentice-Hall.

Gerth, H. H., and C. W. Mills (Eds.)

1958 *From Max Weber: Essays in Sociology.* New York: Oxford.

Gerwin, D.

1976 "A system framework for organizational structural design," in R. H. Kilmann, L. R. Pondy, and D. P. Slevin (Eds.), *The Management of Organization Design: Volume I, Strategies and Implementation.* New York: Elsevier North-Holland.

Ghymn, K.

1974 "Strategic Intelligence System for International Corporations: An Exploratory Study," Ph.D. Thesis, University of Pittsburgh.

Gibson, J. L., J. M. Ivancevich, and J. H. Donnelly, Jr.

1973 *Organizations: Structure, Processes, Behavior.* Dallas: Business Publications.

Gilbreth, F. B.

1914 *Primer of Scientific Management,* 2nd ed. New York: Van Nostrand.

Golembiewski, R. T.

1965 "Small groups and large organizations," in J. G. March (Ed.), *Handbook of Organizations.* Chicago: Rand McNally, 87–141.

1972 *Reviewing Organizations: The Laboratory Approach to Planned Change.* Itasca, Ill.: F. E. Peacock.

Golembiewski, R. T., and A. Blumberg

1968 "The laboratory approach to organization change: 'Confrontation design,' " *Academy of Management Journal*, 2:199–210.

Golembiewski, R. T., and R. Munzenrider

1973 "Persistence and change: A note on the long-term effects of an organization development program," *Academy of Management Journal*, 16:149–153.

Gordon, M. J., and G. Shillinglaw

1964 *Accounting: A Management Approach,* 3rd Ed. Homewood, Ill.: Richard D. Irwin.

Greiner, L. E.

1967 "Patterns of organization change," *Harvard Business Review*, 95:119–130.

Gulick, L.

1969 "Structure and coordination," in J. A. Litterer (Ed.), *Organizations*, vol. I, 2nd ed. New York: Wiley, 107–110.

Gulick, L., and L. Urwick (Eds.)

1937 *Papers on the Science of Public Administration.* New York: Columbia University, Institute of Public Administration.

Hage, J., and M. Aiken

1967 "Relationship of centralization to other structural properties," *Administrative Science Quarterly*, 12:72–92.

Haines, D. B., and W. J. McKeachie

1967 "Cooperative versus competitive discussion methods in teaching introductory psychology," *Journal of Education Psychology*, 58:386–390.

Hammond, L. K., and M. Guildman

1961 "Competition and non-competition and its relationship to individual and group productivity," *Sociometry*, 24:46–60.

Harman, H. H.

1967 *Modern Factor Analysis*, rev. ed. Chicago: University of Chicago Press.

Harrison, R.

1970 "Choosing the depth of organizational intervention," *Journal of Applied Behavioral Science*, 6:181–202.

Harvey, E.

1968 "Technology and the structure of organization," *American Sociological Review*, 33:247–259.

Herbst, P. G.

1962 *Autonomous Group Functioning*. London: Tavistock.

Herzberg, F.

1968 "One more time: How do you motivate employees," *Harvard Business Review*, 46.

Herzberg, F., B. Mausner, and B. B. Snyderman

1959 *The Motivation to Work*. New York: Wiley.

Hickson, D. J., D. S. Pugh, and C. P. Pheysey

1969 "Operations technology and organizational structure: A reappraisal," *Administrative Science Quarterly*, 14:378–397.

Hoffman, L. R., and N. R. F. Maier

1964 "Quality of acceptance of problem solutions by members of homogeneous and heterogeneous groups," in W. E. Vinacke, W. R. Wilson, and G. M. Meredity (Eds.), *Dimensions of Social Psychology*. Chicago: Scott, Foresman, 425–432.

House, R. J.

1968 "Leadership training: some disfunctional consequences," *Administrative Science Quarterly*, 12:556–771.

Hughes, C. L.

1965 *Goal Setting: Key to Individual and Organizational Effectiveness*. New York: American Management Association.

Jackson, D. N., and S. Messick (Eds.)

1967 *Problems in Human Assessment*. New York: McGraw-Hill.

Johnson, R. A., F. E. Kast, and J. E. Rosenzweig

1973 *The Theory and Management of Systems*, 3rd ed. New York: McGraw-Hill.

Julian, J. W., and E. A. Perry

1967 "Cooperation contrasted with intra-group and inter-group competition," *Sociometry*, 30:79–90.

Jung, C. G.

1923 *Psychological Types*. London: Routledge.
1960 *The Structure and Dynamics of the Psyche*. New York: Pantheon.

Kaplan, A.

1964 *The Conduct of Inquiry*. San Francisco: Chandler.

Katz, D., and R. L. Kahn

1966 *The Social Psychology of Organizations*. New York: Wiley.

Keim, R. T., and R. H. Kilmann

1975 "A longitudinal investigation of alternative implementation processes," *Proceedings of the M.I.T. Implementation Conference*. Cambridge, Mass.: Sloan School.

Kilmann, R. H.

1974a "The effect of interpersonal values on laboratory training: An empirical investigation," *Human Relations*, 27:247–265.
1974b "An extension of the risk-shift phenomenon to achievement and affiliation concerns," *Psychological Reports*, 35:845–846.
1974c "The MAPS approach to curriculum innovation," *Proceedings of the Eastern Academy of Management*, May.
1974d "An organic adaptive organization: The MAPS method," *Personnel*, 51:35–47.
1974e "Participative management in the college classroom," *Journal of Applied Psychology*, 59:337–338.
1975a "Designing and developing a 'real' organization in the classroom," *Academy of Management Journal*, 18:143–148.
1975b "A quasi-experimental paradigm for organizational development: Intervention strategies vs. environmental conditions," *Proceedings of the Eastern Academy of Management*, April.

Kilmann, R. H., and K. Ghymn

"Designing strategic intelligence systems for multinational corporations via the MAPS Design Technology: theoretical and empirical perspectives," *Organization and Administrative Sciences,* in press.

Kilmann, R. H., and W. R. King

1975 "Conceptual framework, strategic issues and preliminary illustrations for the management science study," Working paper, Graduate School of Business, University of Pittsburgh.

Kilmann, R. H., and the MAPS Group

1976 "MAPS as a design technology to effectively mobilize resources for social and organizational problem solving," in R. H. Kilmann, L. R. Pondy, and D. P. Slevin (Eds.), *The Management of Organization Design: Volume I, Strategies and Implementation.* New York: Elsevier North-Holland.

Kilmann, R. H., and B. McKelvey

1975 "The MAPS route to better organization design," *California Management Review,* 17:23–31.

Kilmann, R. H., and I. I. Mitroff

1975 "Towards an integrated philosophic–technical methodology for organization design," Working Paper No. 98, Graduate School of Business, University of Pittsburgh.

1976 "Qualitative versus quantitative analysis for management science: Different forms for different psychological types," *Interfaces,* February.

1977 *The Management of Real World Problem Solving: A Social Science Approach.* In preparation.

Kilmann, R. H., and R. Nath

1973 "An organic methodology for the use of behavioral exercises for management development," *Proceedings of the Eastern Academy of Management,* April.

Kilmann, R. H., L. R. Pondy, and D. P. Slevin (Eds.)

1976 *The Management of Organization Design: Volumes I and II.* New York: Elsevier North-Holland.

Kilmann, R. H., and A. Rahim

1975 "The management of conflict through effective organization design: The MAPS approach," Working Paper No. 100, Graduate School of Business, University of Pittsburgh.

Kilmann, R. H., and J. Seltzer

1975 "An experimental test of organization design theory and the MAPS design technology: Homogeneous versus heterogeneous composition of organizational subsystems," *Proceedings of the Eastern Academy of Management*, May.

Kilmann, R. H., and V. Taylor

1974 "A contingency approach to laboratory learning: Psychological types versus experiential norms," *Human Relations*, 27:891–909.

Kilmann, R. H., and K. W. Thomas

1974 "Four perspectives on conflict management," Working Paper No. 86, Graduate School of Business, University of Pittsburgh.

King, D. C., and J. J. Sherwood

1974 "Monitoring the process and evaluating the results of organization development," Institute Paper, Krannert Graduate School of Industrial Administration, Purdue University.

King, W. R.

1965 "A stochastic personnel-assignment model," *Operations Research*, 13.

1974 "Intelligent management information systems," Working Paper No. 35, Graduate School of Business, University of Pittsburgh.

King, W. R., and D. I. Cleland

1973 "Decision and information systems for strategic planning," *Business Horizons*, April, 29–36.

Kish, L.

1961 "Selection of the Sample," in L. Festinger and D. Katz (Eds.), *Research Methods in the Behavioral Sciences*. New York: Holt, Rinehart and Winston.

Koontz, H., and C. O'Donnell

1972 *Principles of Management*, 5th Ed. New York: McGraw-Hill.

Lawrence, P. R.

1973 "Why the change worked," *Journal of Applied Behavioral Science*, 9:636–637.

Lawrence, P. R., and J. W. Lorsch

1967a *Organization and Environment*. Homewood, Ill.: Dorsey-Irwin.

1967b "Differentiation and integration in complex organizations," *Administrative Science Quarterly*, 12:1– 47.

1967c "New management job: The integrator," *Harvard Business Review*, November–December, 142–151.

1969 *Developing Organizations: Diagnosis and Action.* Reading, Mass.: Addison-Wesley.

Leavitt, H. G.

1975 "Applied organizational change in industry: Structural, technological and humanistic approaches," in J. G. March (Ed.), *Handbook of Organizations.* Chicago: Rand McNally, 1144–1170.

Lewin, K.

1947 "Group decision and social change," in J. M. Newcomb and E. L. Hartley (Eds.), *Readings in Social Psychology*, New York: Holt, Rinehart and Winston.

1951 *Field Theory in Social Sciences.* D. Cartwright (Ed.), New York: Harper.

Likert, R.

1961 *New Patterns of Management.* New York: McGraw-Hill.

1967 *The Human Organization.* New York: McGraw-Hill.

1974 "The nature of highly effective groups," in D. A. Kolb, I. M. Rubin, and J. M. McIntyre (Eds.), *Organizational Psychology: A Book of Readings*, 2nd ed. Englewood Cliffs, N.J.: Prentice-Hall, 189–201.

Lippitt, G. L.

1969 *Organization Renewal.* New York: Appleton-Century-Crofts.

1973 *Visualizing Change.* NTL Learning Resources Corporation.

Loevinger, J.

1967 "Objective tests as instruments of psychological theory," in D. M. Jackson and S. Messick (Eds.), *Problems in Human Assessment.* New York: McGraw-Hill.

Lorsch, J. W., and P. R. Lawrence

1970 *Studies in Organization Design.* Homewood, Ill.: Dorsey-Irwin.

MacKinnon, D. W.

1962 "The nature and nurture of creative talent," *American Psychologist*, 17:484–495.

Malone, E. L.

1975 "Non-linear systems, Inc.: An experiment in participative management that failed," *Management Review*, 64:36– 43.

Mann, F. C.

1957 "Studying and creating change: A means to understanding social organization,"*Research in Industrial Human Relations*. Industrial Relations Research Association, 146–167.

March, J. G., and H. A. Simon

1958 *Organizations*. New York: Wiley.

Margulies, N., and A. P. Raia (Eds.)

1972 *Organizational Development: Values, Process, and Technology*. New York: McGraw-Hill.

Marshall, I. N.

1967 "The four functions: A conceptual analysis," *Journal of Analytical Psychology*, 12:1–31.

Maslow, A. H.

1954 *Motivation and Personality*. New York: Harper.
1962 *Toward a Psychology of Being*. New York: Van Nostrand.
1966 *The Psychology of Science: A Reconnaissance*. New York: Harper & Row.

Mason, R. O.

1969 "A dialectical approach to strategic planning," *Management Science*, 15:B403–413.

Mason, R. O., and I. I. Mitroff

1973 "A program for research on management information systems," *Management Science*, 19:475– 487.

Mayo, Elton

1933 *The Human Problems of an Industrial Civilization*. New York: Macmillan.

McClelland, D. C.

1961 *The Achieving Society*. New York: Van Nostrand.

McGregor, D.

1960 *The Human Side of Enterprise*. New York: McGraw-Hill.

McKelvey, B.

1976 "Toward more comprehensive organization design objectives," in R. H. Kilmann, L. R. Pondy, and D. P. Slevin (Eds.),

The Management of Organization Design. Elsevier North-Holland.

McKelvey, B., and R. H. Kilmann

1973 "Participative multivariate differentiation towards purposefulness," *Academy of Management Proceedings,* August, 489–495.

1975 "Organization design: A participative multivariate approach," *Administrative Science Quarterly,* 20:24–36.

McWhinney, W. H.

1971 "Organizational form, decision modalities and the environment," in J. G. Maurer (Ed.), *Readings in Organization Theory: Open Systems Approaches.* New York: Random House, 435–447.

1972 "Open systems and traditional hierarchies," Working Paper, Organization Studies Center, Graduate School of Management, UCLA.

1973 "Phenomenarchy: A suggestion for social redesign," *Journal of Applied Behavioral Science,* 9:163–180.

Milgram, S.

1965 "Some conditions of obedience and disobedience to authority," *Human Relations,* 18:57–76.

Miller, E. J.

1959 "Technology, territory, and time: The internal differentiation of complex production systems," *Human Relations,* 12.

Miller, E. J., and A. K. Rice

1967 *Systems of Organization.* London: Tavistock.

Mitroff, I. I.

1974 *The Subjective Side of Science: A Philosophical Inquiry into the Psychology of the Apollo Moon Scientists.* Amsterdam: Elsevier.

Mitroff, I. I., and T. R. Featheringham

1974 "On systematic problem solving and the error of the third kind," *Behavioral Science,* 19:383–393.

Mitroff, I. I., and R. H. Kilmann

1975a "On evaluating scientific research: The contributions of the psychology of science," *Technological Forecasting and Social Change,* 8:163–174.

1975b "Stories managers tell: A new tool for organizational problem solving," *Management Review,* 64:18–28.

1976 "On organizational stories: An approach to the design and analysis of organizations through myths and stories," in R. H. Kilmann, L. R. Pondy, and D. P. Slevin (Eds.), *The Management of Organization Design: Volume I, Strategies and Implementation.* New York: Elsevier North-Holland.

Mitroff, I. I., and F. Sagasti

1973 "Epistemology as general systems theory: An approach to the design of complex decision-making experiments,"*Philosophy of Social Science,* 3:117–134.

Mitroff, I. I., and M. Turoff

1973a "Technological forecasting and assessment: Science and /or mythology," *Technological Forecasting and Social Change,* 5:113–134.

1973b "The whys behind the hows," *IEEE Spectrum,* March, 62–73.

Mitroff, I. I., J. Williams, and E. Rathlswohl

1972 "Dialectical Inquiring Systems: A New Methodology for Information Science," November–December.

Mogar, R. E.

1969 "Toward a psychological theory of education," *Journal of Humanistic Psychology,* 9:17–52.

Mohr, L. B.

1971 "Organizational technology and organizational structure," *Administrative Science Quarterly,* 16:444–459.

Mooney, J. D.

ı 1969 "The coordinative principle," in J. A. Litterer (Ed.), *Organizations,* vol. II, 2nd ed. New York: Wiley, 105–106.

Mooney, J., and A. Reiley

1931 *Onward Industry,* New York: Harper.

Morse, J. J., and J. W. Lorsch

1970 "Beyond theory Y," *Harvard Business Review,* 48:61–68.

Mott, P. E.

1972 *The Characteristics of Effective Organizations.* New York: Harper & Row.

Murdick, R. G., and J. L. Ross

1971 *Information Systems for Modern Management.* Englewood Cliffs, N.J.: Prentice-Hall.

Myers, I. B., and K. C. Briggs

1962 *Myers-Briggs Type Indicator.* Princeton, N.J.: Educational Testing Service.

Nath, R.

1968a "Dynamics of organizational change: Some effects of a change program on the client system," *Academy of Management Proceedings,* August.

1968b "Managerial problem-solving patterns: An action research program," *Pittsburgh Business Review,* 2:1–8.

Negandhi, A. R., and B. C. Reimann

1972 "A contingency theory of organization re-examined in the context of a developing country," *Academy of Management Journal,* 15:137–146.

Nunnally, J. C.

1967 *Psychometric Theory.* New York: McGraw-Hill.

Odiorne, G.

1965 *Management by Objectives.* New York: Pitman.

Parsons, T.

1960 *Structure and Process in Modern Societies.* New York: Free Press.

Perrow, C.

1967 "A framework for the comparative analysis of organizations," *American Sociological Review,* 32:194–208.

1970 *Organizational Analysis: A Sociological View.* Belmont, Calif.: Wadsworth.

1973 "The short and glorious history of organizational theory," *Organizational Dynamics,* 2:2–15.

Pickle, H., and F. Friedlander

1967 "Seven societal criteria of organizational success," *Personnel Psychology,* 20:165–178.

Pondy, L. R.

1967 "Organizational conflict: Concepts and models," *Administrative Science Quarterly,* 12:296–320.

Pondy, L. R., F. V. Fox, and L. E. Pate

1976 "On the design of responsive processes in organizations," in R. H. Kilmann, L. R. Pondy, and D. P. Slevin (Eds.), *The Management of Organization Design: Volume I, Strategies and Implementation.* New York: Elsevier North-Holland.

Radnor, M., A. H. Rubenstein, and D. A. Tansik

1970 "Implementation of operations research and R & D in government and business organizations," *Operations Research*, 18:967–991.

Raiffa, H.

1968 *Decision Analysis*. Reading, Mass.: Addison-Wesley.

Rappaport, A. (Ed.)

1970 *Information for Decision-Making*. Englewood Cliffs, N.J.: Prentice-Hall.

Raven, G. H., and H. T. Eachus

1963 "Cooperation and competition in means-interdependent trials," *Journal of Abnormal and Social Psychology*, 67:307–316.

Reddin, W. J.

1972 *Effective Management by Objectives*. New York: McGraw-Hill.

Reudi, A., and P. R. Lawrence

1970 "Organizations in two cultures," in J. W. Lorsch and P. R. Lawrence (Eds.), *Studies in Organization Design*. Homewood, Ill.: Dorsey-Irwin, 53–83.

Rice, A. K.

1958 *Productivity and Social Organization: The Ahmedabad Experiment*. London: Tavistock.

Roby, R. B., and J. T. Lanzetta

1958 "Considerations in the analysis of group tasks," *Psychological Bulletin*, 55:88–101.

Roethlisberger, F. J.

1941 *Management and Morale*. Boston: Harvard University Press.

Roethlisberger, F. J., and J. Dickson

1938 *Management and the Worker*. Boston: Harvard University Press.

Rogers, C.

1961 *On Becoming A Person*. Boston: Houghton Mifflin.

Rokeach, M.

1969 *Beliefs, Attitudes, and Values*. San Francisco: Jossey-Bass.

Ross, R.

1973 "Organizational development—for whom," *Journal of Applied Behavioral Science*, 7.

Rubin, J., M. Plovnik, and R. Fry

1974 "Initiating planned change in health care systems," *Journal of Applied Behavioral Science*, 10:107–123.

Sagasti, F. R., and I. I. Mitroff

1973 "Operations research from the viewpoint of general systems theory," *Omega*, 1:695–709.

Schein, E. H.

1969 *Process Consultation: Its Role in Organization Development.* Reading, Mass.: Addison-Wesley.

Schultz, R. L., and D. P. Slevin

1975 "Implementation and organizational validity: An empirical investigation," in R. L. Schultz and D. P. Slevin (Eds.), *Implementing Operations Research/Management Science.* New York: Elsevier North-Holland, 153–182.

Seiler, J. A.

1963 "Diagnosing interdepartmental conflict," *Harvard Business Review*. 41:121–132.

Shaw, M. E.

1962 *Scale Analyses of Group Tasks, Annual Report.* Contract 580, Gainesville: University of Florida Press.

1971 *Group Dynamics.* New York: McGraw-Hill.

Sherif, M.

1958 "Superordinate goals in the reduction of intergroup conflict," *American Journal of Sociology*, 43:349 –356.

Simon, H. A.

1957 *Administrative Behavior.* New York: Free Press.

1962 "The architecture of complexity," *Proceedings of the American Philosophical Society*, 106:467–482.

Skinner, B. F.

1971 *Beyond Freedom and Dignity.* New York: Knopf.

Slevin, D. P.

1973 "The innovation boundary: A specific model and some empirical results," *Administrative Science Quarterly*, 18:71–75.

Smith, A.

1937 *An Inquiry Into the Nature and Causes of the Wealth of Nations.* New York: Modern Library.

Smith, A. J., E. H. Madden, and R. Sobol

1957 "Productivity and recall in cooperative and competitive discussion groups," *Journal of Psychology*, 43:193–204.

Starbuck, W. H.

1965 "Organizational growth and development," in J. March (Ed.), *Handbook of Organizations*. Chicago: Rand-McNally, 451–533.

1976 "Organizations and their environments," in M. Dunnette (Ed.), *Handbook of Industrial and Organizational Psychology*. Chicago: Rand McNally.

Steiner, G. A.

1969 *Top Management Planning*. London: Macmillan.

Stinchcombe, A. L.

1959 "Bureaucratic and craft administration of production: A comparative study," *Administrative Science Quarterly*, 4:168–187.

1965 "Social structure and organizations," in J. March (Ed.), *Handbook of Organizations*. Chicago: Rand McNally, 142–193.

Taylor, D. W., P. C. Berry, and C. H. Block

1958 "Does group participation when using brainstorming facilitate or inhibit creative thinking?," *Administrative Science Quarterly*, 3:23–47.

Taylor, F. W.

1947 *Scientific Management*. New York: Harper.

Terreberry, S.

1971 "The evaluation of organizational environments," in J. G. Maurer (Ed.), *Readings in Organization Theory: Open Systems Approaches*. New York: Random House, 58–73.

Thomas, J. M., and W. G. Bennis

1973 *The Management of Change and Conflict*. Baltimore, Md.: Penguin.

Thomas, K. W.

1976 "Conflict and conflict management," in M. D. Dunnette (Ed.), *The Handbook of Industrial and Organizational Psychology*. Chicago: Rand McNally.

Thomas, K. W., and R. H. Kilmann

1975 "The social desirability variable in organizational research: An alternative explanation for reported findings," *Academy of Management Journal*, 18:471–482.

Thompson, J. D.

1967 *Organizations in Action*. New York: McGraw-Hill.

Toffler, A.

1970 *Future Shock*. New York: Bantam.

Torbert, W. R.

1973 "Selection process for a collaborative organization,"*Journal of Applied Behavioral Science*, 9:331–359.

Trist, E. L., and K. W. Bamforth

1951 "Social and psychological consequences of the Longwall method of coal getting," *Human Relations*, 4:3–38.

Udy, S. H., Jr.

1965 "The comparative analysis of organizations," in J. March (Ed.), *Handbook of Organizations*. Chicago: Rand McNally: 678–709.

Viola, R. H.

1973 The Third Force in Psychology and Its Implications for Management. Fifth Annual Franklin F. Moore Lecture in Management, School of Business Administration, Rider College, Trenton, New Jersey.

Vroom, V. H.

1965 *Motivation in Management*. New York: American Foundation for Management Research.

Wagner, H. M.

1969 *Principles of Operations Research*. Englewood Cliffs, N.J.: Prentice-Hall.

Walker, C. R., and R. H. Guest

1952 *The Man on the Assembly Line*. Cambridge, Mass.: Harvard University Press.

Wall Street Journal

1971 "Strike at its Lordstown, Ohio plant ended," September, 14:6.

Walton, R. E.

1969 *Interpersonal Peacemaking: Confrontations and Third Party Consultation*. Reading, Mass.: Addison-Wesley.

Watson, G.

1966 "Resistance to change," in G. Watson (Ed.), *Concepts for Social Change*. Washington, D.C.: National Training Laboratories.

Weber, M.

1947 *The Theory of Social and Economic Organization*, Trans. by A. M. Handerson and Talcott Parsons. New York: Free Press.

Wheeler, R., and F. L. Ryan

1973 "Effects of cooperative and competitive classroom environments on the attitudes and achievement of elementary school students engaged in social studies inquiry activities," *Journal of Educational Psychology*, 92:402–407.

Weick, K. E.

1969 *Social Psychology of Organizing*. Reading, Mass.: Addison-Wesley.

Weiss, L., and M. Rein

1970 "The evaluation of broad-aim programs: Experimental design, its difficulties, and an alternative," *Administrative Science Quarterly*, 15:97–109.

Wilensky, H. L.

1967 *Organizational Intelligence*. New York: Basic Books.

Wirt, J. G.

1973 *A Proposed Methodology for Evaluating R & D Programs in the Department of Health, Education, and Welfare*. Santa Monica, Calif.: The Rand Corporation.

Wirt, J. G., A. Leiberman, and R. E. Levien.

1974 *R & D Management: Methods Used by Federal Agencies*. Santa Monica, Calif.: The Rand Corporation.

Woodward, J.

1965 *Industrial Organization: Theory and Practice*. London: Oxford.

Yuchtman, E., and S. E. Seashore

1967 "A system resource approach to organizational effectiveness," *American Sociological Review*, 32:891–903.

Zaltman, G., R. Duncan, and J. Holbek

1973 *Innovations and Organizations*. New York: Wiley.

Zand, D. E.

1974 "Collateral organization: A new change strategy," *Journal of Applied Behavioral Science*, 10:63–89.

Ziller, R. C., B. J. Stark, and H. O. Pruden

1969 "Marginality and integrative management positions," *Academy of Management Journal*, 12:487–495.

Author Index

Subject Index

323